W9-BGA-326

POLISH RADIO BROADCASTING IN THE UNITED STATES

BY JOSEPH MIGALA

EAST EUROPEAN MONOGRAPHS, BOULDER
DISTRIBUTED BY COLUMBIA UNIVERSITY PRESS, NEW YORK

1987

EAST EUROPEAN MONOGRAPHS, NO. CCXVI

Maps reprinted with permission from:
Standard Rate and Data Service, Inc.,
Spot Radio Rates and Data, Vol. 62, No. 1, January 1, 1980

Library of Congress Catalog Card Number 86-82812
ISBN 0-88033-112-7

Printed in the United States of America

TABLE OF CONTENTS

PART THREE
The Role of Radio in the Service of American Ethnic Groups

PART FOUR
Analysis of Response to a Public Opinion Survey About Polish Radio in the United States

TO THE READER

I am an American of Polish ancestry, born in the United States, raised and educated in Poland, living my adult life in the United States. I feel that I am a son of Poland, as much as I am a son of the land of my birth.

I have lived an interesting life, perhaps as interesting as the history of Polish Americans. I feel I have the duty to share what I have learned about the people who toiled in Polish-American radio as I did. The years spent working in Polish radio in this nation led me to much information and several observations which I wish to share with the readers of this book. This information and these observations are but one small part of the story of Polish radio in America. As far as I can determine, no one to date has attempted to write such a history, so late in my life, I determined to collect what scattered documents, reports, and all I could assemble on so fleeting a subject as radio.

I presented this work to the Department of Journalisn at the University of Warsaw, Poland, as a doctoral dissertation. As a result, I believe I am the first doctor of mass media studies who broadcasts daily in the Polish language on American radio. My programs are heard on WCEV, Cicero, Illinois, where I am president and general manager.

* * * * *

Dr. Joseph Migala was born in 1913 in Chicago into a family of Polish immigrants. In 1914, he returned to Poland with his mother, Tekla, to her native village Siedliszowice in the Tarnow region. After completing secondary school in Tarnow in 1933, he joined the "Wici" Rural Youth Movement and the Polish Populist Party.

As an American citizen, Mr. Migala voluntarily fought in the September Campaign of World War II in the 20th Infantry Regiment. After being taken prisoner, he managed to escape from a Nazi transport and return to Cracow, to work in the Syndicate of Agricultural Cooperatives. The author was part of the underground peasant resistance movement. He was one of the five leaders of the underground Populist Party "Roch" in the Malopolska Region and Silesia, and a soldier in the Peasant Battalions of the Polish Army of Resistance, later part of the home army. His wartime pseudonym was "Kafar."

After the war, Joseph Migala completed his studies toward a master's degree in economics at the Jagiellonian University in Cracow. He was president of the "Spolem" Agricultural Cooperative for the Province of Cracow from after the war until his return to the United State.

In 1947, he left with his wife and three daughters for the United States. He first was employed as a blue-collar worker, later as an accountant and as a real estate and insurance broker. In 1949, he began to work in Polish radio.

That year he began broadcasting the "Voice of Polonia" program in a weekly quarter-hour, then half-hour show on WLEY-FM in Chicago. In 1950, he moved the "Voice of Polonia" to WCRW-AM as a half-hour program three times a week. In 1951, he switched to WOPA-AM in suburban Oak Park, Illinois, broadcasting the "Voice of Polonia" for half an hour, Monday through Saturday.

The program expanded to an hour daily, then an hour and a half, and finally to two hours a day. One of its features was and is the first radio course of the Polish language in the United States, created by Joseph Migala. In 1957, he founded Europe Travel Bureau, a travel agency in Chicago and served as its president until 1978.

In 1979, he founded WCEV (1450 AM, Cicero, Illinois) as the first ethnic concept station in the United States, broadcasting in a dozen languages. The station has managed to attract some of the oldest, most successful ethnic programs in the country, among them, of course, the "Voice of Polonia."

Joseph Migala has long been active in Polish American community life. He is a long-standing member of the Polish National Alliance and the

Polish Alma Mater. For 15 years he was president of the Cracow Society of the Polish Roman Catholic Union of America. He reorganized the Friends of Polish Village Alliance and served as its president. For 25 years he has been president of the Siedliszowice Club of the Alliance of Polish Clubs. Under his leadership the club built a new school, a community center and a fire house in the village and is in the process of building a parish church there. He was chairman of the fundraising committee of the Wietrzychowice Parish Association (of the Alliance of Polish Clubs) which built a hospital in the village of Wietrzychowice. He organized the Friends of Cracow Club in Chicago in 1980.

Also in 1980, Joseph Migala received a doctor's degree from the Department of Journalism at Warsaw University in Poland.

Dr. Joseph Migala

AUTHOR'S NOTE

Historians and sociologists have been interested in ethnicity for quite some time. Serious scholarly research into the problems of assimilation of ethnic minorities in the United States and ways of solving them have been published due to a second wave of ethnic consciousness of the various minorities in their new country of residence. Even if the ethnicity is not much noticed by others, there exists a strong drive to search for one's roots to find one's ancestors and heritage. This phenomenon is especially evident in multi-ethnic countries where the divisions between "who is who" have been eliminated, but where a crystalized and unified nation has not yet emerged. Perhaps this may already be a unified nation, although its members differ in the degree of their national consciousness, in their understanding of culture in the broad sense, or in the color of their skin. Unity in variety—the United States can certainly be counted as such a nation and country.

This book limits itself to only one ethnic group in the United States—the Poles, and to only one aspect concerning them: radio as a mass medium and its role within that group. It strives to make a small contribution to the history of the Polish American community, known also as Polonia. A small, but nevertheless, important aspect of their life—the history of Polish language radio broadcasting in the United States is the subject of this book.

While undertaking this project, I was fully aware of the difficulties I would encounter and knew that anything I would write would be merely a small part of the history of Polish radio broadcasting in the United States.

I would like to make one point clear at the onset: This subject has remained in the shadows long enough, unnoticed by either historians or sociologists. Thus in the more than 50 years of their existence, Polish radio programs in the United States have had no scholarly study devoted to them, written either by Polish or American historians interested in the Polish ethnic group. While making my arduous search for source materials relating to the history of Polish radio stations in the United States, I became fully aware of the reason for this lack of interest on the part of historians on both sides of the Atlantic. This is simply a very difficult project, as no source materials for it exist in print.

Radio broadcasting is a transient phenomenon; it remains in the memory of listeners for a shorter or longer duration, it may evoke a greater response than the written word, but after a certain time, disappears without leaving a trace. In order to present even a general outline of the history of Polish radio programs in the United States, I had to reach the managers and announcers of those programs in 27 states. My research experience seems to explain to a large degree the seemingly lack of interest in this subject on the part of individual historians, as many of them–if only because of financial reasons–could not spend several months in various Polish-American communities. However, it is difficult to understand the absence of studies in this area by the Committee for Research Into Polonian Affairs of the Polish Academy of Sciences, the Institute for Polonian Studies of the Jagiellonian University in Cracow, or other similar research centers existing at institutions of higher learning in Poland.

No wonder then, that we have not received any book on this subject or even any serious article in the press for that matter. Only occasional brief mention is made, for example, in an article written by A. Miklaszewski and J. Serwanski devoted to the Polonia in Chicago: "Apart from the press, radio programs hold a special place in the Polonian mass media. In 1978, in Chicago, there were 10 weekly radio programs, one Sunday hour-long television program run by Bob Lewandowski. Those programs, broadcasting a total of ten hours, supplemented the daily programs of Lidia Pucinski, the Migala Family and W. Sikora."[1]

While writing this book, I kept asking myself one question: "Why is it that radio programs pass alongside history, in this case the history of the Polish American ethnic community?" There can be only one answer: Radio broadcasting transmits words which go into the air and hence are transient, they are spoken, but not written down, ephemeral. Radio programs are treated as a service, something that has become a part of social life, and hence nobody seems to notice them anymore. On the other hand, everything that has been written down and made public, has a chance of lasting. Words spoken over the radio, but not recorded on tape, do not have such a chance. Few radio programs have their own tape archives with recorded interviews with important people or covering important historical events for the use of future generations.

Therefore it was impossible to find source material to reconstruct the history of Polish radio programs in the United States in the airwaves, but few traces are to be found—as I have already mentioned—in written sources. The ones that I did find were merely brief notes on the contents of programs, short notices found in the daily press on radio programs.

The people who created the history of Polish radio programs in the United States or were witnesses to its creation are now not numerous and very old, which means that in several years time, the last "live" sources will also disappear. High time then to collect their recollections from those days and to safeguard them for use in future generations.

The contribution of the producers of the Polish radio programs to the social life of Polonia has so far remained unacknowledged. The radio programs created and presented by them to Polish listeners had enormous influence on shaping the opinions of Polonia, mobilizing public opinion in matters important for Poland and American Polonia. Hence, one of the aims of this publication is to preserve some of their noble work for posterity.

The question "What light has been shed on this matter by previously published scholarlary works?" will also be addressed.

In Andrew Paczkowski's study, *Prasa polska w latach 1918-1939* (The Polish Press From 1918-1939)[2] the existence of Polish radio programs was not even noted. Bogdan Lewandowski did not devote a single sentence to the shaping of ethnic consciousness or political trends by ethnic radio programs, while he was analyzing the propaganda influence of radio on American society. However he did acknowledge the value of this means of information.[3]

Between August 30 and September 5, 1975, an international conference was held at the Jagiellonian University in Cracow on the state and needs of research into emigration from Polish territory and the communities created by that emigration in various countries around the globe.[4]

Twenty-eight scholars from the United States took part in the conference, and although many problems connected with the life of the Polish ethnic community in the United States was discussed, not even the smallest piece of information on Polish radio broadcasting surfaced.

The results of this international conference were summarized in the book titled *Stan i potrzeby badan nad zbiorowosciami polonijnymi* (Research on Polonian Communities: Its Present State and Future Needs), edited by Hieronim Kubiak and Andrew Pilch and published in 1976 under the auspices of Komitet Badania Polonii Zagranicznej (Committee for the Study of Polonia Abroad) a part of Polska Akademia Nauk (The Polish Academy of Sciences) which published this under its own imprint of PAN.

This important element of Polonian life went unnoticed by Andrew Brozek in his book, *American Polonia 1854-1939* (Interpress, Warsaw, 1977). In chapter VII, in the part devoted to the press, the author discusses the history of Polonian newspapers, but takes no notice of the Polonian radio. After all, in modern times, the word "press" is understood very broadly, and radio and television as news mass media can be included in this category.

The Catholic writer Father John Piekoszewski in his work, *The Catholic Church in Contemporary America* (Veritas Publishers, London, 1967) in the chapter on the press, cites data on American AM and FM radio stations and the number of radio sets in the possession of listeners between 1930-1965, however, not a single word is mentioned about the Polish language radio. He even omits mentioning "The Rosary Hour," a program that was growing in popularity at the time. By 1980, it was transmitted by 47 radio stations in the United States and six in Canada, excellently fulfilling its religious mission, reaching millions of listeners.

The topic of Polish language radio found no room in the work of John Drohojowski,[5] or in the recently published collective work *Poles in the History and Culture of the United States of America.*[6]

Such researchers into Polonian affairs as J. A. Wytrwal,[7] Laura Pilarski,[8] or Theresita Polzin[9] did not touch on this subject either.

Helena Znaniecki Lopata devoted barely one full sentence to Polish radio in her entire book, comparing it to the daily press:

> Although the Polish Americans formed only 12 percent of the people who spoke a non-English tongue, they maintained 22 percent of the foreign press circulation. By contract, the 488 hours of average weekly Polish radio broadcasting were lower than that for other groups, forming only 6.4 percent of all foreign language broadcasting.[10]

Neil C. Sandberg in his book noted that in Los Angeles "there was not a single local radio or television program addressed to the Polish ethnic community."[11]

We could go on and on citing studies and books on problems concerning American Polonia, however, the result of research in the context of Polish radio would be meager. In light of these findings, let us stress that the author of this book did not follow in the footsteps of others and did not use the same source materials.

The guiding thought of this book is to show the importance of having their own mass media—particularly radio—for the Polish ethnic group.

This work has been divided into three sections. To the first belongs the general and then a specific discussion of radio development in the United States, and on this background, the Polish radio audience is discussed. Added to this are the specific remarks about the radio stations which broadcast Polish programs.

In the historical portion of this work when individual programs in various sections of the country are discussed, they are discussed chronologically. The aim of using this method was to demonstrate the quantitative development of Polish radio programs, while completely cognizant of the faulty feature of using this methodology which is the impossibility of avoiding repetition. It was also attempted to present the fluctuation in the number of broadcasts, which was particularly evident during the period of World War II.

The importance of influencing Polish ethnic society by this means of mass transmission are discussed in the chapters dealing with a review of the various states. Some attention is paid to the programs of the "Polka Show" type and to religious programs. The readers are introduced to the pioneers and radio personalities who were particularly instrumental in developing Polish broadcasting. On the basis of my personal experience, I discuss the role of ethnic radio stations.

The final section of this study which was written based on the answers supplied by the respondents of a poll attempts to analyze ways of reaching listeners. The results of the poll proved that good Polish radio broadcasts can create educated people who will work for the commonweal while living among their ethnic group. Only they know the problems of the group which they serve. An intelligent choice of information, and sometimes just ordinary information over the radio can call attention to many problems and sometimes even solve them.

From the results achieved by this study, the importance to the Polish ethnic community of possessing their own mass media, and particularly radio, has been demonstrated. To have Polish radio stations in Polish hands is political power and gives the responsibility of influencing public opinion which counts for a great deal in the United States.

PART ONE

The Position of Polish Radio Programs in The American Broadcasting System

Mr. John M. Lewandowski, of Cleveland, Ohio, the Father of Polish Radio Broadcasting in the United States.

CHAPTER 1

A Historical Sketch of Radio in the United States

An interesting and even an important comparison is made in the preface of Mary Crozier's book *Broadcasting (Sound and Television)*:

> Transmitting news over the radio has sometimes been compared to the invention of print which allowed the publication of many books through which ideas and knowledge were spread, making a contribution to civilization. The growth of radio broadcasting which immeasureably spread the discoveries made in the twentieth century is similar to a revolution. In any case, these are extremely important discoveries; books must be borrowed and then read, and sometimes translated and printed abroad, while radio programs overcome the distance from the broadcasting spot to the destined spot and broadcasting to the people in their own language. In the majority of countries everyone at home is amused by the continual sounds giving pleasure, bringing the news and the occurrences that have taken place, as well as music, politics, and education.[12]

In the United States there was also such a period when without regard to age, taste, material wealth or sex, radio was an attraction from the majority of Americans. Already in the beginning of the 1940s, a radio was found in almost every house.

However, at that time, critical voices regarding the ways of airing radio broadcasts were multiplying. Many radio listeners were of the opinion that radio was too banal and vulgar, since it didn't include in its repertoire enough good music and intellectual discussions. In the opinion of others, radio was too commercialized, although it was not possible to avoid this. In order to safeguard themselves from the undue influence of wealthy sponsors, every radio station ought to be able to have sufficient means at its disposal to counteract outside influences. This was impossible. It is difficult to suit every taste. Radio never attained the heights if it was a qestion of aesthetics; not did it avoid commercialization, but it was an excellent pastime form its earliest years.

Bypassing such experimental radio broadcasts as for example the transmission of Caruso's appearances at the Metropolitan Opera in New York at the beginning of the twentieth century, everything began only on November 20, 1920, in Pittsburgh when station KIKA transmitted the first report of returns from the presidential elections.[13] The older generation still remembers those first radio sets, bought or made by hobbyists. Possession a radio station became a status symbol for many institutions, and even private persons.

Since those beginnings, radio broadcasting became an effective tool in the hands of politicians. The voice of President W. G. Harding was transmitted for the first time in connection with military celebrations in 1921.[14] The Republican National Convention was transmitted over radio almost in full, creating a nationwide political sensation back then. A warm appealing radio voice became an attribute of candidates for high office.

By 1925, Americans spent $430 million on radio equipment purchases, almost twice as much as for sports and music equipment.[15] People began to set their daily schedules according to radio programming.

In 1924, researchers discovered the significant influence of radio on the evolution of the spoken language. They estimated that at least 5000 new words had suddenly been added to spoken English.[16]

Between 1922 and 1925, 1,079 new radio stations came into existence. This dynamic development of broadcasting created new problems, among them how to accumulate financial means for this new industry. Some considered using the methods of European broadcasters who preferred covering operating costs with payments made by listeners or by taxing manufacturers two percent for every radio set made. In 1923, after prolonged discussions, it was decided not to tax manufacturers and this principle has remained in force to this day.

That is when the idea of commercials was born; the idea of paid advertisements and announcements, from which radio stations draw funds for their operation. This system has survived up to now.

In early 1921, there were some 50,000 radio sets in the United States; in just one year, this number grew to one million. That is when conflicts between radio stations began, which often interferred in the reception of their competitors. The new industry lacked regulating legislation. Commerce Secretary Robert Hoover accomplished much in this field and at his initiative in 1927, Congress created the Federal Radio Commission which received broad prerogatives. The commission was to issue licenses and allocate wavelengths to individual radio stations.

A new state in the history of broadcasting began in 1926, with the creation of the first radio network, the National Broadcasting Company (NBC) which emerged from the Radio Corporation of America (RCA) created by David Sarnoff. NBC inaugurated its services on November 15, 1926, broadcasting to a territory from New England to Kansas City. When the second large radio corporation was created in 1927, Columbia Broadcasting Systems (CBS), radio services reached almost all the inhabitants of the United States. The above mentioned David Sarnoff became the first president of NBC, while William S. Paley led CBS. As these chains of radio stations emerged, local stations began to lose their independence in broadcasting individual programs. A process of reliance on NBC and CBS began.

New types of programs began to appear: educational shows for children, poetry programs and of course, entertainment, and in 1929, the famous radio series "Amos 'n' Andy," about two black characters from the suburbs of Chicago. At one point, this series had an audience of 60 percent of all radio listeners in the United States. Producers suddenly realized that as Valentino and Chaplin were attractions for movie-goers, so the heroes of radio series could be for listeners. So two new series: "The Goldbergs" and "The Rudy Valley Show" were created. The latter proved to be even more popular than the big vaudeville shows at the famous Palace Theater in New York.

For several months in 1931, radio broadcasting went through its first crisis. The popularity of serials and the number of listeners steadily began to drop. NBC tried to save the situation by hiring radio plays from the detective stories about Sherlock Holmes, The Adventures of Rin Tin Tin, and others. This crisis could probably be traced to a lack of talent and big names, as film stars and theater actors and actresses shunned the radio.

The lack of popularity forced NBC for financial reasons to put network radio at the disposal of big business. The tradition of broadcast commercials started in October 1923 by WEAD in New York City made a comeback. Gradually, businessmen became the absolute owners of radio stations. By the 1930s the statistics read as follows:[17]

33 percent of the programs were prepared by advertising agencies;
28 percent of the programs were prepared by local radio stations;
20 percent of the programs were prepared by sponsors;
10 percent of the programs were prepared by program producers.

In practical terms, sponsors had radio programs at their disposal for a period of 39 weeks at a time, although contracts were usually written for 13 weeks. The sponsor could delete part of a radio script, or withdraw it completely if the program was a failure from the advertising aspect. Sponsors demanded full information on the response to various programs. As early as 1935, telephone polls were used to ask listeners their opinion of a given program while it was on the air. One company, Hooperating, had branches in 32 cities and called listeners from morning until evening asking their opinion on the content of broadcasts. Later on, listeners were encouraged through contests and other methods to call radio stations if they were listening. With the advent of electronic recording, these calls could be recorded on tape as evidence for sponsors. If a sponsor received information that a particular program was unpopular, he withdrew his financial support from the program.

In this situation, the quality of programing ceased to be most important, its advertising effectiveness was paramount. In some cases, 90 percent of program time was used for commercials, and only 10 percent for other content. Radio had become the tool of big business.

When asked which industry best fulfills social needs, listeners responded as follows:[18]

1.	Auto Industry	43.1 percent
2.	Radio	29.2 percent
3.	Air Transport	9.8 percent
4.	Cinema	9.5 percent

The Research Committee on Social Trends deduced from available data that a significant increase in the number of students could be noted in those schools where sports transmissions were often listened to. It seems that radio had enormous bearing on the breakdown of regionalism in American society. Although local stations transmitted only regional programs, the networks broadcast high quality uniform programming into all the states.

A new radio series, the "Eddie Cantor Show" restored radio its lost popularity.[19] In 1931, radio programming became more mature: music and discussions were broadcast, detective programs, westerns, series of all kinds, soap operas, comedies, operas and serious theater plays. Screen stars began to appear on radio: the Marx Brothers, Jack Benny, Ed Wynn, George Burns, Gracie Allen and others, as well as such popular singers as Bing Crosby and the Boswell Sisters. When Franklin D. Roosevelt became president, his wife, Eleanor, who was very popular, appeared on a regular basis on "Vanity Fair," a variety program sponsored by Pond's Cosmetics. The president himself made 40 speeches over the radio between 1933 and 1935. In this period, the first radio journalists and political commentators emerged.

New heroes of radio–symbols of truth, justice and honor appeared. The number of entertainment programs for children increased. Often in the case of adventure stories the events portrayed were too brutal, which was also openly criticized as for instance in the cases of "Jack Armstrong," "Jungle Jim" and similar programs.[20] As a result, children's programs were launched with the highest ideals of American history. Advertising agencies learned to create programs serving their own self-interest, based on broadcasts of the greatest popularity. Listeners were invited to the studios in order to listen to their remarks and commentary.

The Great Depression found its reflection in radio in the form of numerous discussions with experts. At the same time the ever popular quizzes appeared ("Information Please," "The World Game," "Musical Quiz," etc.). One of them offered a top prize of $1000 and a consolation prize of $100. All you had to do was call the announcer during the program.

With the creation of the Lux Radio Theater big-time Hollywood stars appeared in radio studios: James Stewart, Cary Grant, Humphrey Bogart and others. This state of affairs lasted up to 1955. Radio also promoted unknown actors, such as Orson Welles who began his great career in radio. Later on famous adaptations of novels went on the air, such as the famous "War of the Worlds" by Wells,[21] theater plays by Shakespeare, Hugo, Ibsen, Gogal, Corneille, Eliot, Tolstoi, and many others.

In 1937, Sarnoff–copying CBS–announced the creation of the NBC Symphony Orchestra, and signed A. Toscanini as its conductor. Film directors began to work in radio as well as authors who wrote scripts or novels for radio (Irwin Shaw, Arthur Miller).

Radio became a testing ground for many artists. Arch Oboler invented new sound effects which made it possible to produce radio plays in the form we know today. Oboler became a great advocate of radio, as well as a critic of all dishonest advertising and radio junk.

In the footsteps followed a radio reporter by the name of Norman Corwin, who in the 1940s traveled around the world with his microphone. The result of those journeys was a wonderful series "One World Flight" (1947).[22] By now no scriptwriter or actor could change the character of radio broadcasting. It was a reflection of the culture ans system in which it was created.

During World War II, the speeches of King George, Chamberlain, Roosevelt, and news of victories or defeats were broadcast on radio. American radio tried to remain neutral, broadcasting information and commentaries by E.R. Murrow, Thomas and W. Winchell. Most sympathized with the British and French, only a few local stations presented a pro-fascist position.[23]

Afterward, ceremonies were transmitted from the port of Tokyo, etc. Some thought that American radio ought to condemn the enemy and so programs such as "Adolph and Miss Rumpu," "Hate," "Chicago," "Germany," and others were created.[24]

The patriotism of the war period was also felt in other radio broadcasts. American children experienced the war "glued" to the radio. In the opinion of some, it was thought necessary to introduce the kind of programs which would instill in the youth democratic and anti-military ideals.

The internal unrest of America was tied to fear of censorship. Two types of censorship existed: direct federal censorship and local censorship undertaken by station directors. Radio was subjected for all practical purposes to the latter type. The Federal Communication Commission (FCC) was forbidden from dictating to radio stations the subject matter to be broadcast.

But when the United States entered the war, federal censorship began.[25] The Office of Censorship in 1942 made a list of banned radio programs. Politically neutral programs were broadcast but newscasts were strictly censored. Many radio stations ceased operation and their equipment was turned over to military institutions. A great number of radio employees found employment with the government.

The end of the war brought a great increase in the number of radio stations. Many were rebuilt, others were newly commissioned. Frequency Modulation–FM–radio service was introduced.

Talented Black performers such as Paul Robeson, Juan Hernandes and others returned to radio. New competition began along with the creation of ABC, an FCC decision. ABC changed the name of its main station from WJZ to WABC.[26]

With the end of the war certain ballyhooed programs ceased having any essential meaning.[27] Radio had to rebuild its popularity. The level of programming had to be revamped and improved. Old comedy, quiz and musical programs remained, repeats of old series such as "Amos 'n' Andy" (1953) and "Lux Theater" (1953) returned to the air. Traditional programs were still popular.

Once again, competition between broadcasters appeared. Radio stations openly battled for listeners: if radio was to survive it needed financial support, which came with listenership.

The era of television was coming–an era Americans had waited for since the invention of the medium in 1920. Television would have developed earlier if not for the war. From the late 1940s to 1960, television supplanted radio, especially in the area of entertainments. Radio proceeds dropped by $32 million annually. Oboler himself wrote that television would replace radio as sound films had replaced the silent films.[28]

Certainly, radio broadcasting did not toally disappear by the year 1960. It underwent a metamorphosis. By then, Americans were seeking entertainment from TV. Radio had become a tool of commerical advertising.

Still, in the last 30 years, we have witnessed a serious increase of the number of radio stations in the United States.

At the beginning of 1950, the total number of radio stations was 2,867; in 1965, this number doubled; and in 1979, tripled. This dynamic increase was not steady. The biggest increase took place in the 1960s; the slowest, in the 1970s. This translates into stagnation and the symptom of satisfying the market.

The radio market is dominated by commercial radio stations; however, the number of noncommercial radio stations rises continually. At the time, there have been changes in the proportion between the number of commercial radio stations braoadcasting on AM (long waves) and FM (ultra short waves).

Namely, the growing advantage of the AM radio stations over FM in the 1950s suddenly diminished, arriving at a more and more steady balance. The chart on the next page illustrates this process.

To fully describe the process of development of radio stations in the last 15 years, the trend line is expressed by the following equation:

$$x = a + bt$$

where: "x" represents the number of radio stations of a given type
"t" represents the number of years
"a" "b" represents parameters

The estimate of those parameters was obtained by the method of the smallest squares utilizing the system of following regular equations:

$$\Sigma x = N a + b \Sigma t$$
$$\Sigma tx + a \Sigma t + b \Sigma t^2$$

The data for the above system of equations may be found in charts one, two and three (following pages). Below the charts, one may also find the claculation of the equation based on the method of determinants.

The achieved trends have the following numerical shape:

–commercial AM radio stations
$x = 4024.3324 + 37.3893t$

–commercial FM radio stations
$x = 1266.2095 + 126.9071t$

–noncommercial FM radio stations
$x = 115.7238 + 56.0679t$

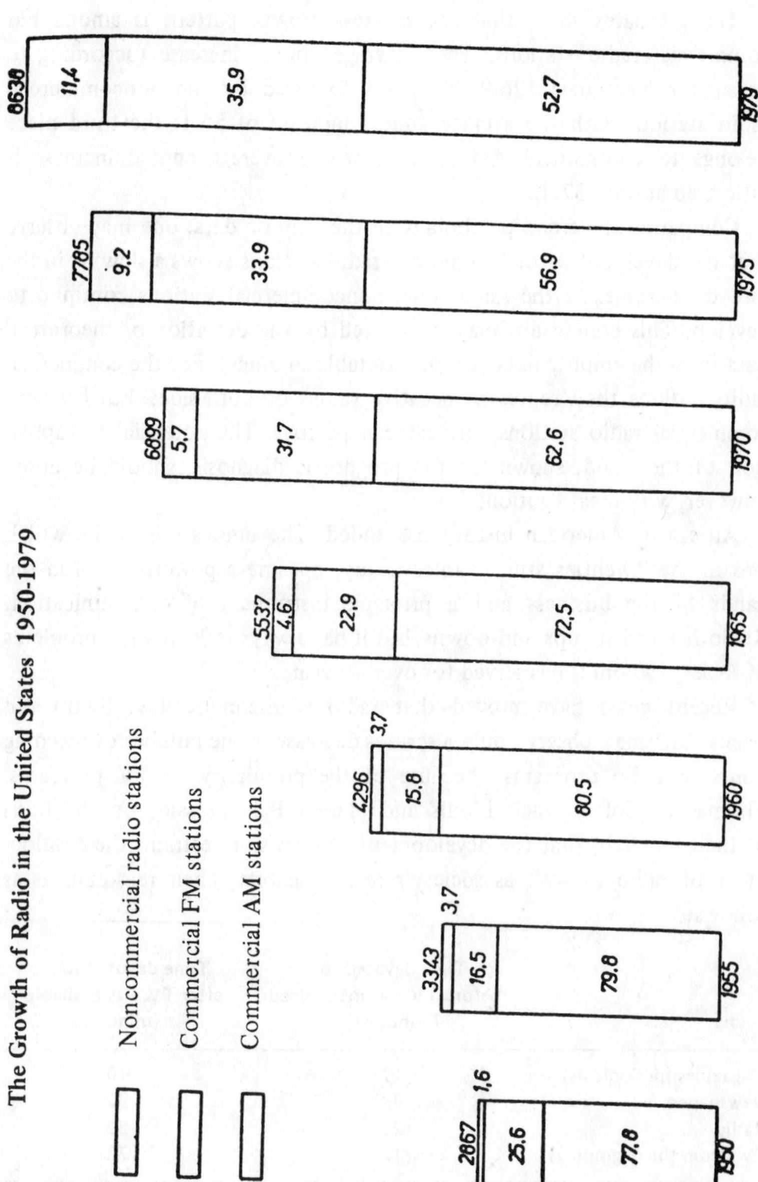

The Growth of Radio in the United States 1950-1979
Noncommercial radio stations
Commercial FM stations
Commercial AM stations
2867
1,6
25.6
77.8
1950
3343
3.7
16.5
79.8
1955
4296
3.7
15.8
80.5
1960
5537
4.6
22.9
72.5
1965
6899
5.7
31.7
62.6
1970
7785
9.2
33.9
56.9
1975
8638
11,4
35.9
52.7
1979

Chart Two illustrates the described trends.

The estimates show that the greatest growth pattern is among FM commercial radio stations. Their average annual increase (according to parameter b) equals 126.9. They are followed by the noncommercial radio stations with the average annual increase of 56.1; the third place belongs to commercial AM stations whose average annual increase is estimated at only 37.4.

Comparing the trend parabola with the empiric data, one may observe that the development of commercial radio stations shows a slowing in the rate of increase. In the same time, noncommercial stations continue to develop. This conclusion may be proved by the deviation of theoretical data from the empiric data (see the last table columns). For the commercial radio stations they represent negative values on both sides, but for noncommercial radio stations, the value is positive. The potential extrapolation of the trend, shown for the prognostic diagnosis, should be done, however, with great caution.

An era of American history has ended. The innovation, radio, which was in the Twenties still a fantastic toy, became a powerful tool in the hands of the business and a principle instrument of communication. Radio has had its ups and downs, but it has always reflected the problems of society, whom it has served for over 40 years.

Recent years have proved that radio is unconquerable. Radio still reigns. One may observe only a serious decrease in the number of listening hours of radio programs because of the popularity of TV programs. Thomas E. Coffin, Jack Lindis and Marvin Baiman said, on the basis of their research, that the development of television restrains the development of radio as well as society's reading habits. Their reasoning is as follows:

Media	Time devoted to it before TV was introduced (minutes)	Time devoted to it after TV was available (minutes)
Magazines (periodicals)	17	10
Newspapers	39	32
Radio	122	52
TV (from the beginning)	12	173
Totals	190	267

Based on: Thomas E. Coffin, Jack Lindis, Marvin Baiman—Strangers Into Customers (New York: International Broadcasting Co., 1955)

TABLE 1
The Empirical and Theoretical Value of Commercial AM Radio Stations from 1965-1979

Lp.	Year	Number of radio stations x	t	t^2	tx	Theoretical x'	Differences x–x'
1.	1965	4012	1	1	4012	4061,7	–49,7
2.	66	4050	2	4	8100	4099,1	–49,1
3.	67	4117	3	9	12351	4136,5	–19,5
4.	68	4171	4	16	16684	4173,9	– 2,9
5.	69	4236	5	25	21180	4211,3	24,7
6.	1970	4319	6	36	25914	4248,7	70,3
7.	71	4323	7	49	30261	4286,1	36,9
8.	72	4355	8	64	34840	4323,5	31,5
9.	73	4393	9	81	39537	4360,9	32,1
10.	74	4422	10	100	44220	4398,2	23,8
11.	1975	4432	11	121	48752	4435,6	– 3,6
12.	76	4463	12	144	53556	4473,0	–10,0
13.	77	4497	13	169	58461	4510,4	–13,4
14.	78	4513	14	196	63182	4547,8	–34,8
15.	79	4549	15	225	68235	4585,2	–36,2
		64852	120	1240	529285		

$$64852 = 15\,a + 120\,b$$
$$529285 = 120\,x + 1240\,b$$

$$a = \frac{\begin{vmatrix} 64852 & 120 \\ 529285 & 1240 \end{vmatrix}}{\begin{vmatrix} 15 & 120 \\ 120 & 1240 \end{vmatrix}} = \frac{16\,902\,280}{4200} = 4024{,}3524$$

$$b = \frac{\begin{vmatrix} 15 & 64852 \\ 120 & 529285 \end{vmatrix}}{\begin{vmatrix} 15 & 120 \\ 120 & 1240 \end{vmatrix}} = \frac{157\,035}{4200} = 37{,}389286$$

TABLE 2
The Empirical and Theoretical Values of Commercial FM Radio Stations from 1965-1979

Lp.	Year	Number of radio stations x	t	t^2	tx	Theoretical x^1	Difference $x-x^1$
1.	1965	1270	1	1	1270	1393,1	−123,1
2.	66	1446	2	4	2892	1520,0	− 74,0
3.	67	1631	3	9	4893	1646,9	− 15,9
4.	68	1779	4	16	7116	1773,8	5,2
5.	69	1944	5	25	9720	1900,7	43,3
6.	1970	2184	6	36	13104	2027,7	156,3
7.	71	2196	7	49	15372	2154,6	41,4
8.	72	2304	8	64	18432	2281,5	22,5
9.	73	2482	9	81	22338	2408,4	73,6
10.	74	2605	10	100	26050	2535,3	69,7
11.	1975	2636	11	121	28996	2662,2	− 26,2
12.	76	2767	12	144	33204	2789,1	− 22,1
13.	77	2873	13	169	37349	2916,0	− 43,0
14.	78	3001	14	196	41014	3042,9	− 41,9
15.	79	3104	15	225	46560	3169,8	− 65,8
		34222	120	1240	309310		

$$34222 = 15\,a + 120\,b$$
$$309310 = 120\,a + 1240\,b$$

$$a = \frac{\begin{vmatrix} 34222 & 120 \\ 309310 & 1240 \end{vmatrix}}{\begin{vmatrix} 15 & 120 \\ 120 & 1240 \end{vmatrix}} = \frac{5\,318\,080}{4200} = 1266{,}2095$$

$$b = \frac{\begin{vmatrix} 15 & 34222 \\ 120 & 309310 \end{vmatrix}}{\begin{vmatrix} 15 & 120 \\ 120 & 1240 \end{vmatrix}} = \frac{533\,010}{4200} = 126{,}90714$$

TABLE 3
The Empirical and Theoretical Values of Noncommercial FM Radio Stations from 1965-1979

Lp.	Year	Number of radio stations x	t	t^2	tx	Theoretical x^1	Difference $x-x^1$
1.	1965	255	1	1	255	171,8	83,2
2.	66	269	2	4	538	227,9	41,1
3.	67	299	3	9	897	283,9	15,1
4.	68	326	4	16	1304	339,9	−13,9
5.	69	362	5	25	1810	396,1	−34,1
6.	1970	396	6	36	2376	452,1	−56,1
7.	71	440	7	49	3080	508,2	−68,2
8.	72	479	8	64	3832	564,3	−85,3
9.	73	625	9	81	5625	620,3	4,7
10.	74	711	10	100	7110	676,4	34,6
11.	1975	717	11	121	7887	732,5	−15,5
12.	76	804	12	144	9648	788,5	15,5
13.	77	870	13	169	11310	844,6	25,4
14.	78	926	14	196	12964	900,7	25,3
15.	79	985	15	225	14775	956,7	28,3
		8464	120	1240	83411		

$$8464 = 15a + 120b$$
$$83411 = 120a + 1240b$$

$$a = \frac{\begin{matrix} 8464 & 120 \\ 83411 & 1240 \end{matrix}}{\begin{matrix} 15 & 120 \\ 120 & 1240 \end{matrix}} = \frac{486\,040}{4200} = 115{,}72381$$

$$b = \frac{\begin{matrix} 15 & 8464 \\ 120 & 83411 \end{matrix}}{\begin{matrix} 15 & 120 \\ 120 & 1240 \end{matrix}} = \frac{235\,485}{4200} = 56{,}067857$$

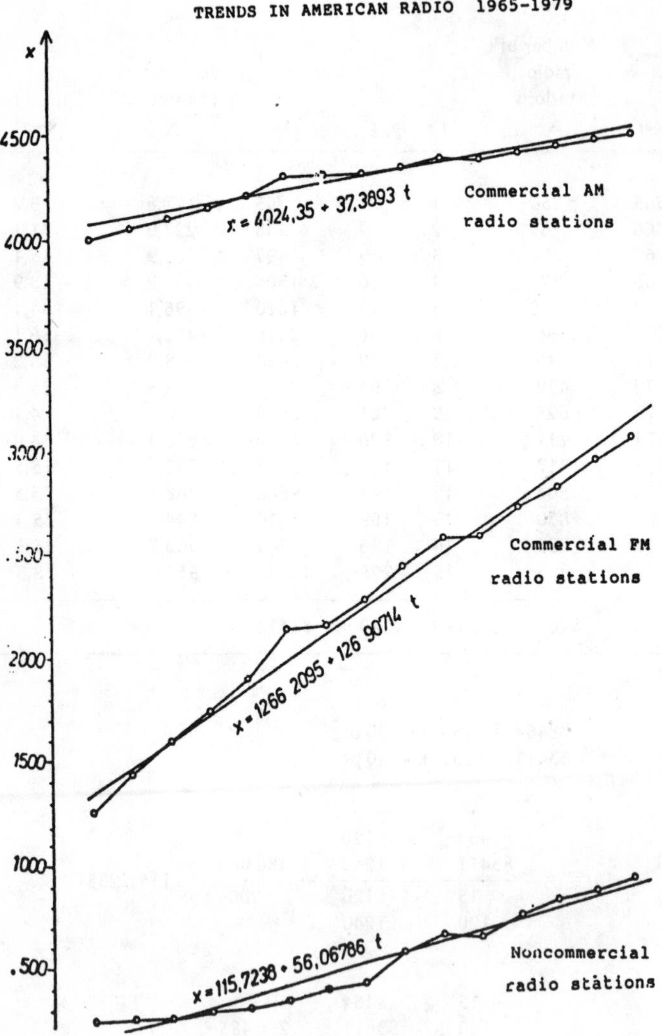
TRENDS IN AMERICAN RADIO 1965-1979
x
4500
4000
3500
3000
2500
2000
1500
1000
500
x = 4024,35 + 37,3893 t
Commercial AM
radio stations
Commercial FM
radio stations
x = 1266 2095 + 126 90714 t
x = 115,7238 + 56,06786 t
Noncommercial
radio stations

The popularity of small transistor radios has brought radio fully into American life. Radio could be found everywhere–from the home to the outdoors. It became a permanent and irreplacable companion of every human being. People listen to the radio while driving, sunbathing, while working, and while relaxing–literally, everywhere! Radio reaches everywhere and is the No. 1 news carrier. Although radio continues its recovery in the mass perception, it is often replaced by TV.

CHAPTER 2

The FCC and the Regulation of Broadcasting in the United States

Unlike most nations on earth, the government of the United States does not own and operate radio and television stations. They are owned and operated by private companies, which base their activities on profits. In some communities there are also radio and TV stations that belong to high schools or colleges, which broadcast educational programs. A completely different category are public radio and TV stations usually operated by not-for-profit community groups. Such stations do not base their profits but are maintained by donations from their audience, contributions from corporations and foundations and funds from the federal government. Such public stations have recently begun experimenting with paid advertising as a revenue source.

The Federal Communications Commission, an independent government agency, oversees all of mass media in the United States, including radio and TV, on behalf of the federal government.

This government agency was created by Congress and reports to it on the basis of a law passed on June 19, 1934.[29]

The Federal Communications Commission (FCC) was established to regulate interstate and foreign radio, television, telegraph, cable and satellite communication.

The FCC has its offices in Washington D.C. and is administered by five commissioners appointed by the president and approved by the

Senate.[30] These people cannot have any financial links with the mass media under the jurisdiction of the FCC, and no more than three of them can belong to a political party. The commissioners are nominated for a period of seven years; the chairman is appointed by the president, who also determines the length of the chairman's office.

The FCC is divided into four operating bureaus: mass media (radio and TV), common carrier (interstate of foreign communications by radio, wire and cable and licensing radio telephone communications), personal radio (such as citizen band radio), and field operations. In this last category, the FCC has numerous offices around the United States which operate mainly in the sphere of technological matters. They inspect radio stations, checking on the technical state of their equipment. They examine the technical staff of radio stations, issue licenses, provide communication equipment for planes and ships used in danger, locate sources of interference and suggest solutions, carry out special government orders, collect and analyze technical data for the use of the FCC. On national and international matters, the FCC cooperates with numerous government agencies connected with the mass media. The FCC employs about 2100 people, of which over 1/4 are local workers in charge of technical work.[31]

The FCC reviews applications for new radio stations, on both the AM and FM frequencies, issues permits for all types of private stations, assigns frequencies, defines operating power of transmitters, time of broadcasting, and call sign of the station. It decides on changes and renewal of licenses, inspects transmitting equipment and issues regulations concerning the use of transmitting equipment by radio and television stations. It does not, however, have any rights in controlling radio communication by the government.

The FCC is barred by law to censor the substance of programming, but it requires the management of radio and television stations to submit assurances that they serve the needs of their community. Licensed operators of radio or television stations are obliged to comply with statutes, regulations and principles guiding the substance of programs, for example, identifying firms advertising their goods or services, announcing the results of state lotteries only in their own or neighboring states, etc.

The FCC also requires licensees to make available equal opportunities for use of broadcast facilities by candidates for political office. It does not allow personal attacks on the air. It enforces rules on fair presentation or controversial issues. It also prohibits broadcasting of false or misleading commercial advertisements.

The FCC leads investigations and applies penalties in case its rules are violated. A licensed company that does not abide by FCC regulations can be fined up to $20,000, and in more serious cases, can lose its right to operate a radio or television station.[22]

The FCC limits the number of broadcasting outlets owned by one person or company to seven AM stations, seven FM stations and seven TV stations (only five of which can be VHF stations). The same person or company cannot operate more than one station of the same kind in the same place.

The right to receive a radio license is restricted to citizens of the United States. Foreigners cannot obtain a license, nor can companies whose board of directors includes citizens of a foreign country, or companies with 1/5 or more of their shares in the hands of a foreigner.

Radio stations have call signs assigned by the FCC. International agreements oblige every radio station to have the first letter of its call sign identify its nationality. For this purpose, countries were assigned various letters of the alphabet. The United States received the letters K, N, W, exclusively, and X, partially.[33]

Under the auspices of the Department of State, the FCC takes part in international conferences that concern matters of international radio communication. The FCC issues radio and cable licenses linking the United States and abroad, and supervises companies servicing those installations. The FCC also issues licenses for radio equipment installed in American planes and ships on international territory, and if requested, inspects radio equipment of foreign ships stationed in American ports.

The FCC, moreover, serves as a mediator in cases of mutual interference between national and foreign stations. FCC principles oblige it to care for the greatest effectivity in the use of radio and wire communications for the protection of life and property.

The FCC has a special task in the national defense system, which is defined by the president. Among others, it informs and instructs the public in the event of an enemy attack or the announcement of a state of emergency.

Having established one of the first, albeit somewhat primitive, remote studios for an ethnic program in Chicago, Estelle, George and Joseph Migala [*left to right*] prepare for a "Voice of Polonia" broadcast. Pictured here at the age of eight, George Migala, currently manager of Radio Station WCEV, was already reading commercials on the air, and reciting poems for holidays and special occasions.

TABLE 1

Territorial Concentration of Population in the United States

State	Population USA in 1979[x]	Area in Square Miles[xx]	Density of Population[xxx]	Structural Succession[xxx] a	Structural Succession[xxx] b	Accumulated Succession[xx/x] a′	Accumulated Succession[xx/x] b′	Calculations[x/xx] ab	Calculations[x/xx] a′b
1. Alaska	414.2	586.040	0.7	0.19	16.21	0.19	16.21	3.08	3.08
2. Wyoming	423.4	97.914	4.3	0.19	2.71	0.38	18.92	0.51	1.03
3. Montana	777.0	147.138	5.3	0.36	4.07	0.74	22.99	1.45	3.01
4. Nevada	670.5	110.540	6.1	0.31	3.06	1.05	26.05	0.95	3.21
5. South Dakota	691.8	77.047	9.0	0.32	2.13	1.37	28.18	0.68	2.92
6. North Dakota	666.9	70.665	9.4	0.31	1.95	1.68	30.13	0.60	3.28
7. New Mexico	1,218.9	121.666	10.0	0.56	3.37	2.24	33.50	1.87	7.55
8. Idaho	889.1	83.557	10.6	0.41	2.31	2.65	35.81	0.95	6.12
9. Utah	1,304.8	84.916	15.4	0.60	2.35	3.25	38.16	1.41	7.64
10. Nebraska	1,576.8	77.227	20.4	0.72	2.14	3.97	40.30	1.54	8.50
11. Arizona	2,384.8	113.909	20.9	1.09	3.15	5.06	43.45	3.43	15.94
12. Oregon	2,430.1	96.981	25.1	1.11	2.68	6.17	46.13	2.97	16.54
13. Colorado	2,719.2	104.247	26.1	1.25	2.88	7.42	49.01	3.60	21.37
14. Kansas	2,342.4	82.276	28.5	1.07	2.28	8.49	51.29	2.37	19.36
15. Maine	1,105.2	33.215	33.3	0.51	0.92	9.00	52.21	0.47	8.28
16. Oklahoma	2,855.3	69.919	40.8	1.31	1.93	10.31	54.14	2.53	19.90
17. Arkansas	2,188.4	53.104	41.2	1.00	1.47	11.31	55.61	1.47	16.63
18. Minnesota	4,009.9	84.068	47.7	1.84	2.33	13.15	57.94	4.29	30.64
19. Texas	13,239.3	267.339	49.5	6.07	7.40	19.22	65.34	44.92	142.23
20. Mississippi	2,420.0	47.716	50.7	1.11	1.32	20.33	66.66	1.47	26.84
21. Vermont	490.0	9.609	51.0	0.22	0.27	20.55	66.93	0.06	5.55
22. Iowa	2,892.4	56.290	51.4	1.33	1.56	21.88	68.49	2.07	34.13
23. Washington	3,710.6	68.192	54.4	1.70	1.89	23.58	70.38	3.21	44.57
24. Missouri	4.746.8	69.674	68.1	2.18	1.93	25.76	72.31	4.21	49.72
25. Alabama	3,739.4	51.609	72.5	1.71	1.43	27.47	73.74	2.45	39.28
26. West Virginia	1,877.5	24.181	77.6	0.86	0.67	28.33	74.41	0.58	18.98
27. Louisana	3,974.8	48.523	81.9	1.82	1.34	30.15	75.75	2.44	40.40
28. Wisconsin	4,695.9	56.154	83.6	2.15	1.55	32.30	77.30	3.33	50.07
29. Kentucky	3,511.2	40.395	86.9	1.61	1.12	33.91	78.42	1.80	37.98
30. Georgia	5,145.7	58.876	87.4	2.36	1.63	36.27	80.05	3.85	59.12

TABLE 1 (Continued)

	State	Population USA in 1979ˣ	Area in Square Milesˣˣ	Density of Populationˣˣˣ	Structural Successionˣˣˣ a	b	Accumulated Successionˣ/ˣˣ a′	b′	Calculationsˣ/ˣˣ ab	a′b
31.	New Hampshire	868.2	9.304	93.3	0.40	0.26	36.67	80.31	0.10	9.53
32.	South Carolina	2,929.3	31.055	94.3	1.34	0.86	38.01	81.17	1.15	32.69
33.	Tennessee	4,359.5	42.244	103.2	2.00	1.17	40.01	82.34	2.34	46.81
34.	North Carolina	5,622.8	52.712	106.7	2.58	1.46	42.59	83.80	3.77	62.18
35.	Virginia	5,219.4	40.815	127.9	2.39	1.13	44.98	84.93	2.70	50.83
36.	California	22,170.5	158.693	139.7	10.16	4.39	55.14	89.32	44.60	242.06
37.	Hawaii	917.1	6.429	142.9	0.42	0.18	55.56	89.50	0.08	10.00
38.	Indiana	5,344.7	36.291	147.3	2.45	1.00	58.01	90.50	2.45	58.01
39.	Florida	8,876.5	58.560	151.6	4.07	1.62	62.08	92.12	6.59	100.57
40.	Michigan	9,162.1	58.216	157.4	4.20	1.61	66.28	93.73	6.76	106.71
41.	Illinois	11,265.8	56.400	199.7	5.16	1.56	71.44	95.29	6.05	111.45
42.	Ohio	10,707.5	41.222	259.8	4.91	1.14	76.35	96.43	5.60	87.04
43.	Pennsylvania	11,802.8	45.333	206.4	5.41	1.25	81.76	97.68	6.76	102.20
44.	Delaware	591.4	2.057	287.5	0.27	0.06	82.03	97.74	0.02	4.92
45.	New York	17,844.0	49.576	359.9	8.18	1.37	90.21	99.11	11.21	123.59
46.	Maryland	4,186.7	10.577	395.8	1.92	0.29	92.13	99.40	0.56	26.72
47.	Connecticut	3,123.9	5.009	623.7	1.43	0.14	93.56	99.54	0.20	13.10
48.	Massachusetts	5,836.5	8.257	706.9	2.67	0.23	96.23	99.77	0.61	22.13
49.	Rhode Island	932.4	1.214	768.0	0.43	0.23	96.66	99.80	0.01	2.90
50.	New Jersey	7,345.9	7.836	937.5	3.37	0.22	100.03	100.02	0.74	22.01
	TOTALS	218,220.0	3,614.777		100.03	100.02			208.87	1,979.28

Sources: x—Spot Radio Rates and Data. Standard Rate Data Service Inc., Skokie, January 1, 1980.
xx—The USA F.E. Compton Company, Chicago 1953.
xxx—Personal Calculations

CHAPTER 3

The Distribution of Radio Stations in the United States

Area and population density are the basic quantities on which local radio stations are distributed. From this point of view, the continent on which the United States is found is extremely varied. There are terrains like the Rocky Mountains or Alaska which are very extensive and lightly populated, as well as industrialized urban regions with extreme density of population in a small space.

To more easily characterize this phenomenon, measures of territorial concentrations were used. To this end, the states were arranged according to population density, then to the percentage of each state in the general territorial area and then to the calculated general population census.

From the obtained indicators of the structure, the following cumulative series was constructed which illustrates the distribution of concentration of the studied quantity. The calculations are placed in Table 1.

In comparing both series, it turns out that the least populated states whose density does not exceed 40 inhabitants per square mile, occupy 52.2 percent of the total area of the country, and have barely 9.0 percent of the total population. In turn, median density populated states having from 40 to 200 inhabitants per square mile, occupy 43.1 percent of the total area and constitute a concentration of 61.4 percent of the total population. On the other hand, the most populous states with a density of more than 200 inhabitants per square mile occupy a mere 4.9 percent of the land and carry 28.6 percent of the total population of the country.

The territorial concentration is shown graphically in Figure 3.

The points situated below the diagonal representing the line of uniform distribution create a curve. Where the curve is the sharpest, it represents

Diagram: Concentration of Population in the United States

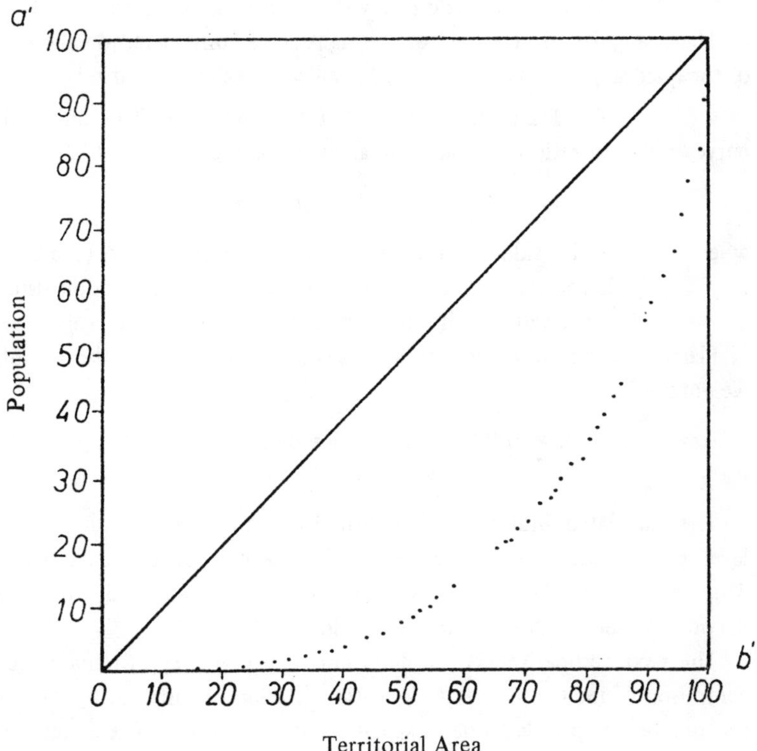

the greatest degree of concentration. From examining this concentration, it turns out that the earlier high rate of area growth is ceded to the ever increasing tempo of population growth on the point furthest from the line of equal division.

The concentration indicator which is illustrated on the basis of the equation below is the measure of the degree of concentration:

$$K = \frac{P - Q}{P}$$

where K is the concentration indicator;
P is the triangular surface field below the line of equal distribution;
Q is the surface field below the concentration curve.

The triangular surface field of the right angle constructed on the sides of the quadrangle with a length of 100 can easily be calculated as:

$P = 1/2\ (100 \times 100) = 5000$ –while the field under the curve of concentration is depicted in an approximate way as:

$$Q = a'b - 1/2\ ab$$

where "a" is the value of the structural series with traits A (the area);
"b" is the value of the structural series with traits B (population);
"a′" is the value of the cumulative series with traits A.

Placing the numbers from the correct columns of Table 1 to the formula, we obtain:[34]

$$K = \frac{5000 - 1{,}874{,}845}{5000} = 0.625$$

The calculated indicator of territorial concentration indicates a high level of concentrated population in the makeup of particular states. This testifies to the unequal conditions of development of the radio network on the territory of the United States.

The next comparison is the determination of the level of spatial concentration of radio stations. As a spatial criterion of distributing stations, the number of people living in specific states was taken. The states were arranged according to the number of stations per 100,000 population in Table 2.

From the analysis of the cumulative series, the states with the least number of stations, i.e., those that don't exceed 20 stations per 1 million inhabitants comprise 30.0 percent of the country's population, while concentrating only 14.9 percent of the network. In turn, in the states equipped with 20 to 50 stations per 1 million inhabitants lives 52.0

percent of the population, which comprises, 52.7 percent of the network. Finally, in the most highly equipped states having more than 50 stations per 1 million inhabitants lives 18.1 percent of the population which has 30.8 percent of the radio network.

Graphically, these concentrations are depicted in Diagram 4.

From an examination of the situated points it turns out that the spatial distribution of radio stations from the point of view of population density is evenly distributed. The concentration indicator, after taking the correct numbers from Table 2, comes to:

$$K = \frac{5000 - 3613.8696}{5000} = 0.277$$

Comparing this indicator with the previous indicator of the concentration of spatial population, we notice that the main determinant of allotting radio stations is the population distribution in the individual states.

Detailed maps of the distribution of radio stations along with the designation of stations broadcasting Polish programs are given in the following pages. Each map is preceded by a description of the stations broadcasting Polish programs along with the broadcast times in a weekly schedule.[35]

Diagram: The General Concentration of Radio Stations

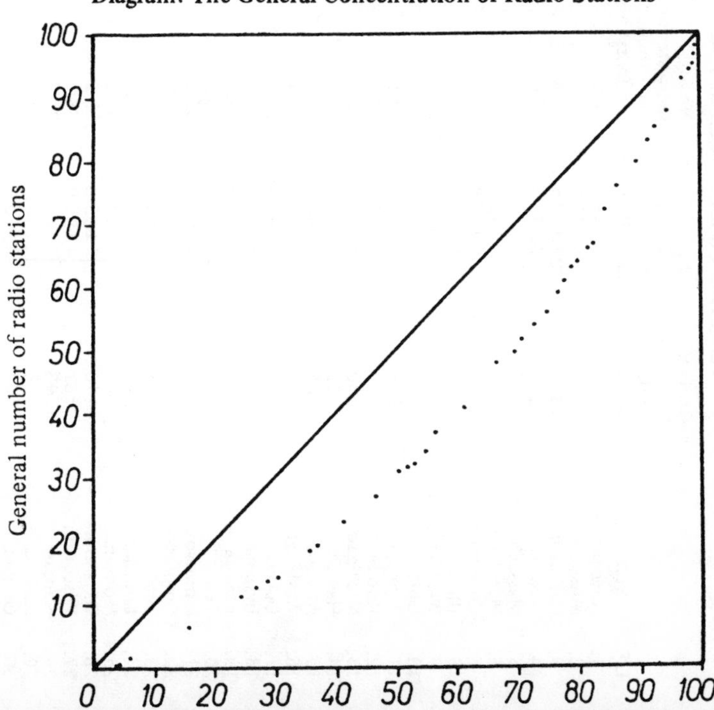

TABLE 2

Territorial Concentration of Radio Networks in the United States

Lp.	State	General Number of Radio Stations[x]	U.S. Population in 1979[xx] in millions	No. of radio stations per 1 million residents[xxx]	Structure a	Structure b	Cumulative Columns[xxx] a′	Cumulative Columns[xxx] b′	Calculations[xxx] ab	Calculations[xxx] a′b
1.	New Jersey	51	7,345.9	6.9	0.76	3.37	0.76	3.37	2.56	2.56
2.	Missouri	73	4,746.8	15.4	1.08	2.18	1.84	5.55	2.35	4.01
3.	California	341	22,170.5	15.4	5.06	10.16	6.90	15.71	51.41	70.10
4.	New York	296	17,844.0	16.6	4.39	9.18	11.29	23.89	35.91	92.35
5.	Massachusetts	103	5,836.5	17.6	1.53	2.68	12.82	26.57	4.10	34.36
6.	Maryland	79	4,186.7	18.9	1.17	1.92	13.99	28.49	2.25	26.86
7.	Connecticut	59	3,123.9	18.9	0.87	1.43	14.86	29.92	1.24	21.25
8.	Illinois	254	11,265.8	22.5	3.77	5.16	18.63	35.08	19.45	56.13
9.	West Virginia	44	1,877.5	23.4	0.65	0.86	19.28	35.94	0.56	16.58
10.	Ohio	253	10,707.5	23.6	3.75	4.91	23.03	40.85	18.41	113.08
11.	Pennsylvania	289	11,802.8	24.5	4.29	5.41	27.32	46.26	23.21	147.80
12.	Rhode Island	23	932.4	24.7	0.34	0.43	27.66	46.69	0.15	11.89
13.	Michigan	230	9,162.1	25.1	3.41	4.20	31.07	50.89	14.32	130.49
14.	Hawaii	23	917.1	25.1	0.34	0.42	31.41	51.31	0.14	13.19
15.	Arizona	65	2,348.8	27.3	0.96	1.09	32.37	52.40	1.05	35.28
16.	Washington	119	3,710.6	32.1	1.76	1.70	34.13	54.10	2.99	58.02
17.	Delaware	19	591.4	32.1	0.28	0.27	34.41	54.37	0.08	9.29
18.	Indiana	181	5,344.7	34.1	2.70	2.45	37.11	56.82	6.62	90.92
19.	Florida	303	8,876.5	34.1	4.49	4.07	41.60	60.89	18.27	169.31
20.	Texas	456	13,239.3	34.4	6.76	6.07	48.36	66.96	41.03	293.55
21.	Minnesota	141	4,009.9	35.2	2.09	1.84	50.45	68.80	3.85	92.83
22.	Colorado	98	2,719.2	36.0	1.45	1.25	51.90	70.05	1.81	64.88
23.	Utah	48	1,304.8	36.8	0.71	0.60	52.61	70.65	0.43	31.57
24.	Louisiana	147	3,974.8	37.0	2.18	1.82	54.79	72.47	3.97	99.72
25.	Montana	29	777.0	37.3	0.43	0.36	55.22	72.83	0.15	19.88
26.	Oklahoma	110	2,855.3	38.5	1.63	1.31	56.85	74.14	2.14	74.47
27.	Wisconsin	181	4,695.9	38.5	2.68	2.15	59.53	76.29	5.76	127.99
28.	Kansas	93	2,342.4	39.7	1.38	1.07	60.91	77.36	1.48	65.17
29.	Nevada	28	670.5	41.7	0.42	0.31	61.33	77.67	0.13	19.01
30.	Oregon	104	2,430.1	42.8	1.54	1.11	62.87	78.78	1.71	69.79

TABLE 2 (Continued)

Lp.	State	General Number of Radio Stations[x]	U.S. Population in 1979[xx] in millions	No. of radio stations per 1 million residents[xxx]	Structure a	Structure b	Cumulative Columns[xxx] a′	Cumulative Columns[xxx] b′	Calculations[xxx] ab	Calculations[xxx] a′b
31.	Alaska	18	414.2	43.5	0.27	0.19	63.14	78.97	0.05	12.00
32.	Nebraska	69	1,576.8	43.5	1.02	0.72	64.16	79.69	0.73	46.20
33.	Iowa	129	2,892.4	44.6	1.91	1.33	66.07	81.02	2.54	87.87
34.	Idaho	42	889.1	47.2	0.62	0.41	66.69	81.43	0.25	27.34
35.	New Mexico	59	1,218.9	48.4	0.87	0.56	67.56	81.99	0.49	37.83
36.	North Carolina	288	5,622.8	51.2	4.27	2.58	71.83	84.57	11.02	185.32
37.	Georgia	264	5,145.7	51.3	3.91	2.36	75.74	86.93	9.23	178.75
38.	New Hampshire	45	868.2	51.8	0.67	0.40	76.41	87.33	0.27	30.56
39.	Tennessee	230	4,359.5	52.8	3.41	2.00	79.82	89.33	6.82	159.64
40.	Vermont	26	490.0	53.1	0.39	0.22	80.21	89.55	0.09	17.65
41.	Alabama	204	3,739.4	54.6	3.02	1.71	83.23	91.26	5.16	142.32
42.	South Carolina	163	2,929.3	55.7	2.42	1.34	85.65	92.60	3.24	114.77
43.	Kentucky	197	3,511.2	56.1	2.92	1.61	88.57	94.21	4.70	142.60
44.	Arkansas	123	2,188.4	56.2	0.18	1.00	88.75	95.21	0.18	88.75
45.	Virginia	297	5,219.4	56.9	4.40	2.39	93.15	97.60	10.52	222.63
46.	South Dakota	40	691.8	57.8	0.59	0.32	93.74	97.92	0.19	30.00
47.	North Dakota	39	666.9	58.5	0.58	0.31	94.32	98.23	0.18	29.24
48.	Maine	73	1,105.9	66.0	1.08	0.51	95.40	98.74	0.55	48.65
49.	Mississippi	164	2,420.0	67.8	2.43	1.11	97.83	99.85	2.70	108.59
50.	Wyoming	33	423.4	78.0	0.49	0.19	98.32	100.04	0.09	18.68
	TOTALS	6,744	218,220.0		98.32	100.04			322.55	3,775.14

Sources: x, xx, Spot Radio Rates and Data. Standard Rate Data Service Inc., Skokie, January 1, 1980.
xxx Personal Calculations

CHAPTER 4

Radio Stations Airing Polish Radio Programs

Radio Stations Broadcasting Polish Programs in Arizona

1. Radio Station KTUC-AM
   1511 East 16th Street
   Tuscon, Arizona

   One hour weekly

   Only one radio station broadcast Polish programs in Arizona.

   Total number of hours of Polish programming:

   One hour weekly.

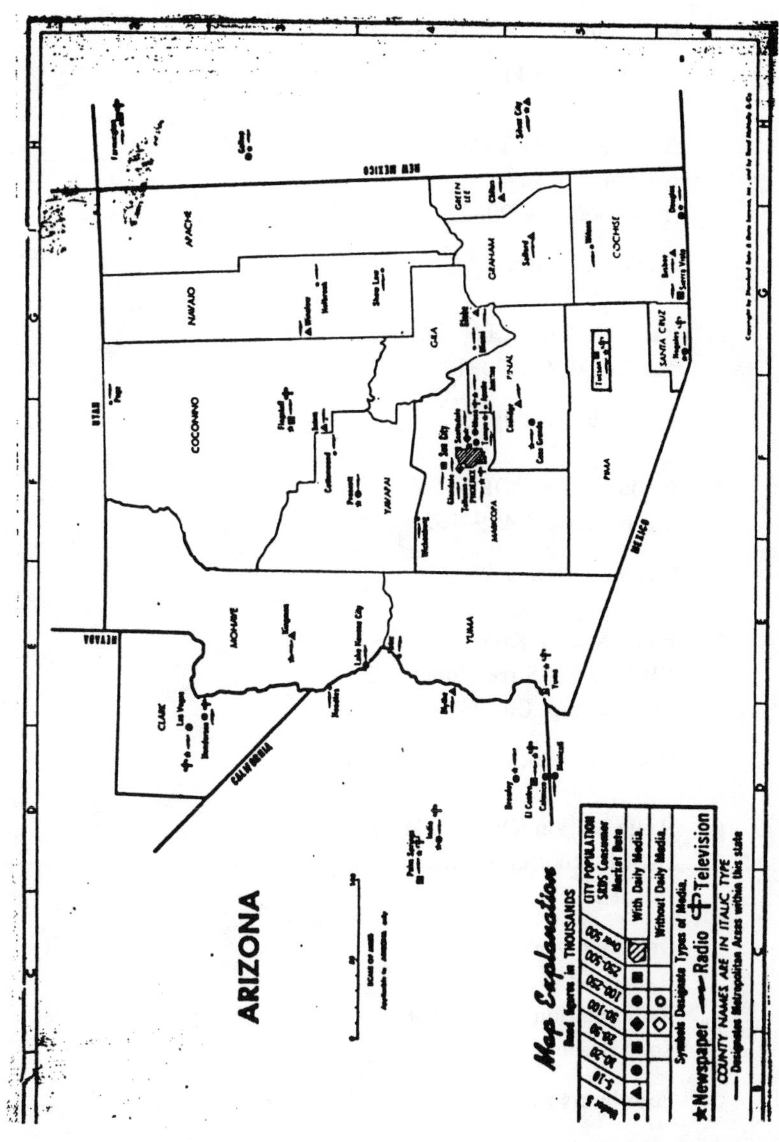
ARIZONA
Map Explanation
CITY POPULATION
With Daily Media.
Without Daily Media.
Symbols Designate Types of Media.
Newspaper
Radio
Television
COUNTY NAMES ARE IN ITALIC TYPE
UTAH
NEVADA
CALIFORNIA
NEW MEXICO
MEXICO
CLARK
MOHAVE
COCONINO
NAVAJO
APACHE
YAVAPAI
GILA
GRAHAM
GREENLEE
MARICOPA
PINAL
PIMA
SANTA CRUZ
COCHISE
YUMA

Radio Stations Broadcasting Polish Programs in California

1. Radio Station KKUP–FM
   Cupertino, CA 95014

   Two hours weekly

2. Radio Station KTYM
   6803 West Blvd.
   Inglewood, CA 90802

   One hour weekly

3. Radio Station KCEN–FM
   Northridge, CA 90913

   Two hours weekly

4. Radio Station KQED–FM
   San Francisco, CA 94103

   One hour weekly

5. Radio Station KBRG–FM
   1355 Market Street, Suite 152
   San Francisco, CA 94103

   One hour weekly

6. Radio Station KMAX–FM ARCADIA
   3844 E. Roothill Blvd.
   Pasadena, CA 91107

   One hour weekly

7. Radio Station KLON–FM
   Long Beach, CA

   Four hours weekly

Radio Stations Broadcasting Polish Programs in California
(cont.)

8. Radio Station KLIT
Pomona, CA

One hour weekly

Eight radio stations broadcast Polish programs in California.

Total number of hours of Polish programming:

13 hours weekly

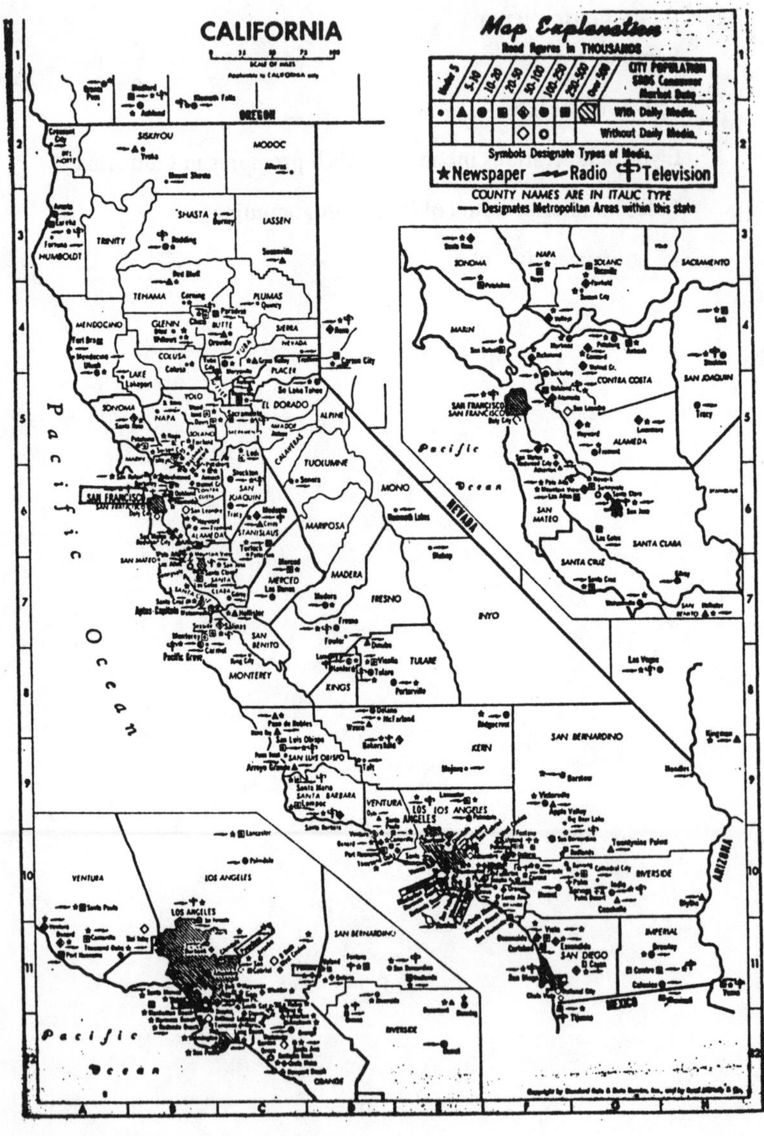

CALIFORNIA
Map Explanation
Read figures in THOUSANDS
CITY POPULATION
SRDS Consumer
Market Data
With Daily Media.
Without Daily Media.
Symbols Designate Types of Media.
★Newspaper
Radio
Television
COUNTY NAMES ARE IN ITALIC TYPE
— Designates Metropolitan Areas within this state
OREGON
NEVADA
ARIZONA
MEXICO
Pacific Ocean
SISKIYOU
MODOC
SHASTA
LASSEN
TRINITY
HUMBOLDT
TEHAMA
PLUMAS
GLENN
BUTTE
MENDOCINO
SIERRA
NEVADA
COLUSA
PLACER
LAKE
YOLO
EL DORADO
SONOMA
NAPA
ALPINE
SAN FRANCISCO
TUOLUMNE
MONO
SAN JOAQUIN
STANISLAUS
MARIPOSA
SAN MATEO
MADERA
MERCED
FRESNO
INYO
SAN BENITO
MONTEREY
TULARE
KINGS
KERN
SAN BERNARDINO
SAN LUIS OBISPO
SANTA BARBARA
VENTURA
LOS ANGELES
RIVERSIDE
SAN DIEGO
IMPERIAL
MARIN
CONTRA COSTA
ALAMEDA
SANTA CLARA
SANTA CRUZ
SACRAMENTO
ORANGE

Radio Stations Broadcasting Polish Programs in Colorado

1. Radio Station KLMO
   Longmont–Boulder, CO

   One hour weekly

   Only one radio station broadcasts Polish programs in Colorado.

   Total number of hours of Polish programming:

   One hour weekly

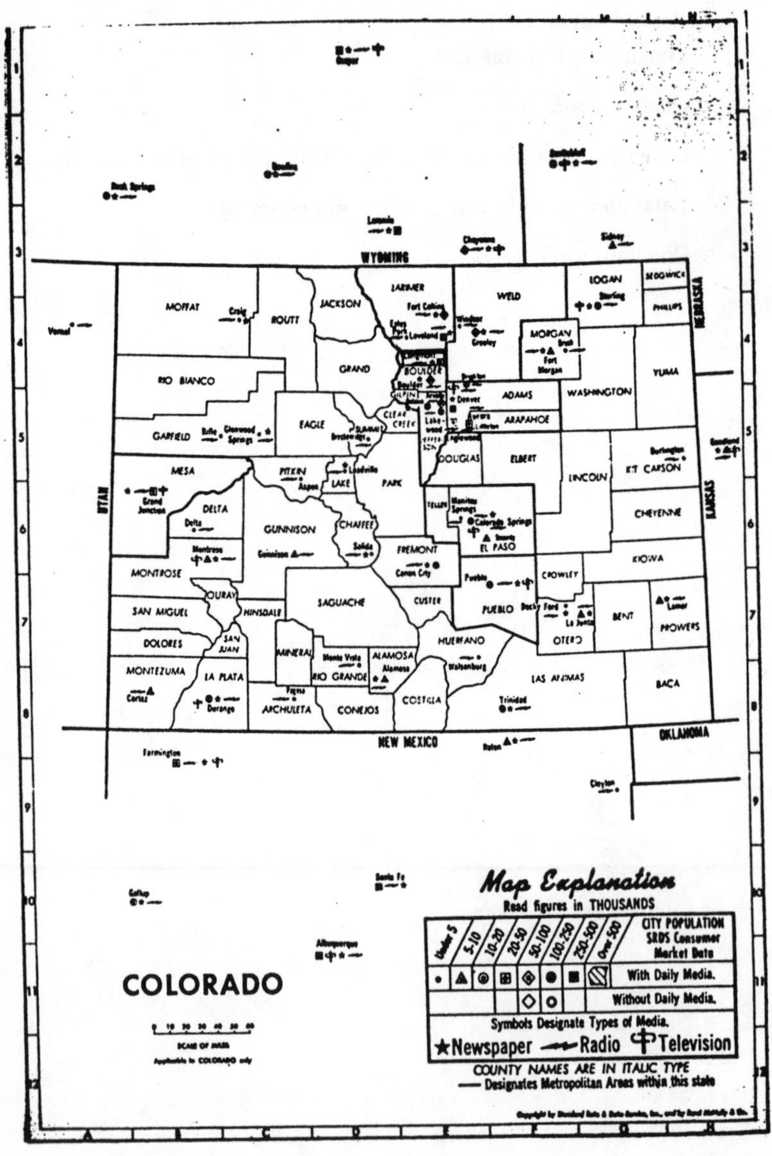
WYOMING
NEBRASKA
KANSAS
OKLAHOMA
NEW MEXICO
UTAH
MOFFAT
ROUTT
JACKSON
LARIMER
WELD
LOGAN
SEDGWICK
PHILLIPS
MORGAN
GRAND
BOULDER
RIO BLANCO
ADAMS
WASHINGTON
YUMA
GARFIELD
EAGLE
CLEAR CREEK
ARAPAHOE
MESA
PITKIN
LAKE
PARK
DOUGLAS
ELBERT
LINCOLN
KIT CARSON
DELTA
GUNNISON
CHAFFEE
TELLER
EL PASO
CHEYENNE
MONTROSE
FREMONT
CROWLEY
KIOWA
OURAY
SAGUACHE
CUSTER
PUEBLO
BENT
PROWERS
SAN MIGUEL
HINSDALE
HUERFANO
OTERO
DOLORES
SAN JUAN
MINERAL
ALAMOSA
MONTEZUMA
LA PLATA
RIO GRANDE
LAS ANIMAS
BACA
ARCHULETA
CONEJOS
COSTILLA
COLORADO
SCALE OF MILES
Applicable to COLORADO only
Map Explanation
Read figures in THOUSANDS
Under 5
5-10
10-20
20-50
50-100
100-250
250-500
Over 500
CITY POPULATION SRDS Consumer Market Data
With Daily Media.
Without Daily Media.
Symbols Designate Types of Media.
★Newspaper Radio Television
COUNTY NAMES ARE IN ITALIC TYPE
— Designates Metropolitan Areas within this state

Radio Stations Broadcasting Polish Programs in Connecticut

1. Radio Station WADS
366 Main St.
Ansonia, CT 06401
One hour weekly

2. Radio Station WBIS
1021 Farmington Ave.
Bristol, CT 06010
Two hours weekly

3. Radio Station WVOF-FM
Box R
Fairfield, CT 06430
Two hours weekly

4. Radio Station WGCH
Box 1490, 1490 Dayton Ave.
Greenwich, CT 06830
One and a half hours weekly

5. Radio Station WSUB
1064 Powuonock Road
Groton, CT 06340
Two and a half hours weekly

6. Radio Station WCCC
11 Asylum Street
Hartford, CT 06103
One hour weekly

7. Radio Station WMMW
21 Colony St.
Meriden, CT 06450
Two hours weekly

8. Radio Station WCNX
Box 359 River Road
Middleton, CT 06457
Two hours weekly

9. Radio Station WMNR
Monroe, CT 06468
Two hours weekly

10. Radio Station WRYM
1056 Willard Ave.
Newington, CT 06111
12 hours weekly

11. Radio Station WHAY
New Britain, CT
One hour weekly

12. Radio Station WSTC
117 Prospect St.
Stamford, CT 06901
One hour weekly

13. Radio Station WIOF-FM
Box 2719
Waterbury, CT 06720
Two and a half hours weekly

14. Radio Station WILI
Box 496
Quillimatic, CT 06226
Two hours weekly

15. Radio Station WSOR
Windsor, CT

One hour weekly

16. Radio Station WATR
1 Broadcast Lane
Waterbury, CT 06702

Two and a half hours weekly

17. Radio Station WNHC
129 College St.
New Haven, CT 06510

One hour weekly

18. Radio Station WICH
Box 551
Norwich, CT 06360

One hour weekly

19. Radio Station WEXT
West Hartford, CT 06107

One-half hour weekly

20. Radio Station WMLB
630 Oakwood Ave.
West Hartford, CT 06110

Three hours weekly

Twenty radio stations broadcast Polish programs in Connecticut.

Total number of hours of Polish programming:

43½ hours weekly

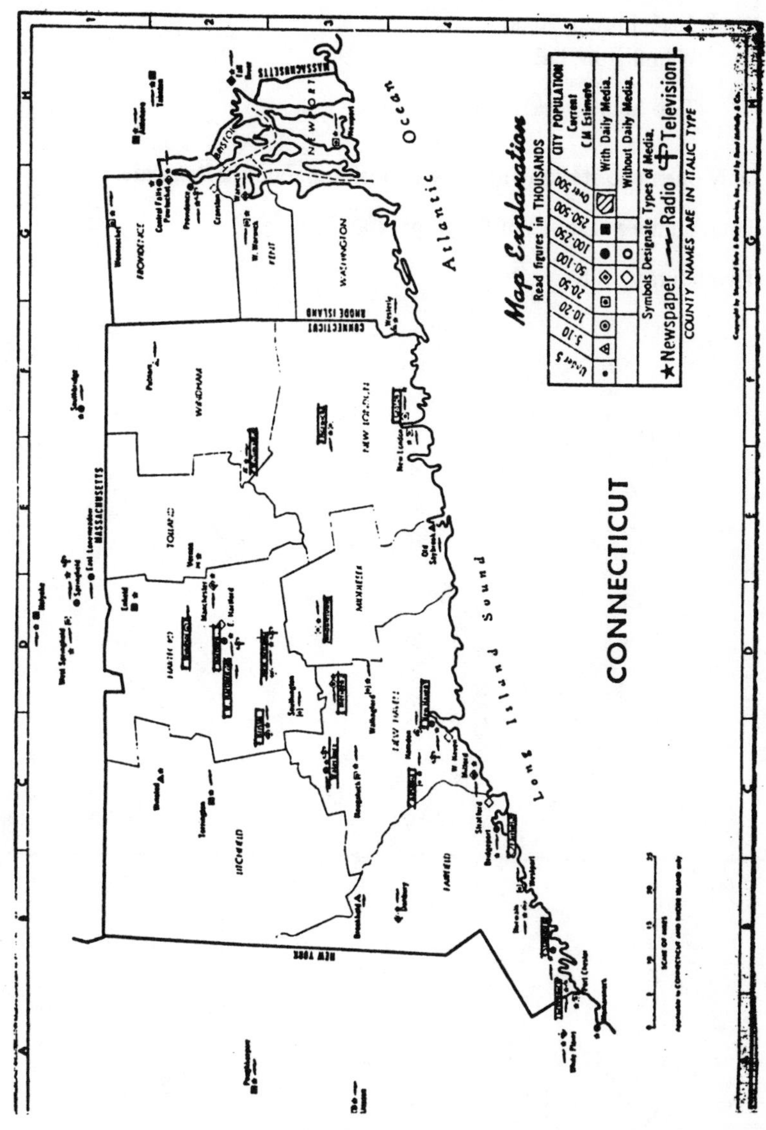
CONNECTICUT
Map Explanation
Read figures in THOUSANDS
CITY POPULATION
Current
CM Estimate
With Daily Media.
Without Daily Media.
Symbols Designate Types of Media.
★Newspaper —Radio Television
COUNTY NAMES ARE IN ITALIC TYPE
Atlantic Ocean
Long Island Sound
MASSACHUSETTS
RHODE ISLAND
CONNECTICUT
NEW YORK

Radio Stations Broadcasting Polish Programs in Delaware

1. Radio Station WJBR
   2617 Ebright Road
   Wilmington, DE 19810

   Two hours weekly

Only one radio station broadcasts Polish programs in Delaware.

Total number of hours of Polish programming:

Two hours weekly

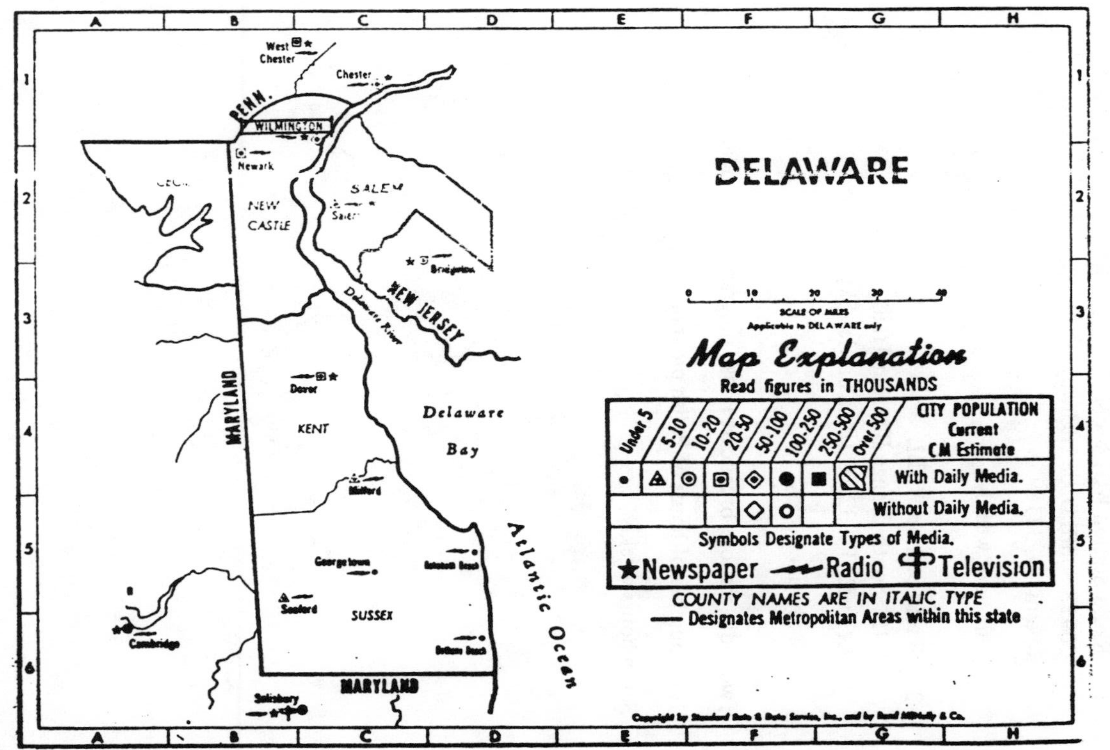
DELAWARE
SCALE OF MILES
Applicable to DELAWARE only
Map Explanation
Read figures in THOUSANDS
CITY POPULATION
Current
C M Estimate
Under 5
5-10
10-20
20-50
50-100
100-250
250-500
Over 500
With Daily Media.
Without Daily Media.
Symbols Designate Types of Media.
Newspaper
Radio
Television
COUNTY NAMES ARE IN ITALIC TYPE
— Designates Metropolitan Areas within this state
Atlantic Ocean
Delaware Bay
NEW JERSEY
Delaware River
MARYLAND
MARYLAND
PENN.
WILMINGTON
Newark
NEW CASTLE
West Chester
Chester
SALEM
Salem
Bridgeton
KENT
Dover
Milford
SUSSEX
Georgetown
Seaford
Salisbury
Cambridge

Radio Stations Broadcasting Polish Programs in Florida

1. Radio Station WGLY-FM
   20938 South Dixie Highway
   Miami, FL 33189

   One hour weekly

2. Radio Station WHBL
   8421 South Orange Blossom Trail
   Orlando, FL 32809 (Pine Castle–Skylake)

   Six hours weekly

Two radio stations broadcast Polish programs in Florida.

Total number of hours of Polish programming:

Seven hours weekly

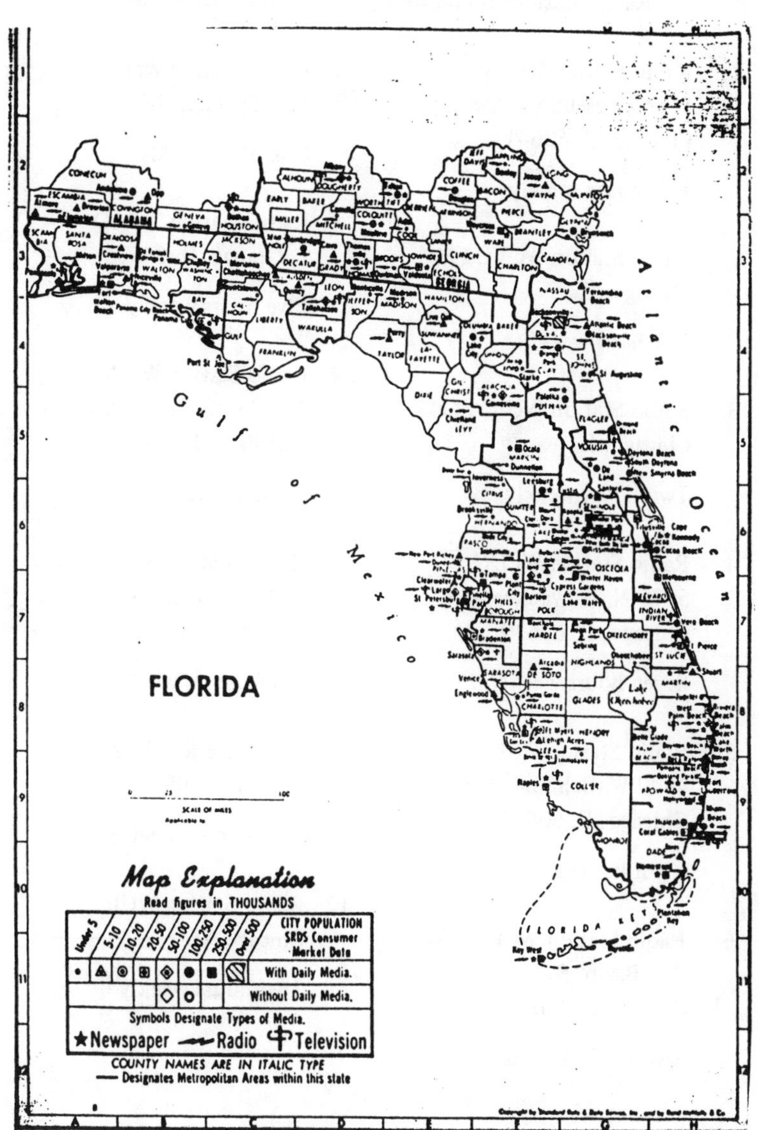
FLORIDA
Gulf of Mexico
Atlantic Ocean
Map Explanation
Read figures in THOUSANDS
Under 5
5-10
10-20
20-50
50-100
100-250
250-500
Over 500
CITY POPULATION SRDS Consumer Market Data
With Daily Media.
Without Daily Media.
Symbols Designate Types of Media.
★Newspaper Radio Television
COUNTY NAMES ARE IN ITALIC TYPE
— Designates Metropolitan Areas within this state
FLORIDA KEYS
Key West
A
B
C
D
E
F
G
H

Radio Stations Broadcasting Polish Programs in Illinois

1. Radio Station WCEV
5356 W. Belmont Ave.
Chicago, IL 60641

15½ hours weekly

2. Radio Station WCYC-FM
Chicago, IL

One hour weekly

3. Radio Station WUIC-FM
Chicago, IL

Two hours weekly

4. Radio Station WEDC
5475 N. Milwaukee Ave.
Chicago, IL 60630

Seven hours weekly

5. Radio Station WSBC
4949 W. Belmont Ave.
Chicago, IL 60641

Eight hours weekly

6. Radio Station WCBW-FM
211 Beaird St.
Columbia, IL 62236

Two hours weekly

7. Radio Station WMRY
East St. Louis 622

One hour weekly

8. Radio Station WTAQ
LaGrange, IL 60525

Five hours weekly

9. Radio Station WOPA
408 South Oak Park Ave.
Oak Park, IL 60203

13 hours weekly

10. Radio Station WIVQ-FM
1727½ Fourth Street
Peru, IL 61354

Three hours weekly

11. Radio Station WKZN
Zion, IL 60099

Three hours weekly

12. Radio Station WUIC
Chicago, IL

Two hours weekly

Twenty radio stations broadcast Polish programs in Illinois.

Total number of hours of Polish programming:

60½ hours weekly

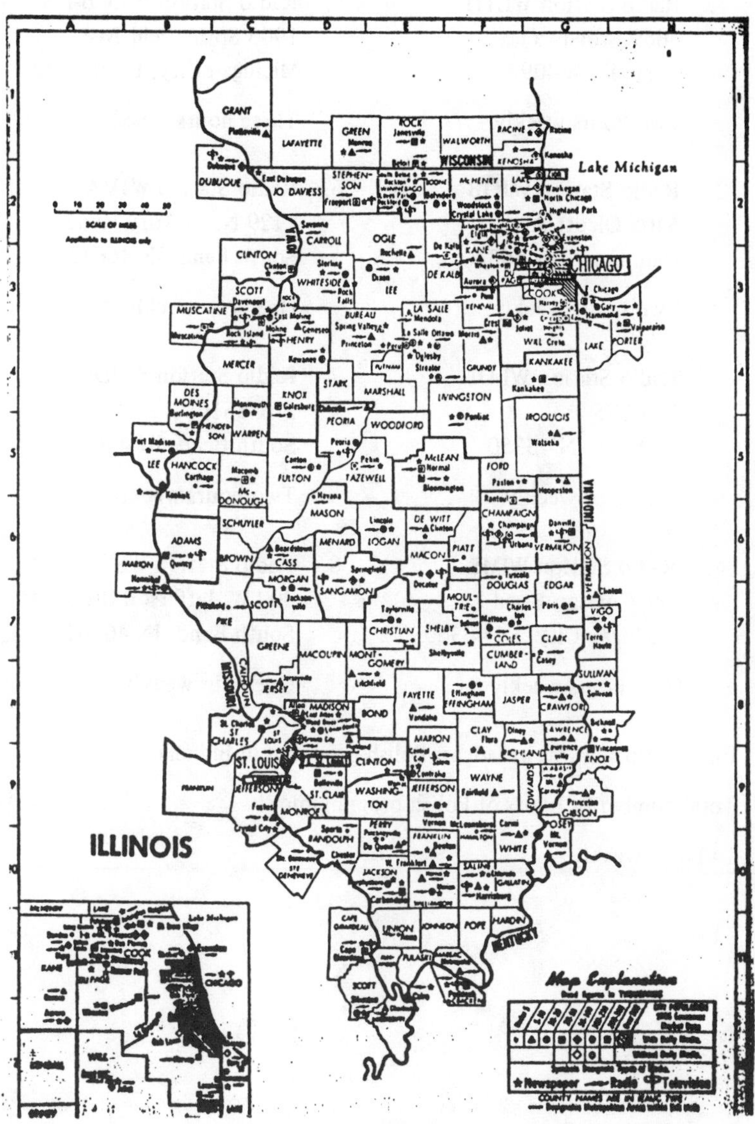
ILLINOIS
Lake Michigan
CHICAGO
WISCONSIN
INDIANA
KENTUCKY
MISSOURI
ST. LOUIS
GRANT
LAFAYETTE
GREEN
ROCK
WALWORTH
RACINE
KENOSHA
DUBUQUE
JO DAVIESS
STEPHENSON
McHENRY
LAKE
CARROLL
OGLE
CLINTON
SCOTT
WHITESIDE
LEE
DE KALB
KANE
COOK
MUSCATINE
BUREAU
HENRY
LA SALLE
MERCER
KANKAKEE
WILL
KNOX
STARK
MARSHALL
LIVINGSTON
IROQUOIS
PEORIA
WOODFORD
DES MOINES
WARREN
HANCOCK
FULTON
TAZEWELL
McLEAN
FORD
MASON
SCHUYLER
DE WITT
CHAMPAIGN
VERMILION
ADAMS
BROWN
CASS
MENARD
LOGAN
MACON
PIATT
MARION
MORGAN
SANGAMON
DOUGLAS
EDGAR
SCOTT
PIKE
CHRISTIAN
SHELBY
COLES
CLARK
VIGO
GREENE
MACOUPIN
MONTGOMERY
CUMBERLAND
JERSEY
FAYETTE
EFFINGHAM
JASPER
CRAWFORD
SULLIVAN
MADISON
BOND
ST. CHARLES
CLAY
RICHLAND
LAWRENCE
KNOX
CLINTON
MARION
WAYNE
JEFFERSON
WASHINGTON
ST. CLAIR
MONROE
GIBSON
POSEY
RANDOLPH
PERRY
FRANKLIN
WHITE
JACKSON
SALINE
GALLATIN
UNION
JOHNSON
POPE
HARDIN
PULASKI
Map Explanation
Newspaper
Radio
Television

Radio Stations Broadcasting Polish Programs in Indiana

1. Radio Station WLTH
   3669 Broadway
   Gary, IN 46409

   Two hours weekly

2. Radio Station WJOB
   6405 Olcott Ave.
   Hammond, IN 46320

   Two hours weekly

3. Radio Station WLOI
   Box 385
   LaPorte, IN 46350

   One hour weekly

4. Radio Station WIMS
   Old Chicago Road
   Michigan City, IN 46360

   Two hours weekly

5. Radio Station WMCB-FM
   1903 Springfield Ave.
   Michigan City, IN 46360

   Three hours weekly

6. Radio Station WJVA
   1129 N. Hickory Road
   South Bend, IN 46615

   One hour weekly

7. Radio Station WNDU
   Box 1616
   South Bend, IN 46624

   Two hours weekly

8. Radio Station WSBT
   300 W. Jefferson Blvd.
   South Bend, IN 46601

   One hour weekly

Eight radio stations broadcast Polish programs in Indiana.

Total number of hours of Polish programming:

14 hours weekly

Lake Michigan
CHICAGO
INDIANA
MICHIGAN
ILLINOIS
OHIO
KENTUCKY
Map Explanation
Read figures in THOUSANDS
Under 5
5-10
10-20
20-50
50-100
100-250
250-500
Over 500
CITY POPULATION
SRDS Consumer
Market Data
With Daily Media.
Without Daily Media.
Symbols Designate Types of Media.
★Newspaper
Radio
Television
COUNTY NAMES ARE IN ITALIC TYPE
— Designates Metropolitan Areas within this state

Radio Stations Broadcasting Polish Programs in Iowa

1. Radio Station KRCB
   Box 586
   Council Bluffs, IA 51501

   Four hours weekly

Only one radio station broadcasts Polish programs in Iowa.

Total number of hours of Polish programming:

Four hours weekly

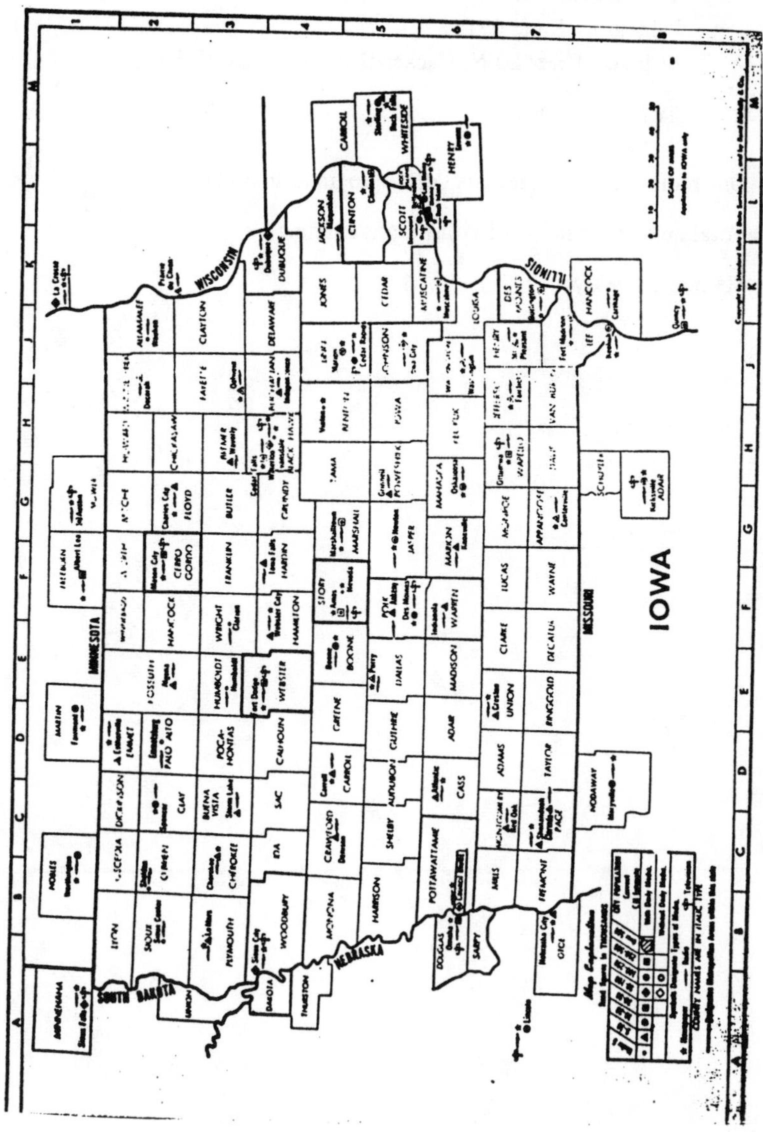
IOWA
MINNESOTA
WISCONSIN
ILLINOIS
MISSOURI
NEBRASKA
SOUTH DAKOTA

Radio Stations Broadcasting Polish Programs in Kansas

1. Radio Station KLEY
   Wellington, Kan., 67152
   Business office: 20 N. Wacker Drive, Chicago, IL 60606

   Six hours weekly

One radio station broadcasts Polish programs in Kansas.

Total number of hours of Polish programming:

Six hours weekly

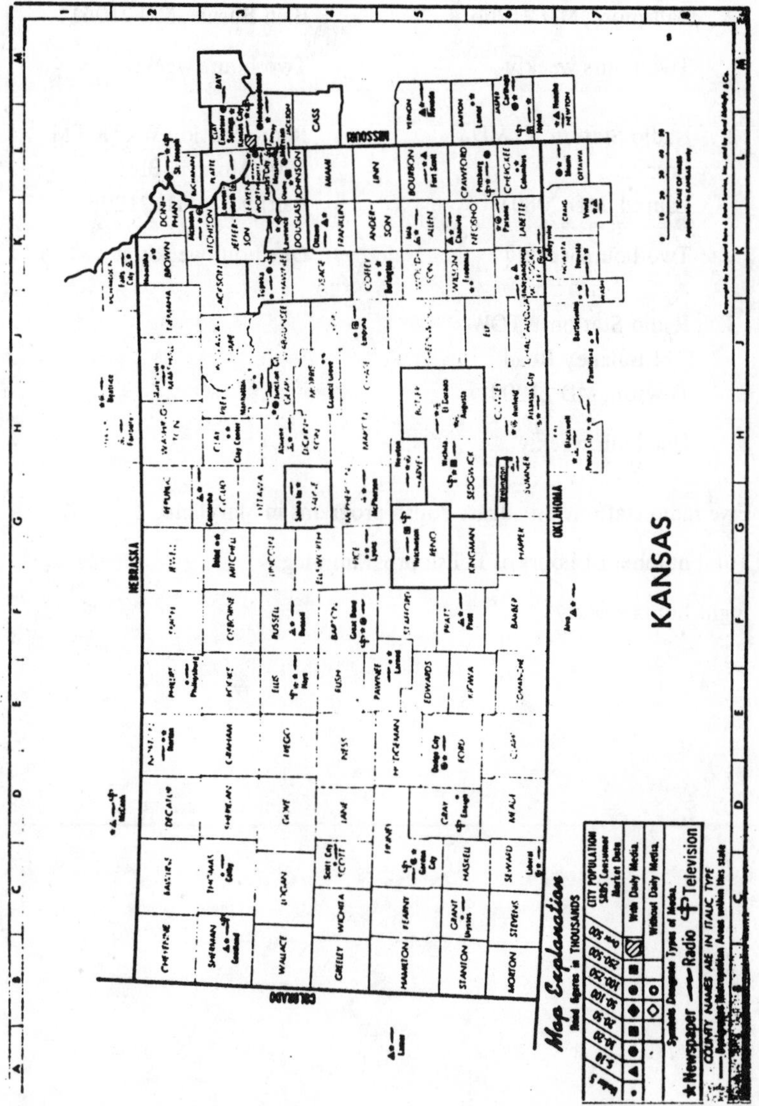
KANSAS
NEBRASKA
OKLAHOMA
MISSOURI
COLORADO
Map Explanation
Newspaper
Radio
Television

Radio Stations Broadcasting Polish Programs in Maryland

1. Radio Station WBMD
   5200 Moravia Blvd.
   Baltimore, MD 21206

   Two hours weekly

2. Radio Station WLMD
   Box 42
   Laurell, MD 20801

   Two hours weekly

3. Radio Station WTOW
   724 Bulaney Road
   Towson, MD 21204

   One hour weekly

4. Radio Station WJRO
   Box 159
   Blen Burnie, MD 21061

   Two hours weekly

5. Radio Station WKTK-FM
   5200 Moravia Blvd.
   Baltimore, MD 21206

   One hour weekly

Five radio stations broadcast Polish programs in Maryland.

Total number of hours of Polish programming:

Eight hours weekly

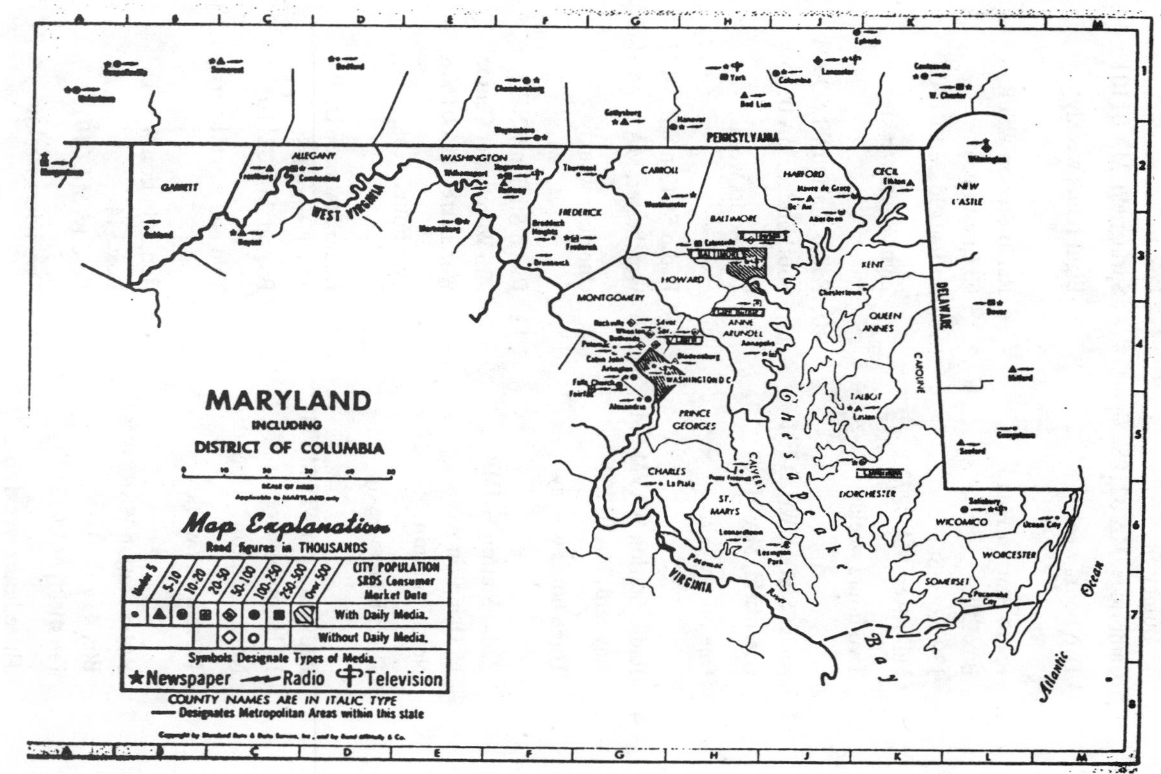
MARYLAND
INCLUDING
DISTRICT OF COLUMBIA
Map Explanation
Read figures in THOUSANDS
Under 5
5-10
10-20
20-50
50-100
100-250
250-500
Over 500
CITY POPULATION
SRDS Consumer
Market Data
With Daily Media.
Without Daily Media.
Symbols Designate Types of Media.
★Newspaper —Radio Television
COUNTY NAMES ARE IN ITALIC TYPE
— Designates Metropolitan Areas within this state
PENNSYLVANIA
DELAWARE
NEW CASTLE
WEST VIRGINIA
VIRGINIA
GARRETT
ALLEGANY
WASHINGTON
FREDERICK
CARROLL
BALTIMORE
HARFORD
CECIL
KENT
QUEEN ANNES
CAROLINE
TALBOT
DORCHESTER
WICOMICO
WORCESTER
SOMERSET
HOWARD
MONTGOMERY
ANNE ARUNDEL
PRINCE GEORGES
CALVERT
CHARLES
ST. MARYS
WASHINGTON D.C.
Chesapeake Bay
Potomac River
Atlantic Ocean

Radio Stations Broadcasting Polish Programs in Massachusetts

1. Radio Station WHRB
45 Quincy St.
Cambridge, MA 02138

   Two hours weekly

2. Radio Station WALE
Box 208
130 Rock St.
Fall River, MA 02722

   Two hours weekly

3. Radio Station WHAI-FM
Greenfield, MA 01301

   One hour weekly

4. Radio Station WAVM-FM
Maynard, MA 01754

   Three hours weekly

5. Radio Station WHMP
15 Hampton Ave.
Northhampton, MA 01060

   Three hours weekly

6. Radio Station WHPM-FM
15 Hampton Ave.
Northhampton, MA 01060

   Three hours weekly

7. Radio Station WBRK-FM
Box 413
Fittsfield, MA 01211

   Three hours weekly

8. Radio Station WACE
Box 1
Springfield, MA 01101

   Eight hours weekly

9. Radio Station WSPR
63 Chestnut St.
Springfield, MA 01303

   Eight hours weekly

10. Radio Station WESO-FM
Southbridge, MA 01550

    Two hours weekly

11. Radio Station WICN-FM
Worchester, MA

    One hour weekly

12. Radio Station WNEB
236 Worchester Center
Worchester, MA 01608

    Two hours weekly

13. Radio Station WUNR
275 Tremont St.
Boston, MA 02116

    Two and a half hours weekly

14. Radio Station WBVD
Box 344
Beverly, MA 01915

    Two hours weekly

15. Radio Station WLDM
249 Union St.
Westfield, MA 01085

One and a half hours weekly

16. Radio Station WMYS-FM
737 County St.
New Bedford, MA 02740

Two hours weekly

17. Radio Station WBET
60 Main St.
Brockton, MA 20431

One and a half hours weekly

18. Radio Station WREB
Box 507
560 Dwight St.
Holyokh, MA 01040

Two hours weekly

Eighteen radio stations broadcast Polish programs in Massachusetts.

Total number of hours of Polish programming:

49½ hours weekly

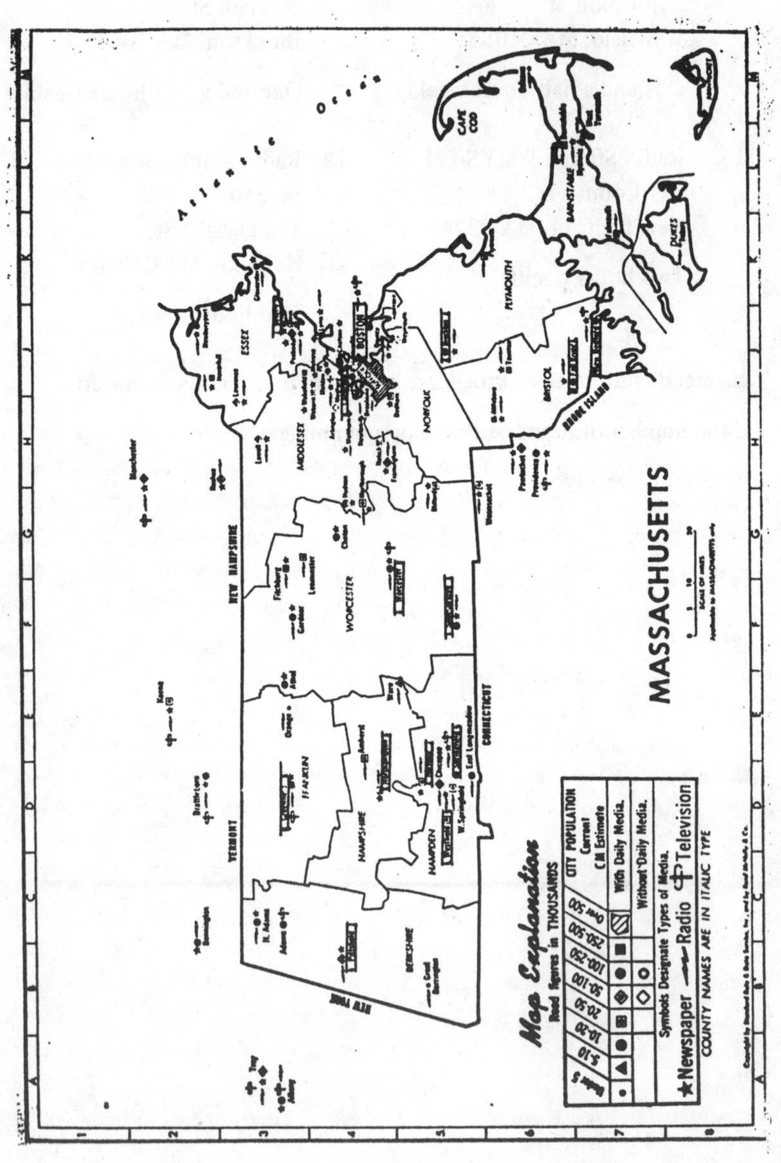
MASSACHUSETTS
Atlantic Ocean
CAPE COD
BOSTON
ESSEX
MIDDLESEX
NORFOLK
PLYMOUTH
BRISTOL
BARNSTABLE
DUKES
WORCESTER
FRANKLIN
HAMPSHIRE
HAMPDEN
BERKSHIRE
NEW HAMPSHIRE
VERMONT
NEW YORK
CONNECTICUT
RHODE ISLAND
Map Explanation
Road figures in THOUSANDS
CITY POPULATION Current C.M. Estimate
Under 5
5-10
10-20
20-50
50-100
100-250
250-500
Over 500
With Daily Media.
Without Daily Media.
Symbols Designate Types of Media.
Newspaper
Radio
Television
COUNTY NAMES ARE IN ITALIC TYPE

Radio Stations Broadcasting Polish Programs in Michigan

1. Radio Station WATZ
   Alpena, MI 49707

   Two hours weekly

2. Radio Station WLEW
   Bad Axe, MI 48413

   Two hours weekly

3. Radio Station WMZK-FM
   2010 Woodward Tower
   Detroit, MI 48226

   One hour weekly

4. Radio Station WFDF
   Flint, MI 48502

   One hour weekly

5. Radio Station WIID
   325 Park Lane
   Garden City, MI 48135

   Nine hours weekly

6. Radio Station WATC
   Gaylord, MI 49735

   Four hours weekly

7. Radio Station WEHB-FM
   Grand Rapids, MI

   Three hours weekly

8. Radio Station WIKB
   I. R. National Bank Building
   Iron River, MI 49935

   Five hours weekly

9. Radio Station WIBM
   Box 1450-2511 Kibby Road
   Jackson, MI 49204

   Two hours weekly

10. Radio Station WHAK
    Rogers City, MI 49779

    Five hours weekly

11. Radio Station WMIC
    Snadusky, MI 48471

    Four hours weekly

12. Radio Station WJOR
    South Haven, MI 49090

    Two hours weekly

13. Radio Station WSTR
    Sturgis, MI 49091

    Four hours weekly

14. Radio Station WBMB
    P. O. Box 85
    West Branch, MI 48661

    Two hours weekly

15. Radio Station WDJD
161 W. Michigan City Hall
Jackson, MI 49201

One hour weekly

16. Radio Station WQRS-FM
1200 Sixth Avenue
Detroit, MI 48226

One hour weekly

17. Radio Station WKCQ-FM
Box 1776
200 Whittier
Saginaw, MI 48605

Nine hours weekly

Seventeen radio stations broadcast Polish programs in Michigan.

Total number of hours of Polish programming:

57 hours weekly

Map Explanation
Road figures in THOUSANDS
Under 5
5-10
10-20
20-50
50-100
100-250
250-500
Over 500
CITY POPULATION
SRDS Consumer Market Data
With Daily Media.
Without Daily Media.
Symbols Designate Types of Media.
★Newspaper
Radio
Television
COUNTY NAMES ARE IN ITALIC TYPE
— Designates Metropolitan Areas within this state
Lake Superior
MICHIGAN
Lake Michigan
Lake Huron
WISCONSIN
ONTONAGON
GOGEBIC
HOUGHTON
BARAGA
IRON
MARQUETTE
ALGER
SCHOOL-CRAFT
LUCE
CHIPPEWA
MACKINAC
DELTA
MENOMINEE
DICKINSON
Marquette
Ishpeming
Iron Mountain
Kingsford
Escanaba
Menominee
Marinette
Newberry
Manistique
St. Ignace
Sault Ste Marie
EMMET
CHEBOYGAN
PRESQUE ISLE
CHARLEVOIX
Petoskey
Cheboygan
ANTRIM
OTSEGO
MONTMORENCY
ALPENA
LEELANAU
BENZIE
GRAND TRAVERSE
Traverse City
KALKASKA
CRAWFORD
Grayling
OSCODA
ALCONA
MANISTEE
Manistee
WEXFORD
Cadillac
MISSAUKEE
ROSCOMMON
Houghton Lake
OGEMAW
IOSCO
Tawas City
ARENAC
MASON
Ludington
LAKE
OSCEOLA
CLARE
HURON
Bad Axe
OCEANA
NEWAYGO
MECOSTA
Big Rapids
Mount Pleasant
ISABELLA
Midland
TUSCOLA
SANILAC
Fremont
MONTCALM
Alma
SAGINAW
Muskegon
Whitehall
KENT
Greenville
GENESEE
LAPEER
ST. CLAIR
Port Huron
Grand Haven
Rockford
Grand Rapids
IONIA
Ionia
St. Johns
CLINTON
OTTAWA
Holland
Wyoming
OAKLAND
Pontiac
Birmingham
Royal Oak
MACOMB
Mt. Clemens
St. Clair Shores
ALLEGAN
Hastings
BARRY
Charlotte
EATON
Lansing
East Lansing
DETROIT
WAYNE
Garden City
Inkster
Dearborn
Lincoln Park
Battle Creek
Marshall
Albion
Kalamazoo
KALAMAZOO
Portage
CALHOUN
JACKSON
Ann Arbor
Ypsilanti
Windsor
CANADA
Benton Harbor
St. Joseph
VAN BUREN
BERRIEN
Niles
CASS
Dowagiac
ST. JOSEPH
Three Rivers
BRANCH
Coldwater
HILLSDALE
Hillsdale
LENAWEE
Adrian
MONROE
Monroe
Michigan City
La Porte
South Bend
Elkhart
Goshen
INDIANA
Bryan
OHIO
Toledo
SCALE OF MILES
A B C D E F G H
1 2 3 4 5 6 7 8 9 10 11 12

Radio Stations Broadcasting Polish Programs in Minnesota

1. Radio Station WKLK-FM
   15 Tenth Street
   Cloquet, MN 55720

   One hour weekly

2. Radio Station KUXL-AM
   5730 Duluth Street
   Minneapolis, MN 55422

   One hour weekly

Two radio stations broad Polish programs in Minnesota.

Total number of hours of Polish programming:

Two hours weekly

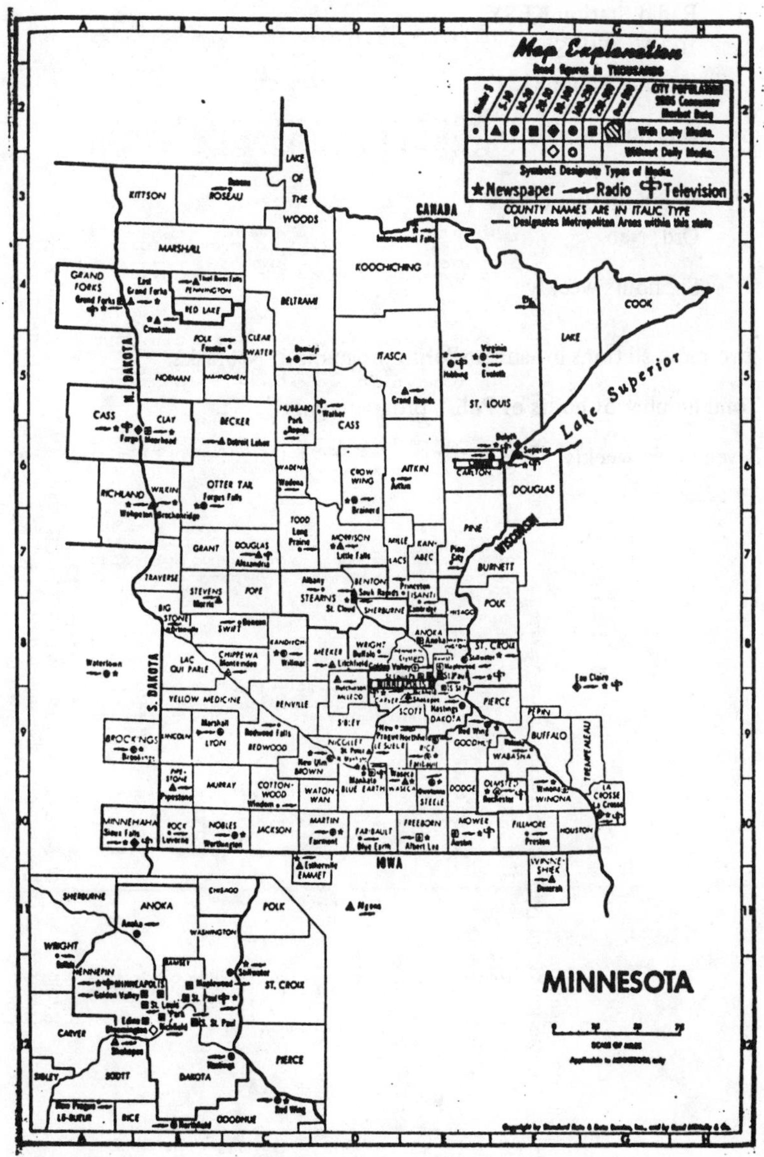
Map Explanation
Newspaper
Radio
Television
COUNTY NAMES ARE IN ITALIC TYPE
CANADA
KITTSON
ROSEAU
LAKE OF THE WOODS
MARSHALL
KOOCHICHING
GRAND FORKS
BELTRAMI
COOK
LAKE
ITASCA
ST. LOUIS
Lake Superior
CASS
CLAY
BECKER
AITKIN
CARLTON
DOUGLAS
OTTER TAIL
RICHLAND
WILKIN
CROW WING
PINE
GRANT
DOUGLAS
BURNETT
TRAVERSE
STEVENS
POPE
STEARNS
BENTON
POLK
ANOKA
ST. CROIX
LAC QUI PARLE
CHIPPEWA
YELLOW MEDICINE
RENVILLE
PIERCE
S. DAKOTA
N. DAKOTA
BROOKINGS
LYON
BUFFALO
MURRAY
COTTONWOOD
WATONWAN
BLUE EARTH
DODGE
STEELE
WINONA
MINNEHAHA
ROCK
NOBLES
JACKSON
MARTIN
FARIBAULT
FREEBORN
MOWER
FILLMORE
HOUSTON
IOWA
EMMET
WINNESHIEK
ANOKA
POLK
WRIGHT
ST. CROIX
CARVER
SCOTT
DAKOTA
PIERCE
RICE
GOODHUE
MINNESOTA

Radio Stations Broadcasting Polish Programs in Nebraska

1. Radio Station KESY
   102 N. 48th Street
   Omaha, Neb. 68131

   One hour weekly

2. Radio Station KNLV
   Ord, Neb.

   Six hours weekly

Two radio stations broadcast Polish programs in Nebraska.

Total number of hours of Polish programming:

Seven hours weekly

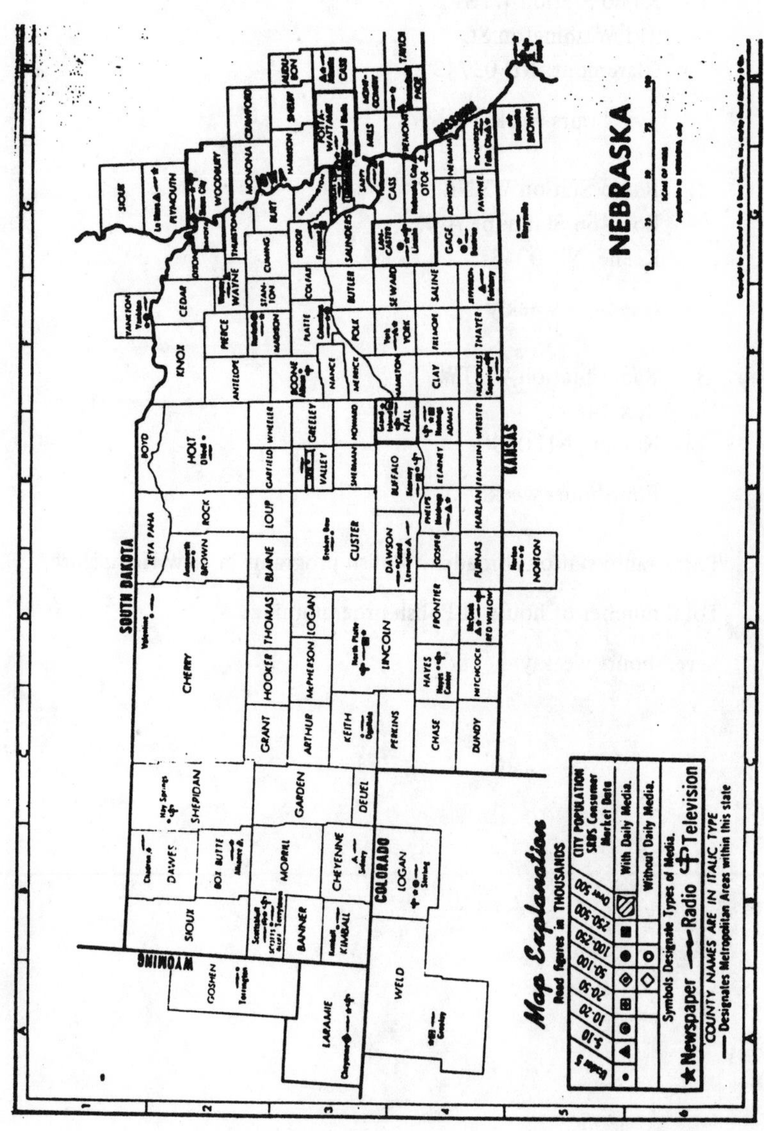
NEBRASKA
SOUTH DAKOTA
KANSAS
COLORADO
WYOMING
IOWA
Map Explanation
Read figures in THOUSANDS
CITY POPULATION
SRDS Consumer Market Data
With Daily Media.
Without Daily Media.
Symbols Designate Types of Media.
Newspaper
Radio
Television
COUNTY NAMES ARE IN ITALIC TYPE
— Designates Metropolitan Areas within this state

Radio Stations Broadcasting Polish Programs in New Hampshire

1. Radio Station WTSV
   211 Washington St.
   Olaremont, NH 03743

   Two hours weekly

2. Radio Station WKNE
   Box 466 Stanhope Ave.
   Keene, NH 03431

   One hour weekly

3. Radio Station WOTW
   Box 448
   Nashau, NH 03061

   Four hours weekly

Three radio stations broadcast Polish programs in New Hampshire.

Total number of hours of Polish programming:

Seven hours weekly

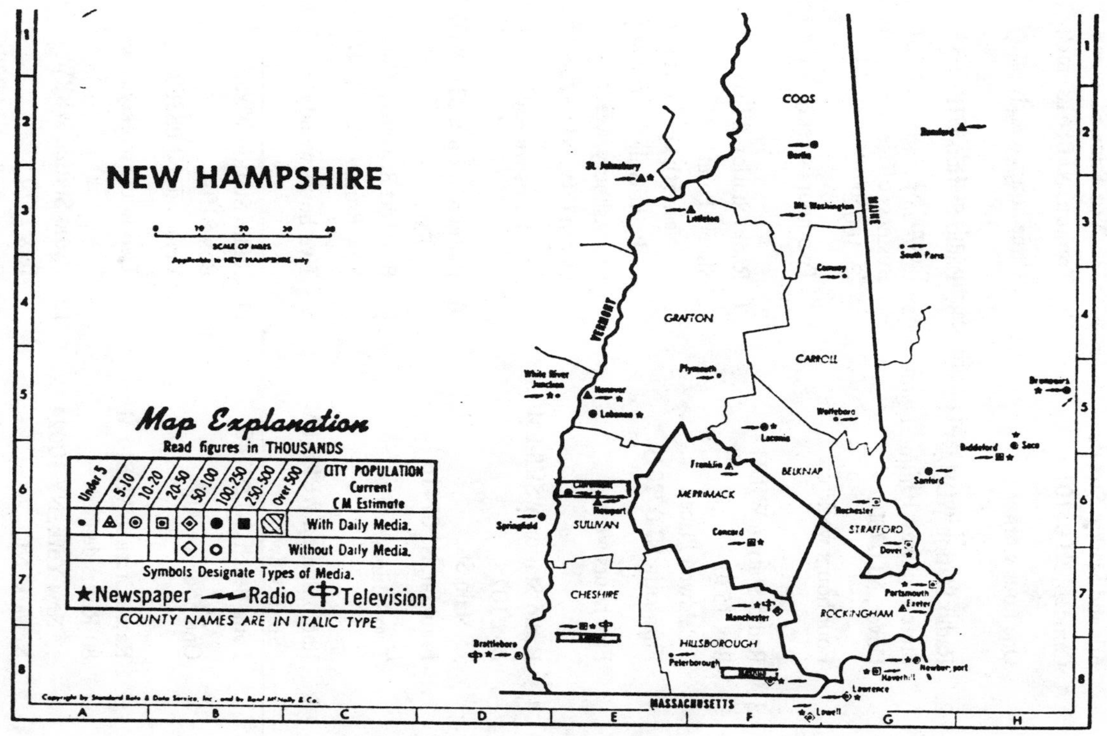
NEW HAMPSHIRE
SCALE OF MILES
Map Explanation
Read figures in THOUSANDS
Under 5
5-10
10-20
20-50
50-100
100-250
250-500
Over 500
CITY POPULATION
Current
CM Estimate
With Daily Media.
Without Daily Media.
Symbols Designate Types of Media.
★Newspaper Radio Television
COUNTY NAMES ARE IN ITALIC TYPE
COOS
GRAFTON
CARROLL
BELKNAP
STRAFFORD
MERRIMACK
SULLIVAN
CHESHIRE
HILLSBOROUGH
ROCKINGHAM
MAINE
VERMONT
MASSACHUSETTS
St. Johnsbury
Berlin
Littleton
Mt. Washington
South Paris
Conway
White River Junction
Hanover
Lebanon
Plymouth
Wolfeboro
Laconia
Franklin
Biddeford
Saco
Sanford
Newport
Springfield
Concord
Rochester
Dover
Portsmouth
Exeter
Manchester
Brattleboro
Peterborough
Newburyport
Haverhill
Lawrence
Lowell

Radio Stations Broadcasting Polish Programs in New Jersey

1. Radio Station WCAM
6th and Market Streets
Camden, NJ 08101

One hour weekly

2. Radio Station WDHA-FM
State Highway 10
Dover, NJ 07801

Four hours weekly

3. Radio Station WJDM
Box 1530
9 Caldwell Place
Elizabeth, NJ 07201

Five hours weekly

4. Radio Station WSUS-FM
Box 102
75 Main St.
Franklin, NJ 07416

Two hours weekly

5. Radio Station WRLB-FM
156 Broadway
Long Beach, NJ 07740

One hour weekly

6. Radio Station WHBI-FM
80 Riverside Park =
New York, NY 10024
Newark, NJ

Two hours weekly

7. Radio Station WTTM
333 West State St.
Trenton, NJ 08618

Three hours weekly

8. Radio Station WJIC
Salem, NJ
Business office: New York, NY 10029

Two hours weekly

9. Radio Station WIBG
Simers Point:
Near 5th Green Samers Point Golf Course
957 Ashbury Ave.
Ocean City, NJ 08226

???? hours weekly

10. Radio Station WCTC-WQMR-FM
Box 100 Broadcast Center
New Brunswick, NJ 08903

Two hours weekly

11. Radio Station WWSZ
Box 810
Vineland, NJ 08360

Two hours weekly

12. Radio Station WBRW
Box 1170
Sommerville, NJ 08876

One hour weekly

Twelve radio stations broadcast Polish programs in New Jersey.

Total number of hours of Polish programming:

26 hours weekly.

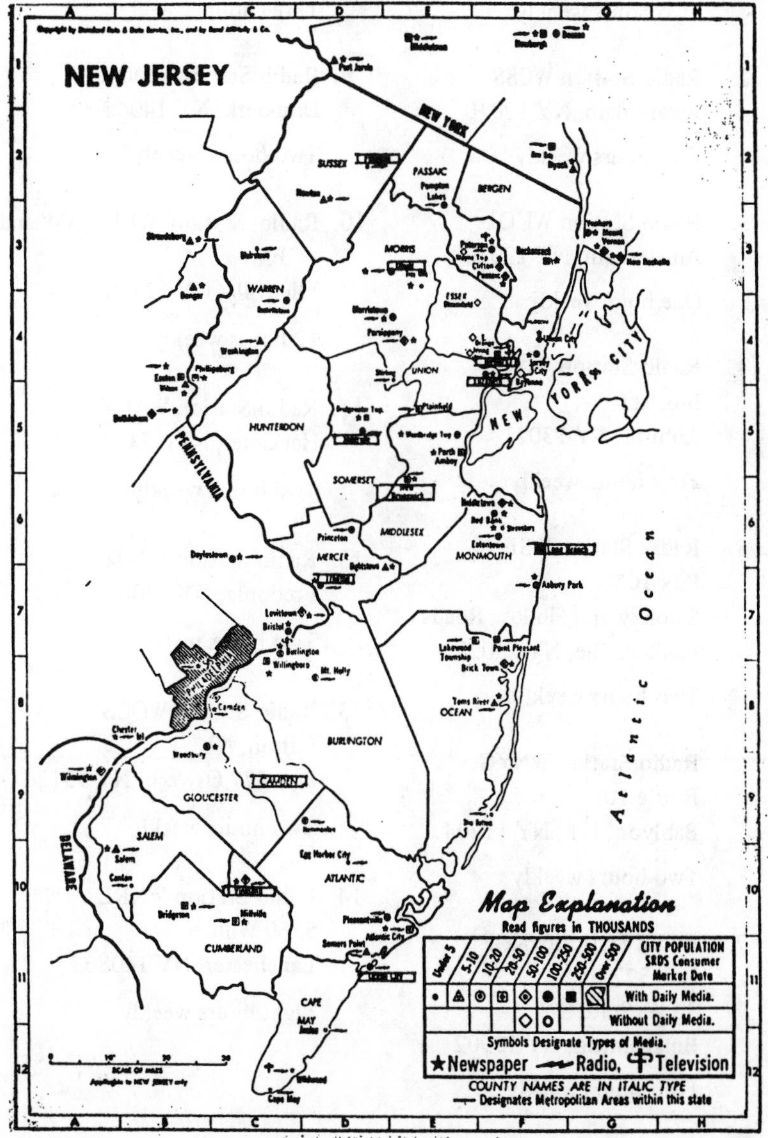

Radio Stations Broadcasting Polish Programs in New York

1. Radio Station WQBK
Box 1300
Albany, NY 12201

Two hours weekly

2. Radio Station WCSS
Amsterdam, NY 12010

Two hours weekly

3. Radio Station WKOL
Amsterdam, NY 12010

One hour weekly

4. Radio Station WAUB
Box 160
Auburn, NY 13021

Four hours weekly

5. Radio Station WSEN
Box 1050
Smokey and Hollow Roads
Baldwinville, NY 13027

Two hours weekly

6. Radio Station WNYG
Route 109
Bablyon, L.I., NY 11704

Two hours weekly

7. Radio Station WKOP
Box 527
32 W. State St.
Binghamton, NY 13902

Four hours weekly

8. Radio Station WNIA
2900 Genesee St. Buffalo, NY
Cheektowaga, NY

Three hours weekly

9. Radio Station WDOE
Dunkierk, NY 14048

Two hours weekly

10. Radio Station WELV-AM and FM
Ellenville, NY 12428

12 hours weekly

11. Radio Station WALY
Herkimer, NY 13350

Two hours weekly

12. Radio Station WBUZ
Fredonia, NY 14063

Two hours weekly

13. Radio Station WOCS
Fulton, NY
Box 177 Oswego, NY 13126

Two hours weekly

14. Radio Station WXRL
5360 William St.
Lanchester, NY 14086

Eight hours weekly

15. Radio Station WVHC-FM
Hemstead, NY 11550

Four hours weekly

16. Radio Station WTHE
265 Kaple Place
Mineola, NY 11501

Two hours weekly

17. Radio Station WLFH
Little Falls, NY 13365

Five hours weekly

18. Radio Station WHUC
Hudson, NY 12534

One hour weekly

19. Radio Station WKNY
212 Fair St.
Kingston, NY 12401

One hour weekly

20. Radio Station WALL
1 Broadcast Plaza
Middletown, NY 10940

Two hours weekly

21. Radio Station WJJL
1224 Main St.
Niagara Falls, NY 14302

One hour weekly

22. Radio Station WHLD
Box 398
Niagara Falls, NY 14302

Six hours weekly

23. Radio Station WVOX
One Broadcast Forum
New Rochelle, NY 10801

Two hours weekly

24. Radio Station WSOQ
North Syracuse, NY 13212

Two hours weekly

25. Radio Station WPOW
305 E. 40th St.
New York, NY 10016

Five hours weekly

26. Radio Station WOSC
Box 177
Oswego, NY 13126

One hour weekly

27. Radio Station WEOK
Box 416
Ponoe Road
Poughkeepsie, NY 12602

One hour weekly

28. Radio Station WKAL-AM
Road 1 Lower South Jay St.
Rome, NY 13440

Two hours weekly

29. Radio Station WRIV
Riverhead, NY 11901

Three hours weekly

30. Radio Sation WVOR-FM
Box 40340
333 Midtown Tower
Rochester, NY 14604

Two hours weekly

31. Radio Station WGGO
Salamanca, NY 14779

One hour weekly

32. Radio Station WWWD
Schenectady, NY 12505
422 Liberty St.

One hour weekly

33. Radio Station WNDR
Box 1212
Syracuse, NY 13201

One hour weekly

34. Radio Station WKAL
Road 1, Lower S. Jay
Utica, NY 13440

Two hours weekly

35. Radio Station WBVN
Box 1550 Genesse St.
Utica, NY 13503

Four hours weekly

36. Radio Station WIBX
Utica, NY 13503

Five hours weekly

37. Radio Sation WWWG
Box 40360
50 Chestnut Plaza
Rocherster, NY 14604

Two hours weekly

38. Radio Station WEVD
1700 Broadway
New York, NY 10019

One hour weekly

39. Radio Station WOKO
1450 Western Ave.
Albany, NY 12203

Two hours weekly

40. Radio Station WTBQ
Warwick, NY 10990

Two hours weekly

41. Radio Station WABY
855 Central Ave.
Albany, NY 12206

One hour weekly

42. Radio Station WBRV Boonville
Box 1170
Sommerville, NY

One hour weekly

43. Radio Station WBTF-FM
33 Main St.
Attica, NY 14011

Two hours weekly

44. Radio Station WVCR-FM
Loudonville, NY

Two hours weekly

45. Radio Station WFUV-FM
New York

Five hours weekly

Forty-five radio stations broadcast Polish programs in New York.

Total number of hours of Polish programming:

100 hours weekly

Map Explanation
Read figures in THOUSANDS
CITY POPULATION
SRDS Consumer Market Data
With Daily Media.
Without Daily Media.
Symbols Designate Types of Media.
★Newspaper Radio Television
COUNTY NAMES ARE IN ITALIC TYPE
— Designates Metropolitan Areas within this state
NEW YORK
Lake Ontario
Lake Erie
BUFFALO
CANADA
PENNSYLVANIA
NEW JERSEY
NEW YORK CITY
Atlantic Ocean
ST. LAWRENCE
FRANKLIN
CLINTON
ESSEX
JEFFERSON
LEWIS
HAMILTON
WARREN
ONEIDA
FULTON
SARATOGA
WASHINGTON
NIAGARA
ORLEANS
MONROE
WAYNE
ONTARIO
CAYUGA
MADISON
CHENANGO
OTSEGO
SCHOHARIE
ALBANY
RENSSELAER
GREENE
COLUMBIA
DELAWARE
ULSTER
SULLIVAN
ORANGE
PUTNAM
SUFFOLK
STEUBEN
YATES
WYOMING
ERIE
LIVINGSTON
CATTARAUGUS
ALLEGANY
CHAUTAUQUA
SUSQUEHANNA
VERMONT
MASSACHUSETTS
CONNECTICUT

Radio Stations Broadcasting Polish Programs in Ohio

1. Radio Station WAUP-FM
   Akron, OH 44309

   Four hours weekly

2. Radio Station WOMP
   Box 448 Woodmont Hill
   Bellaire, OH 43906

   ??? hours weekly

3. Radio Station WZAK-FM
   1303 Prospect Ave.
   Cleveland, OH 44115

   23½ hours weekly

4. Radio Station WERE
   1500 Chester Ave.
   Cleveland, OH 44114

   One hour weekly

5. Radio Station WCSB-FM
   Cleveland, OH 44101

   Two hours weekly

6. Radio Station WZZP
   2644 St. Claire Ave.
   Cleveland, OH 44114

   Two hours weekly

7. Radio Station WBOE-FM
   Cleveland, OH 44101

   One hour weekly

8. Radio Station WLYT-FM
   2156 Lee Road
   Cleveland, OH 44118

   One hour weekly

9. Radio Station WCWA
   604 Jackson St.
   Toledo, OH 43604

   Two hours weekly

10. Radio Station WLRO
    939 Brodway
    Lorain, OH 44052

    Three hours weekly

11. Radio Station WZLE-FM
    214 Sheffield Center
    Lorain, OH 44055

    Three hours weekly

12. Radio Station WNIO
    Box 625
    Niles, OH 44406

    Four hours weekly

13. Radio Station WPNM
    Ottawa, OH 45875

    Three hours weekly

14. Radio Station WLIT
    Box 1798
    2620 Sunset Blvd.
    Staubenville, OH 43952

    One hour weekly

15. Radio Station WKTL-FM
Struthers, OH 44471

One hour weekly

16. Radio Station WGON
6695 Jackman Road
Toledo, OH 43612

Four hours weekly

17. Radio Station WTOD
3225 Arlington Ave.
Toledo, OH 43614

Four hours weekly

18. Radio Station WIOT-FM
604 Jackson St.
Toledo, OH 43612

One hour weekly

19. Radio Station WAXC-FM
Box 146
Wapa Kometa, OH 45895

Two hours weekly

20. Radio Station WHHH
Market and Main Avenues
Warren, OH 44481

One hour weekly

21. Radio Station WTCL
1295 Lane West Road S.W.
Warren, OH 44481

Two hours weekly

22. Radio Station WFAR
610 Hazelwood
Youngstown, OH 44509

One hour weekly

23. Radio Station WTCL
1295 Lane West Road S.W.
Warren, OH

Two hours weekly

Twenty-three radio stations in Ohio broadcast Polish programs.

Total number of hours of Polish programming:

72½ hours weekly

Lake Erie
MICHIGAN
PENNSYLVANIA
INDIANA
KENTUCKY
WEST VIRGINIA
WILLIAMS
FULTON
LUCAS
DEFIANCE
HENRY
WOOD
SANDUSKY
LORAIN
GEAUGA
ASHTABULA
TRUMBULL
PORTAGE
SUMMIT
MEDINA
MAHONING
PAULDING
PUTNAM
HANCOCK
SENECA
HURON
VAN WERT
ALLEN
HARDIN
WYANDOT
CRAWFORD
RICHLAND
ASHLAND
WAYNE
STARK
COLUMBIANA
MERCER
AUGLAIZE
MARION
MORROW
HOLMES
TUSCARAWAS
CARROLL
LOGAN
SHELBY
UNION
DELAWARE
KNOX
COSHOCTON
HARRISON
DARKE
CHAMPAIGN
LICKING
GUERNSEY
BELMONT
MIAMI
CLARK
MADISON
FRANKLIN
FAIRFIELD
PERRY
MUSKINGUM
NOBLE
MONROE
PREBLE
GREENE
FAYETTE
PICKAWAY
HOCKING
MORGAN
WASHINGTON
CLINTON
ROSS
VINTON
ATHENS
HIGHLAND
MEIGS
BROWN
ADAMS
PIKE
SCIOTO
JACKSON
GALLIA
LAWRENCE
CLERMONT
CINCINNATI
WETZEL
WOOD
WIRT
MASON
CABELL
WAYNE
BOYD
GREENUP
ERIE
CRAWFORD
MERCER
LAWRENCE
DE KALB
ALLEN
ADAMS
JAY
RANDOLPH
WAYNE
OHIO
Map Explanation
Read figures in THOUSANDS
Under 5
5-10
10-20
20-50
50-100
100-250
250-500
Over 500
CITY POPULATION
SRDS Consumer
Market Data
With Daily Media.
Without Daily Media.
Symbols Designate Types of Media.
★Newspaper
Radio
Television
COUNTY NAMES ARE IN ITALIC TYPE
Designates Metropolitan Areas within this state
SCALE OF MILES
Applicable to OHIO only
A
B
C
D
E
F
G
H
1
2
3
4
5
6
7
8
9
10
11
12

Radio Stations Broadcasting Polish Programs in Oklahoma

1. Radio Station KCRO
   End, Oklahoma

   One hour weekly

One radio station broadcasts Polish programs in Oklahoma.

Total number of hours of Polish programming:

One hour weekly

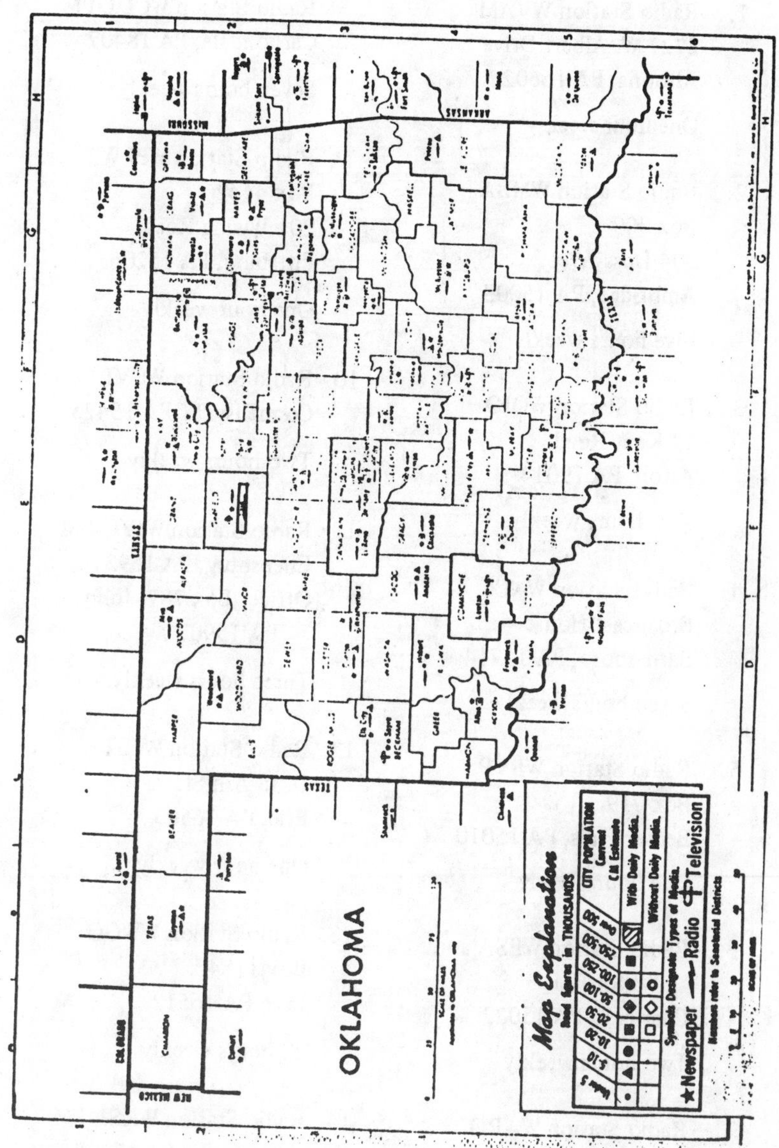
OKLAHOMA
KANSAS
MISSOURI
ARKANSAS
TEXAS
NEW MEXICO
COLORADO
Map Explanation
Bold figures in THOUSANDS
CITY POPULATION
With Daily Media.
Without Daily Media.
Symbols Designate Types of Media.
Newspaper
Radio
Television
Numbers refer to Sanatistical Districts

Radio Stations Broadcasting Polish Programs in Pennsylvania

1. Radio Station WVAM
2727 W. Albert Drive
Altoona, PA 16602

One hour weekly

2. Radio Station WMBA
Box 309
304 Duss Ave.
Ambridge, PA 15003

Five hours weekly

3. Radio Station WQIQ
12 Kent Road
Aston, PA 19014

Two hours weekly

4. Radio Station WNCC
Broadcast House
Barnesboro, PA 15714

Seven hours weekly

5. Radio Station WBVP
Box 719
Beaver Falls, PA 15010

One hour weekly

6. Radio Station WESA and WESA-FM
Charleroi, PA 15022

Two hours weekly

7. Radio Station WARO
Box 191
Canonsburg, PA 15317

Five hours weekly

8. Radio Station WCDL-FM
Carbondale, PA 18407

Seven hours weekly

9. Radio Station WPLW
Box 4442
201 Wwing Road
Pittsburg, PA 15205

One hour weekly

10. Radio Station WCVI
Connellsville, PA 15425

Two hours weekly

11. Radio Station WIYQ-FM
Ebensburg, PA 15931
Office: Box 787, Johnston, PA 15907

Three hours weekly

12. Radio Station WJET
1635 Ash St.
Erie, PA 16503

One hour weekly

13. Radio Station WWGO
Box 1184
Erie, PA 16512

22 hours weekly

14. Radio Station WKSL-FM
Greencastle, PA 17225

Five hours weekly

15. Radio Station WOXU-FM
Greensburg, PA 15601

Two hours weekly

16. Radio Station WDNH
Honesdale, PA 18431

One hour weekly

17. Radio Station WBCW
Jeannette, PA 15644

Four hours weekly

18. Radio Station WIBF-FM
Jenkintown, PA 19064

Two hours weekly

19. Radio Station WCRO
605 Main St.
Johnstown, PA 15901

Two hours weekly

20. Radio Station WLSH
Lansford, PA 18232

Two hours weekly

21. Radio Station WQTW
Latrobe, PA 15650

Five hours weekly

22. Radio Station WTRA
Latrobe, PA 15650

Four hours weekly

23. Radio Station WAMQ
Loretto, PA 15940

Two hours weekly

24. Radio Station WEDO
414 Fifth Ave.
Miltown Plaza Mall
McKeesport, PA 15132

One hour weekly

25. Radio Station WEDI-FM
McKean, PA 16426

Two hours weekly

26. Radio Station WMGW
Meadville, PA 16335
Downtown Mall

Two hours weekly

27. Radio Station WPSL
Monroeville, PA 15146

Two hours weekly

28. Radio Station WNAK
40 E. Main St.
Nanticoke, PA 18634

Two hours weekly

29. Radio Station WKST
219 Savanar-Gardner Rd.
New Castle, PA 16101

Two hours weekly

30. Radio Station WKPA
New Kensington, PA 15068

Two hours weekly

31. Radio Station WOYL
Oil City, PA 16301

Two hours weekly

32. Radio Station WRJS
Oil City, PA 16301

Two hours weekly

33. Radio Station WTEL
4140 Old York Road
Philadelphia, PA 19140

Eight hours weekly

34. Radio Station WPPA
212 S. Centre St.
Pottsville, PA 17901

One hour weekly

35. Radio Station WPAM
Pottsville, PA 17901

Two hours weekly

36. Radio Station WPAZ
638 Maucers Mill Road
Pottstown, PA 19464

Two hours weekly

37. Radio Station WPME-AM/FM
Bob Curry
Box 38
Punxsutawney, PA 15767

Three hours weekly

38. Radio Station WRML
Portage, PA 15946

Eight hours weekly

39. Radio Station WISL and WISL-FM
Shamokin, PA 17872

Six hours weekly

40. Radio Station WMBT
Shenandoah, PA 17976

Three hours weekly

41. Radio Station WTTO
Towanda, PA 18848

Two hours weekly

42. Radio Station WCTL-FM
Union City, PA 16438

One hour weekly

43. Radio Station WMBS
82 W. Fayette St.
Union Town, PA 15401

One hour weekly

44. Radio Station WYZZ-FM
156 Prospect St.
Wilkes Barre, PA 18702

Three hours weekly

45. Radio Station WMBR
Windser, PA 15963

Six hours weekly

46. Radio Station WCED-AM/FM
DuBois, PA 15801

Two hours weekly

47. Radio Station WICK
1049 Sekol Rd.
Scanton, PA 18504

Two hours weekly

48. Radio Station WHYP-FM
North East, PA 16428

Three hours weekly

49. Radio Station WKEG
Box 86 McLane Road
Washington, PA 15301

Five hours weekly

50. Radio Station WPHB
Phillipsburg, PA 16866

Three hours weekly

51. Radio Station WAZL
Hazleton National Bank Bldg.
Hazleton, PA 18201

Two hours weekly

52. Radio Station WIXZ
Box 1360
400 Lincoln Highway
East McKeesport, PA 15035

Two hours weekly

53. Radio Station WZPR-FM
Downtown Mall
Meadville, PA 16335

Three hours weekly

Fifty-three radio stations broadcast Polish programs in Pennsylvania.

Total number of hours of Polish programming:

173 hours weekly

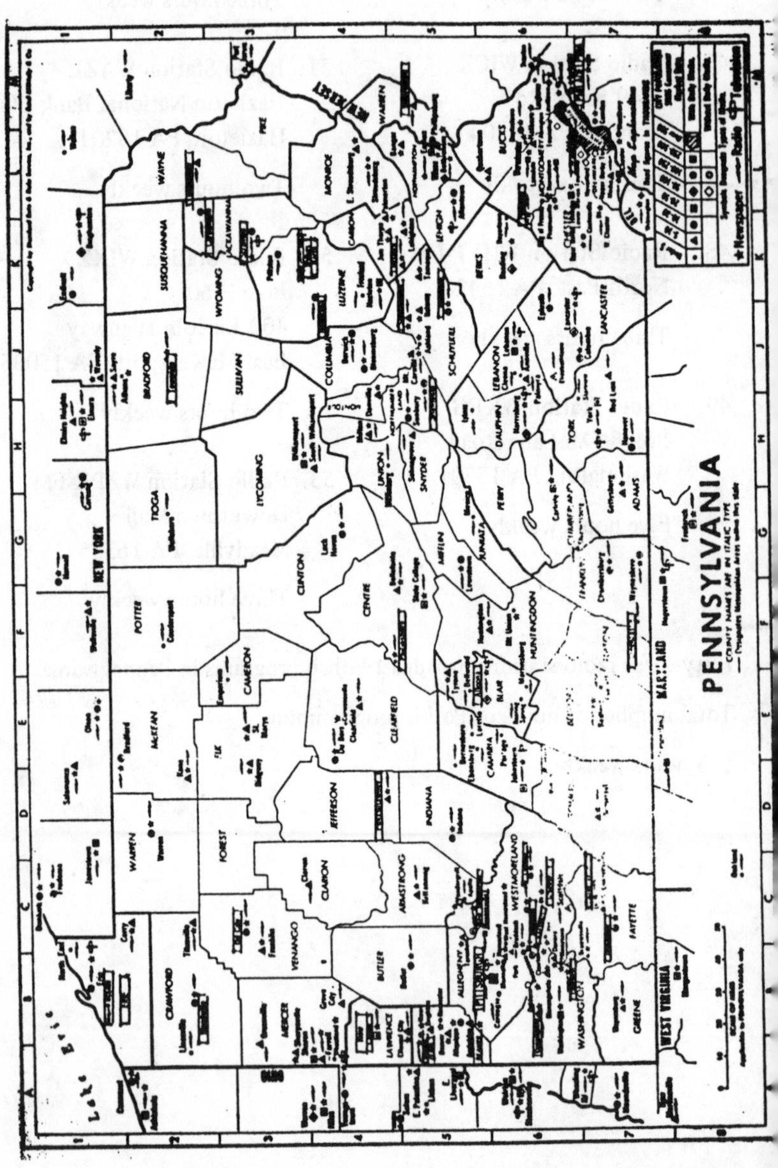
PENNSYLVANIA
NEW YORK
NEW JERSEY
MARYLAND
WEST VIRGINIA
Lake Erie
ERIE
CRAWFORD
WARREN
McKEAN
POTTER
TIOGA
BRADFORD
SUSQUEHANNA
WAYNE
PIKE
WYOMING
SULLIVAN
LYCOMING
CLINTON
CAMERON
ELK
FOREST
VENANGO
MERCER
LAWRENCE
BUTLER
CLARION
JEFFERSON
CLEARFIELD
CENTRE
UNION
SNYDER
COLUMBIA
LUZERNE
MONROE
CARBON
NORTHAMPTON
LEHIGH
BUCKS
BERKS
SCHUYLKILL
LEBANON
DAUPHIN
LANCASTER
YORK
ADAMS
PERRY
JUNIATA
MIFFLIN
HUNTINGDON
BLAIR
CAMBRIA
INDIANA
ARMSTRONG
ALLEGHENY
WESTMORELAND
WASHINGTON
FAYETTE
GREENE
CHESTER
MONTGOMERY

Radio Stations Broadcasting Polish Programs in Rhode Island

1. Radio Station WHIM/WHJY-FM
   115 Eastern Ave.
   Providence, RI 02914

   ??? hours weekly

2. Radio Station WKRI
   1501 Main St.
   West Warnick, RI 02893

   One hour weekly

3. Radio Station WKFD
   Washington County
   Wickford, RI

   One hour weekly

4. Radio Station WNRI
   786 Diamond Hill Road
   Woonsocket, RI 02895

   One hour weekly

5. Radio Station WWON
   986 Gentchell Ave.
   Woonsocket, RI 02895

   One hour weekly

6. Radio Station WRIB
   Water Street
   East Providence, RI 02915

   One hour weekly

7. Radio Station WGNG
   100 John St.
   Cumberland, RI

   Six hours weekly

Seven radio stations broadcast Polish programs in Rhode Island.

Total number of hours of Polish programming:

12 hours weekly

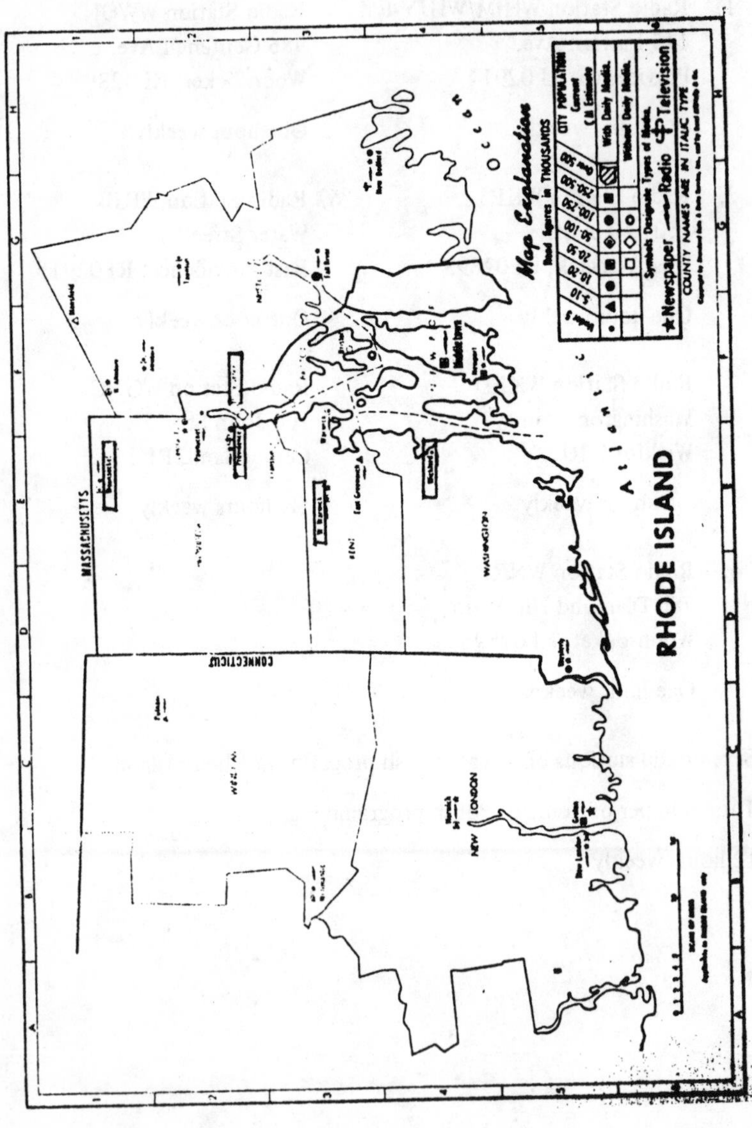
RHODE ISLAND
MASSACHUSETTS
CONNECTICUT
WASHINGTON
NEW LONDON
Map Explanation
Bold figures in THOUSANDS
CITY POPULATION
Current
With Daily Media.
Without Daily Media.
Symbols Designate Types of Media.
★Newspaper —— Radio Television
COUNTY NAMES ARE IN ITALIC TYPE

Radio Stations Broadcasting Polish Programs in Texas

1. Radio Station WGTN
   Georgetown, TX 78626

   Two hours weekly

One radio station broadcasts Polish programs in Texas.

Total number of hours of Polish programming:

Two hours weekly

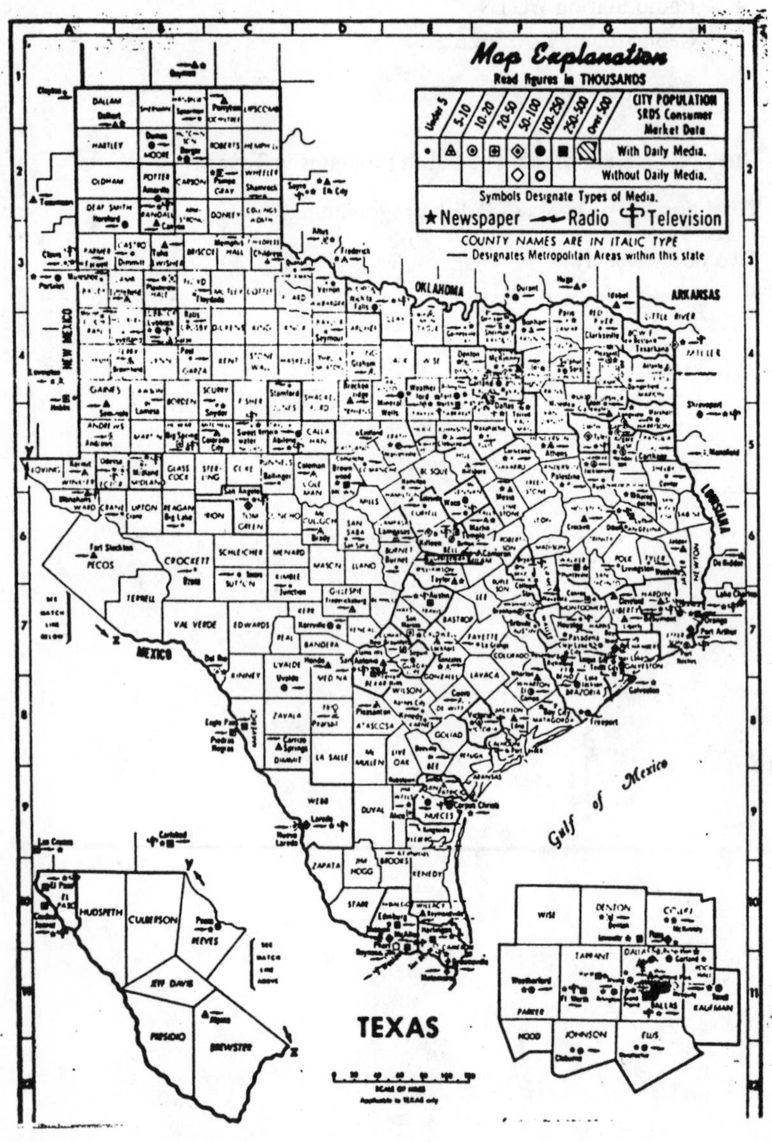
Map Explanation
Read figures in THOUSANDS
Under 5
5-10
10-20
20-50
50-100
100-250
250-500
Over 500
CITY POPULATION
SRDS Consumer
Market Data
With Daily Media.
Without Daily Media.
Symbols Designate Types of Media.
★Newspaper
Radio
Television
COUNTY NAMES ARE IN ITALIC TYPE
— Designates Metropolitan Areas within this state
OKLAHOMA
ARKANSAS
NEW MEXICO
LOUISIANA
MEXICO
Gulf of Mexico
TEXAS

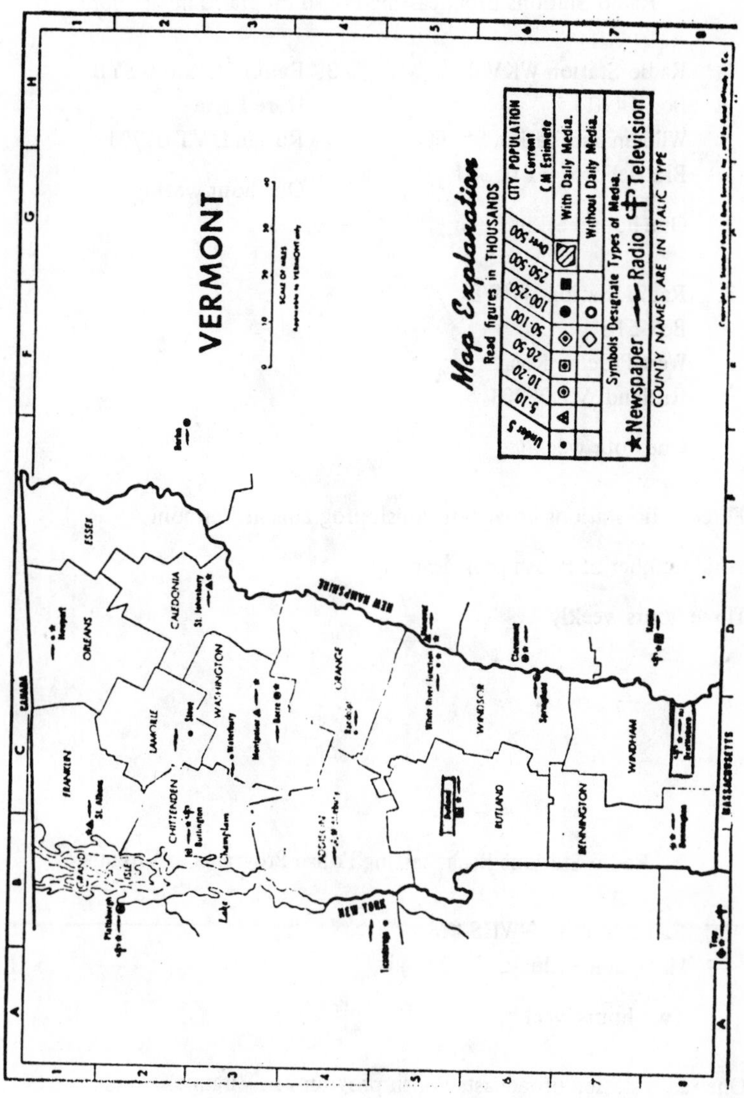
VERMONT
Map Explanation
Read figures in THOUSANDS
CITY POPULATION
Current
C M Estimate
With Daily Media.
Without Daily Media.
Symbols Designate Types of Media.
Newspaper
Radio
Television
COUNTY NAMES ARE IN ITALIC TYPE
CANADA
NEW HAMPSHIRE
NEW YORK
MASSACHUSETTS
FRANKLIN
ORLEANS
ESSEX
CALEDONIA
LAMOILLE
WASHINGTON
CHITTENDEN
ORANGE
WINDSOR
RUTLAND
BENNINGTON
WINDHAM
GRAND ISLE

Radio Stations Broadcasting Polish Programs in Vermont

1. Radio Station WKVT
Box 1490
William and Larkin Streets
Brattleboro, VT 05301

   One hour weekly

2. Radio Station WHWB
Box 518
West Proctor Road
Rutland, VT 05301

   One hour weekly

3. Radio Station WSYB
Dore Drive
Rutland, VT 05701

   One hour weekly

Three radio stations broadcast Polish programs in Vermont.

Total number of Polish programming:

Three hours weekly

Radio Stations Broadcasting Polish Programs in Virginia

1. Radio Station WWHS-FM
Hampden Sydney, VA 23943

   Two hours weekly

One radio station broadcasts Polish programs in Virginia.

Total number of hours of Polish programming:

Two hours weekly

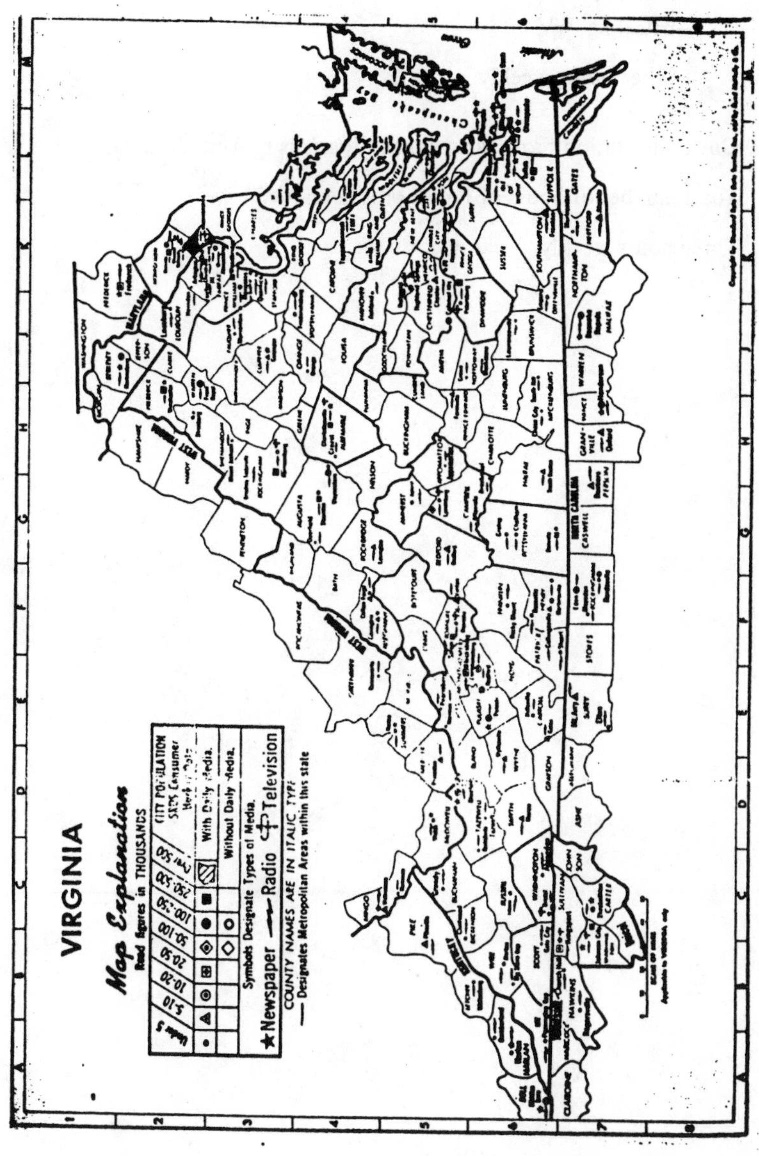
VIRGINIA
Map Explanation
CITY POPULATION
With Daily Media
Without Daily Media
Symbols Designate Types of Media.
Newspaper
Radio
Television
COUNTY NAMES ARE IN ITALIC TYPE
— Designates Metropolitan Areas within this state

1. Radio Station WOMP
   Box 448
   Wheeling, WV

   Three hours weekly

One radio station broadcasts Polish programs in West Virginia.

Total number of hours of Polish programming:

Three hours weekly

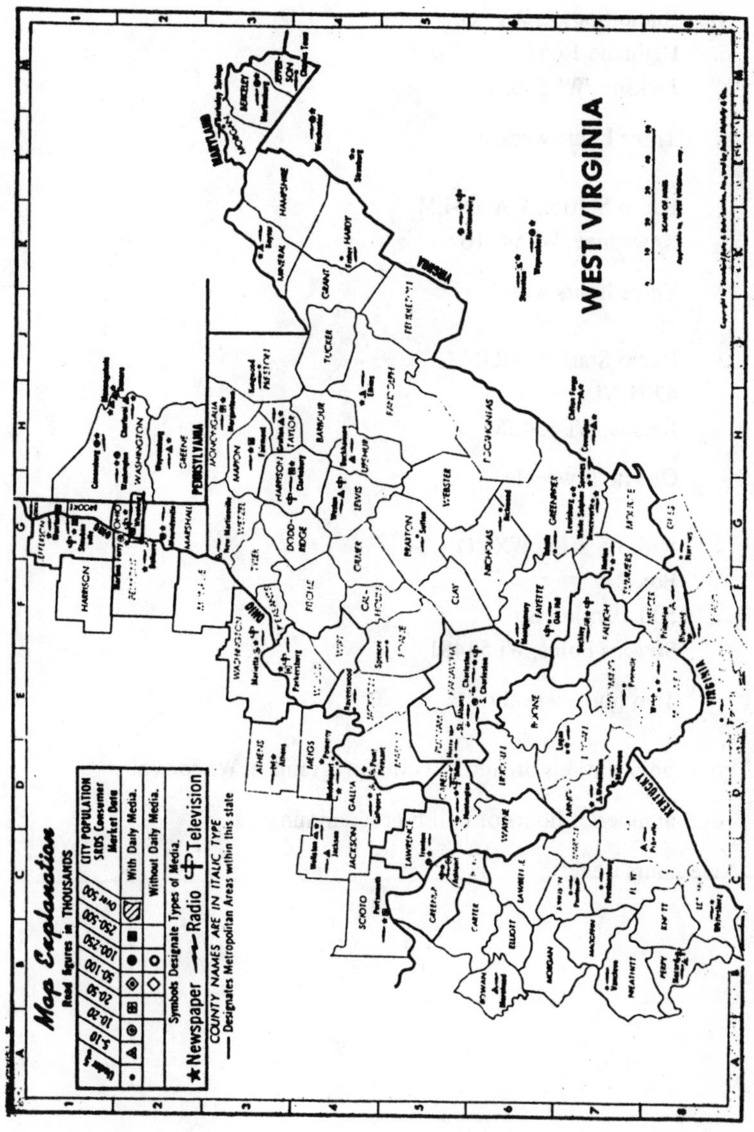
Map Explanation
Read figures in THOUSANDS
CITY POPULATION SRDS Consumer Market Data
With Daily Media.
Without Daily Media.
Symbols Designate Types of Media.
Newspaper
Radio
Television
COUNTY NAMES ARE IN ITALIC TYPE
— Designates Metropolitan Areas within this state
WEST VIRGINIA
PENNSYLVANIA
MARYLAND
VIRGINIA
KENTUCKY
OHIO

Radio Stations Broadcasting Polish Programs in Wisconsin

1. Radio Station WYLO
   Highland Road
   Jackson, WI 53037

   Three hours weekly

2. Radio Station WAUN-FM
   Kewaunee, WI 54216

   Three hours weekly

3. Radio Station WRJN
   4201 Victory Ave.
   Racine, WI 53405

   One hour weekly

4. Radio Station WXYQ
   Box 247
   500 Division St.
   Stevens Point, WI 54481

   Two hours weekly

Four radio stations broadcast Polish programs in Wisconsin.

Total number of hours of Polish programming:

Nine hours weekly

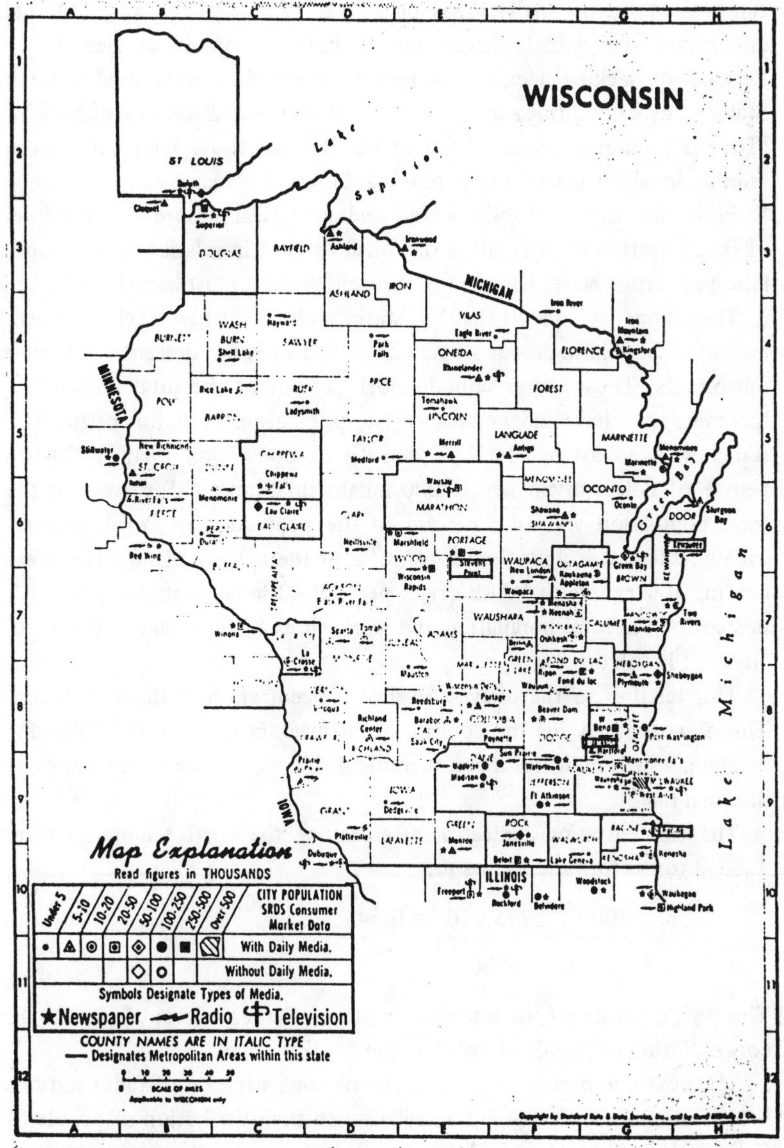
WISCONSIN
Lake Superior
MICHIGAN
MINNESOTA
IOWA
ILLINOIS
Lake Michigan
Green Bay
ST LOUIS
DOUGLAS
BAYFIELD
ASHLAND
IRON
VILAS
ONEIDA
FLORENCE
FOREST
MARINETTE
OCONTO
DOOR
BROWN
WAUPACA
WAUSHARA
CALUMET
ADAMS
DODGE
JEFFERSON
ROCK
WALWORTH
KENOSHA
GRANT
IOWA
LAFAYETTE
TAYLOR
MARATHON
LANGLADE
PORTAGE
WOOD
Map Explanation
Read figures in THOUSANDS
Under 5
5-10
10-20
20-50
50-100
100-250
250-500
Over 500
CITY POPULATION
SRDS Consumer
Market Data
With Daily Media.
Without Daily Media.
Symbols Designate Types of Media.
★Newspaper Radio Television
COUNTY NAMES ARE IN ITALIC TYPE
— Designates Metropolitan Areas within this state
SCALE OF MILES
Applicable to WISCONSIN only

Radio stations broadcasting in Polish do not constitute a separate category and therefore have to be analyzed in the context of all American stations. This analysis has been performed through an additional dimension: the spatial distribution of Polish communities (see chart). Because of lacking adequate statistics, census data were used (United States Census) published in *The World Almanac and Book of Facts, 1975.* (The list contains persons born in Poland and those who come from families in which at least one parent was born in Poland.)

Following the previously introduced analytical procedures, the level of concentration of population of Polish descent in relation to the population of certain states has been researched. A chart illustrates this relation.

The comparison shows that the states with the highest level of concentration of populatin do not surpass 20 people of Polish descent per 10,000 inhabitants. Those states contain 30.1 percent of the total population; however, they have 2.6 percent of the population of Polish origin. The states with an average level of density of population, that is, 20-100 people of Polish origin per 10,000 inhabitants, hold 31.9 percent of the total population and 14.7 percent of the population of Polish descent. Finally, the states with the lowest ratio of the density of population exceeding 100 people of Polish origin per 10,000 inhabitants comprise 38.1 percent of the total population and as much as 82.9 percent of the population of Polish descent.

This testifies to the uneven level of concentration of this population. This is confirmed by the concentration diagram given in the following diagram, which indicates a considerable distancing of the points from the diagonal line.

The concentration indicator, after taking the correct numbers from Table 3 to the formula, comes to:

$$K = \frac{5000 - 2275.9262 = 0.545}{5000}$$

The high quantity of the indicator confirms the large level of population concentration of people of Polish origin.

The next comparison is the analysis of concentration of radio stations broadcasting Polish programs in relation to the distribution of people of Polish origin. Table 4 with the pertinent data presents the states according

CONCENTRATION OF POLONIA IN THE UNITED STATES ACCORDING TO

1). INDIVIDUALS OF POLISH DECENT (FOR EVERY 10,000 RESIDENTS) AND

2). INDIVIDUALS BORN IN POLAND OR RAISED IN A FAMILY IN WHICH AT LEAST ONE PARENT WAS BORN IN POLAND.

BELOW 10

10-50

50-100

100-200

ABOVE 200

TABLE 3
Territorial Concentration of People of Polish Descent in the United States

	State	Polish population in the U.S. 1975x	U.S. population in mln in 1979xx	No. of Poles per 10 thousand of U.S. pop.xxx	Structurexxx		Cumulated columnsxxx		Calculationxxx	
					a	b	a'	b'	ab	a'b
1.	Mississippi	730	2,420.0	3.0	0.03	1.11	0.03	1.11	0.03	0.03
2.	N. Carolina	3.037	5,622.8	5.4	0.13	2.57	0.16	3.68	0.33	0.41
3.	Alabama	2.097	3.739.4	5.6	0.09	1.71	0.25	5.39	0.15	0.42
4.	S. Carolina	1.701	2,929.3	5.8	0.07	1.34	0.32	6.73	0.09	0.43
5.	Arkansas	1,331	2,188.4	6.1	0.06	1.00	0.38	7.73	0.06	0.38
6.	Kentucky	2,417	3,511.2	6.1	0.09	1.60	0.47	9.33	0.14	0.75
7.	Tennessee	2,789	4,359.5	6.4	0.12	1.99	0.59	11.32	0.24	1.17
8.	Utah	904	1,304.8	6.9	0.04	0.60	0.63	11.92	0.02	0.38
9.	Louisiana	2,771	3,974.8	7.0	0.12	1.82	0.75	13.74	0.22	1.37
10.	Idaho	687	889.1	7.7	0.03	0.41	0.78	14.15	0.01	0.32
11.	Hawaii	115	917.1	8.5	0.03	0.42	0.81	14.57	0.01	0.34
12.	Georgia	4,574	5,145.7	8.9	0.19	2.35	1.00	16.92	0.45	2.35
13.	Oklahoma	2,670	2,885.3	9.4	0.11	1.30	1.11	18.22	0.14	1.44
14.	Iowa	3,323	2,892.4	11.5	0.14	1.32	1.25	19.34	0.18	1.65
15.	N. Mexico	1,422	1,218.9	11.7	0.06	1.56	1.31	20.10	0.03	0.73
16.	Texas	16,328	13,239.3	12.3	0.69	6.05	2.00	26.15	4.17	12.10
17.	S. Dakota	1,052	691.8	15.2	0.04	0.32	2.04	26.47	0.01	0.65
18.	Kansas	4,046	2,342.4	17.3	0.17	1.07	2.21	27.54	0.18	2.36
19.	Virginia	9.432	5,219.4	18.1	0.40	2.38	2.61	29.92	0.95	6.21
20.	Alaska	765	414.2	18.5	0.03	0.19	2.64	30.11	0.01	0.50
21.	Oregon	4,855	2,430.1	20.0	0.20	1.11	2.84	31.22	0.22	3.19
22.	Maine	2,532	1,105.9	22.9	0.11	0.51	2.95	31.73	0.06	1.50
23.	Montana	1,781	777.0	22.9	0.08	0.35	3.03	32.08	0.03	1.00
24.	Nevada	1,578	670.5	23.5	0.07	0.31	3.10	32.39	0.02	0.90

TABLE 3 (Continued)

26.	Washington	9.821	3,710.6	26.5	0.41	1.70	3.55	34.28	0.70	6.04
27.	Colorado	7,882	2,719.2	29.0	0.33	1.24	3.88	35.52	0.41	4.81
28.	N. Dakota	1,952	666.9	29.3	0.08	0.30	3.96	35.82	0.02	1.19
29.	Missouri	15,469	4,746.8	32.6	0.65	2.17	4.61	37.99	1.41	10.00
30.	Arizona	7,930	2,384.8	33.3	0.33	1.09	4.94	39.08	0.36	5.38
31.	W. Virginia	6,360	1,877.5	33.9	0.27	0.86	5.21	39.94	0.23	4.48
32.	District of Columbia	2,787	691.7	40.3	0.12	0.32	5.33	40.26	0.04	1.71
33.	California	115,833	22,170.5	52.2	4.88	10.13	10.21	50.39	49.43	103.43
34.	Nebraska	8,888	1,576.8	52.8	0.35	0.72	10.56	51.11	0.25	7.60
35.	Florida	50,591	8,876.5	57.0	2.13	4.05	12.69	55.16	6.63	51.39
36.	Vermont	2,797	490.0	57.1	0.12	0.22	12.81	55.38	0.03	2.82
37.	Indiana	34,590	5,344.7	64.7	1.46	2.44	14.27	57.82	3.56	34.82
38.	Minnesota	26,931	4,009.9	67.2	1.13	1.83	15.40	59.65	2.07	28.18
39.	N. Hampshire	6,886	868.2	79.3	0.29	0.40	15.69	60.05	0.12	6.28
40.	Maryland	39,334	4,186.7	93.9	1.66	1.91	22.25	66.85	23.96	33.14
41.	Ohio	116,262	10,707.5	108.6	4.90	4.89	22.25	67.12	0.08	108.80
42.	Delaware	7,263	591.4	122.8	0.31	0.27	22.56	67.12	0.08	6.09
43.	Rhode Island	13,389	932.4	143.6	0.56	0.43	23.12	67.55	0.24	9.94
44.	Wisconsin	71,534	4,695.9	152.3	3.01	2.15	26.13	69.70	6.47	56.18
45.	Massachusetts	117,992	5,836.5	202.2	4.97	2.67	31.10	72.37	13.27	83.04
46.	Pennsylvania	243,752	11,802.8	206.5	10.27	5.39	41.37	77.75	55.36	222.98
47.	Michigan	214.085	9,162.1	233.7	9.02	4.19	50.39	81.95	37.79	211.13
48.	Illinois	299.316	11.265.8	265.7	12.61	5.15	63.00	87.10	64.94	324.45
49.	N. Jersey	217.509	7,345.9	296.1	9.16	3.36	72.16	90.46	30.78	242.46
50.	N. York	557.478	17.844.0	312.4	23.49	8.15	95.64	98.61	191.36	779.47
51.	Connecticut	103.820	3,123.9	332.3	4.37	1.43	100.01	100.04	6.25	143.01
	TOTALS	2,374.244	218,911.7		100.01	100.04			508.38	2,530.11

X: Represents Poles born in Poland or reared in families in which at least one parent was born in Poland.

Sources: x/World Almanac and Book of Facts 1975.

xx/Spot Radio Rates and Data. Standard Rate Data Service, Inc., Skokie, January 1, 1980.

xxx/Calculated by the author

TABLE 4
Territorial Concentration of Radio Stations Broadcasting Polish Programs in Polish-American Communities in the United States

	State	No. of radio stations broad-casting Polish programs x	No. of[x] people of Polish descent[xx]	No. of radio stations per 10 thousand of Polish population xxx	Structure[xxx] a	b	Cumulated columns[xxx] a'	b'	Calculations[xxx] ab	a'b
1.	Florida	2	50.591	0.40	0.79	2.20	0.79	2.20	1.74	1.74
2.	Illinois	12	299.316	0.40	4.74	13.01	5.53	15.21	61.67	71.94
3.	N. Jersey	12	217.509	0.55	4.74	9.46	10.27	24.67	44.84	97.15
4.	Wisconsin	4	71.543	0.56	1.58	3.11	11.85	27.78	4.91	36.85
5.	Texas	1	16.328	0.61	0.40	0.71	12.25	28.45	0.28	8.70
6.	California	8	115.833	0.69	3.16	5.04	15.41	33.53	15.93	77.67
7.	Minnesota	2	26.931	0.74	0.79	1.17	16.20	34.70	0.92	18.95
8.	Michigan	17	214.085	0.79	6.72	9.31	22.92	44.01	62.56	213.39
9.	N. York	45	557.478	0.81	17.79	24.24	40.71	68.25	431.23	986.81
10.	Virginia	1	9.423	1.06	0.40	0.41	41.11	68.66	0.16	16.86
11.	Arizona	1	7.930	1.26	0.40	0.34	41.51	69.00	0.14	14.11
12.	Colorado	1	7.882	1.27	0.40	0.34	41.91	69.34	0.14	14.25
13.	Maryland	5	39.334	1.27	1.98	1.71	43.89	71.05	3.39	75.05
14.	Delaware	1	7.263	1.38	0.40	0.32	44.29	71.37	0.13	14.17
15.	Massachusetts	18	117.992	1.53	7.11	5.13	51.40	76.50	36.47	263.68
16.	Connecticut	20	103.820	1.93	7.91	4.51	59.31	81.01	35.67	267.49
17.	Ohio	23	116.262	1.98	9.09	5.05	68.40	86.06	45.90	345.42
18.	Pennsylvania	53	243.752	2.17	20.95	10.60	89.35	96.66	222.07	947.11
19.	Indiana	8	34.590	2.31	3.16	1.50	92.51	98.16	4.74	138.77

TABLE 4 (Continued)

	State	No. of radio stations broad-casting Polish programs x	No. of[x] people of Polish descent[xx]	No. of radio stations per 10 thousand of Polish population xxx	Structure[xxx] a	b	Cumulated columns[xxx] a'	b'	Calculations[xxx] ab	a'b
21.	Kansas	1	4.046	2.47	0.40	0.18	93.70	98.70	0.07	16.87
22.	Iowa	1	3.323	3.01	0.40	0.14	94.10	98.84	0.06	13.17
23.	Oklahoma	1	2.670	3.75	0.40	0.12	94.50	98.96	0.05	11.34
24.	New Hampshire	3	6.885	4.36	1.19	0.30	95.69	99.26	0.36	28.71
25.	Rhode Island	7	13.389	5.23	2.77	0.58	98.46	99.84	1.61	57.11
26.	Vermont	3	2.797	10.73	1.19	0.12	99.65	99.96	0.14	11.96
27.	Mississippi	1	730	13.70	0.40	0.03	100.05	99.99	0.01	3.00
	TOTALS	253	2,300.027		100.05	99.99			975.47	3,518.47

x: Represents Poles born in Poland or reared in families in which at least one parent was born in Poland.

Source: x/Spot Radio Rates and Data. Standard Rate, Data Service, Inc., Skokie, January 1, 1980. Ores Broadcasting Yearbook, Broadcasting Publications, Inc. Washington 1980.

xx/World Almanac and Book of Facts 1975.

xxx/Calculation by the author.

Diagram: Individuals of Polish Ancestry

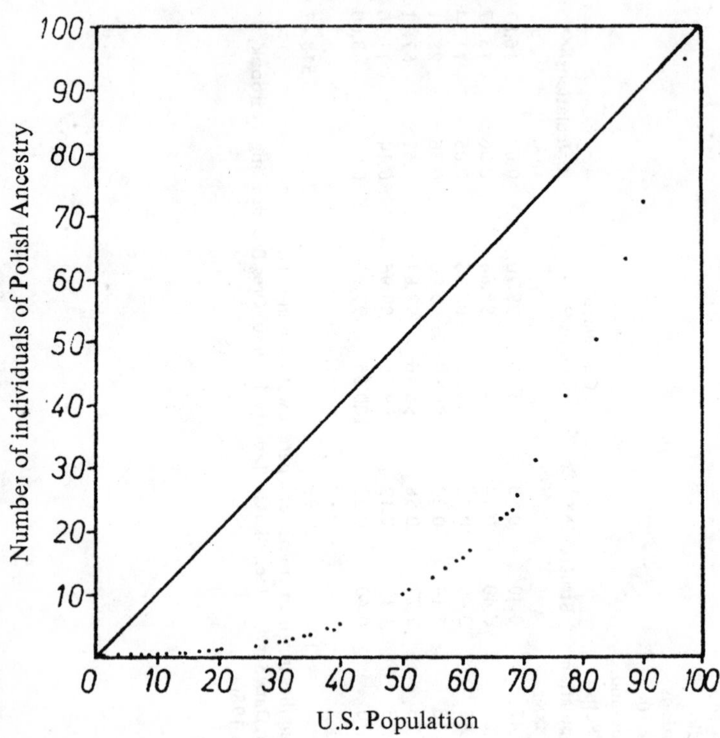

to the density of the radio stations which broadcast Polish programs in Polish centers. In comparing the cumulative series, it turns out that the states with thelowest density indicator do not go above one radio station per 10,000 people of Polish origin, concentrating 68.3 percent of the listeners in 40.7 percent of the stations. In turn, states with a median density of radio stations having one to 10 stations per 10,000 residents of Polish background concentrate 31.6 percent of the listeners in 57.8 percent of the radio stations. Finally, states with the highest density indicator which exceeds 10 stations per 10,000 residents have 0.2 percent of the listeners in 1.6 percent of all the stations broadcasting Polish programs.

It turns out that the spatial distribution of radio stations in relation to the number of listeners is rather equal. This is also confirmed by the diagrammed concentration which is represented in the following diagram, which indicates a rather even distribution of points.

Diagram: The Number of Radio Stations Broadcasting Polish Programs in Relation to the Distribution of Individuals of Polish Ancestry

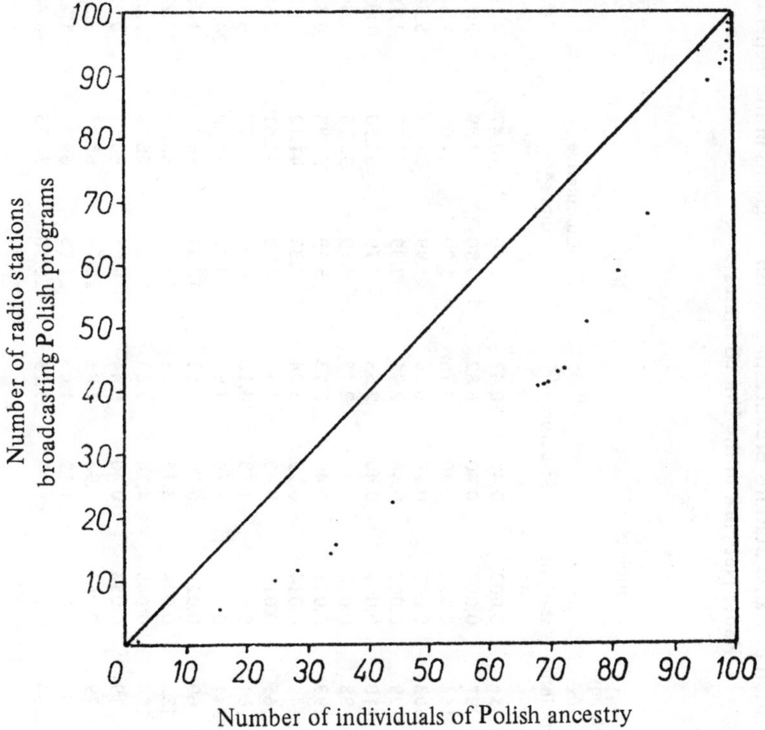

The concentration indicator after taking the right numbers from Table 4 comes to:

$$K = \frac{5000 - 3030.7375}{5000} = 0.394$$

Comparing this indicator with the concentration indicator of the general radio network, we can confirm that the radio stations which broadcast

TABLE 5
Territorial Concentration of Radio Stations Broadcasting Polish Programs in the General Radio Network in the United States

	State	No. of radio stations broad-casting Polish programs[x]	No. of radio stations [xx]	Groupings indicator for radio stations [xxx]	Structure[xxx] a	b	Cumulative columns[xxx] a'	b'	Calculations[xxx] ab	a'b
1.	Texas	1	456	0.002	0.40	10.47	0.40	10.47	4.19	4.19
2.	Virginia	1	297	0.003	0.40	6.82	0.80	17.29	2.73	5.46
3.	Mississippi	1	164	0.006	0.40	3.76	1.20	21.05	1.50	4.51
4.	Florida	2	303	0.007	0.79	6.96	1.99	28.01	5.50	13.85
5.	Iowa	1	129	0.008	0.40	2.96	2.39	30.97	1.18	7.07
6.	Oklahoma	1	110	0.009	0.40	2.53	2.79	33.50	1.01	7.06
7.	Colorado	1	98	0.010	0.40	2.25	3.19	35.75	0.90	7.18
8.	Kansas	1	93	0.011	0.40	2.13	3.59	37.88	0.85	7.65
9.	Minnesota	2	141	0.014	0.79	3.24	4.38	41.12	2.56	14.19
10.	Arizona	1	65	0.015	0.40	1.49	4.78	42.61	0.60	7.12
11.	Wisconsin	4	181	0.022	1.58	4.16	6.36	46.77	6.57	26.46
12.	California	8	341	0.023	3.16	7.83	9.52	54.60	24.74	74.54
13.	Nebraska	2	69	0.029	0.79	1.58	10.31	56.18	1.25	16.29
14.	Indiana	8	182	0.044	3.16	4.18	13.47	60.36	13.21	56.30
15.	Illinois	12	254	0.048	4.74	5.83	18.21	66.19	27.63	106.16
16.	Delaware	1	19	0.053	0.40	0.44	18.61	66.63	0.18	8.19
17.	Maryland	5	79	0.063	1.98	1.81	20.59	68.44	3.58	37.27
18.	N. Hampshire	3	45	0.967	1.19	1.03	21.78	69.47	1.23	22.43
19.	Michigan	17	230	0.074	6.72	5.23	28.50	74.75	35.48	150.48

TABLE 5 (Continued)

	State	No. of radio stations broad-casting Polish programs[x]	No. of radio stations [xx]	Groupings indicator for radio stations [xxx]	Structure[xxx] a	b	Cumulative columns[xxx] a'	b'	Calculations[xxx] ab	a'b
20.	Ohio	23	253	0.091	9.09	5.81	37.59	80.56	52.81	218.40
21.	Vermont	3	26	0.115	1.19	0.60	38.78	81.16	0.71	23.27
22.	New York	45	296	0.152	17.79	6.80	56.57	87.96	120.97	822.60
23.	Massachusetts	18	103	0.175	7.11	2.36	63.68	90.32	16.78	150.28
24.	Pennsylvania	53	289	0.183	20.95	6.63	84.63	96.95	138.90	561.10
25.	N. Jersey	12	51	0.235	4.74	1.17	89.37	98.12	5.55	104.56
26.	Rhode Island	7	23	0.304	2.77	0.53	92.14	98.65	1.47	48.83
27.	Connecticut	20	59	0.339	7.91	1.35	100.05	100.00	10.68	135.07
	TOTALS	253	4,356						482.76	2,510.41

Sources: x/Spot Radio Rates and Data. Standard Rate Data Service, Inc., Skokie, January 1, 1980
Ores Broadcasting Yearbook, Broadcasting Publications, Inc. Washington 1980.
xx/Spot Radio Rates and Data. Standard Rate Data Service Inc., Skokie, January 1, 1980.
xxx/Calculated by the author.

Polish programs are less well-adjusted to Polonian concentrations than the general radio network is to population concentrations in the United States.

Finally, the last comparison will be the analysis of concentration of radio stations broadcasting Polish programs in relatin to the entire radio network in the United States. Table 5 (see preceding pages) contains the states in order according to the above criterion.

Comparing the appropriate cumulative series, we note that the states with the lowest indicator do not exceed the value 0.01 accumulate 35.8 percent of the general radio network and 3.19 percent of the stations broadcasting Polish programs. In turn, states with a median share coming to a value of 0.011 – 0.100 concentrate 44.8 percent of the general network and 3.4 percent of the radio stations with Polish programs. Finally, states with the highest share of radio stations exceeding a value of 0.100 concentrate 19.4 percent of the general radio network and 62.9 pecent of the stations broadcasting Polish radio programs.

The concentration diagram shown in the following diagram is the graphic depiction of the territorial concentration of the radio network. From the distribution points it turns out that the course of concentration of the population of Polish background is practically identical to the general population. This would indicate a certain irrelevane to the placement of the radio stations broadcasting Polish programs within the whole radio network system.

The value of the concentration indicator after entering basic appropriate data from the diagram equals:

$$K = \frac{5000 - 2269.0295 = 0.546}{5000}$$

In order to study the degree of interrelatedness between location of radio stations and population density, it is best to use a correlative analysis. Accordingly, an appropriate correlative diagram was drawn up, bringing into the scale the appropriate coordinating values which correlated qualities on the basis of data discussed earlier in Table 1 through 5, thus drawing up Tables 9, 10, 11 and 12. From the distribution of points on the coordinated scale, one can make conclusions regarding the strong interdependence between the studied variables.

Diagram: Radio Stations Broadcasting Polish Programs in Relation to the Distribution of Radio Stations in the United States

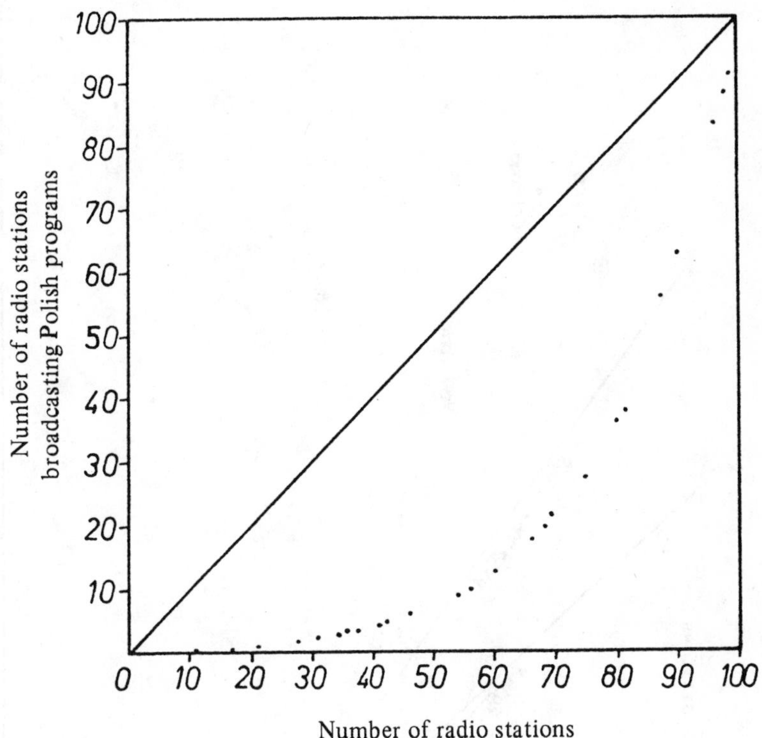

The graphic presentation of interdependence, seen in the regressive lines, express a linear tie between the values of one variable (independent) and corresponding to them the median described in the equations:[36]

$$Y = a + bX$$
$$X = a' + b'X$$

For the evaluation of the regressive coefficients the method of the smallest squares is applied and that leads to the solution of the normal equations given below:

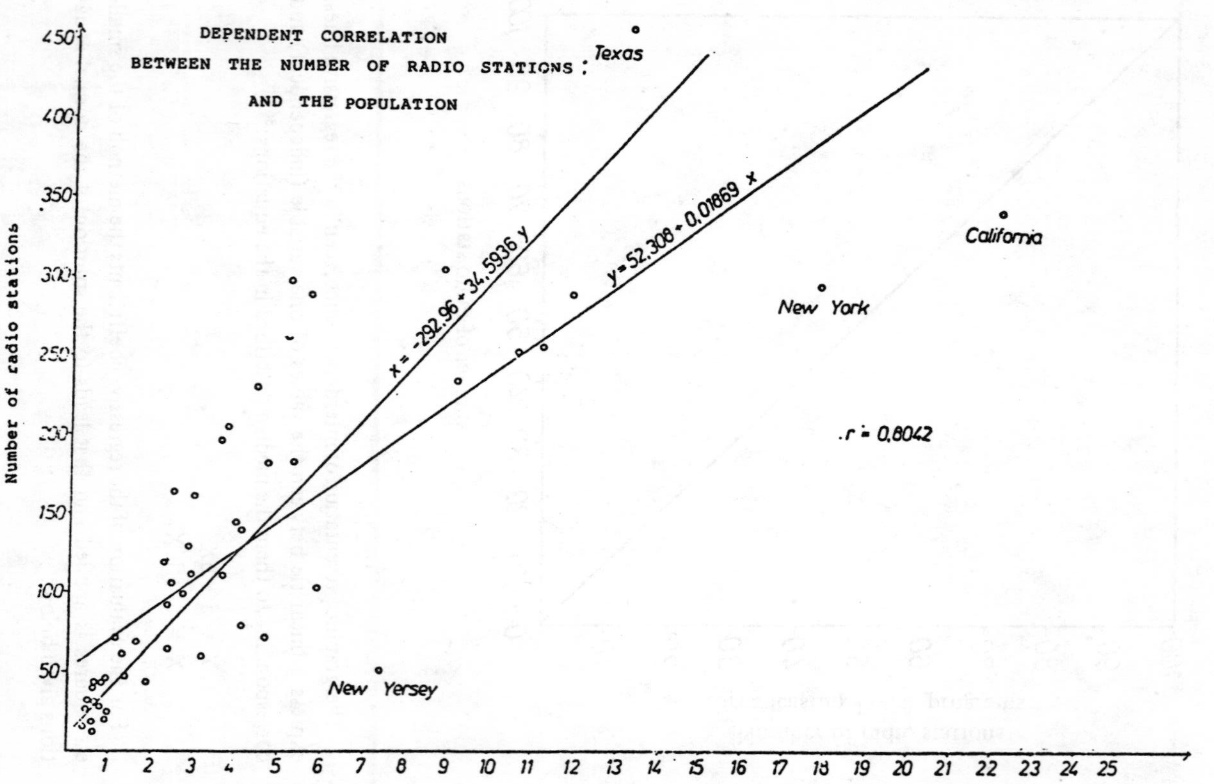
DEPENDENT CORRELATION
BETWEEN THE NUMBER OF RADIO STATIONS :
AND THE POPULATION
Texas
California
New York
New Yersey
r = 0,8042
x = -292,96 + 34,5936 y
y = 52,308 + 0,01869 x
Number of radio stations

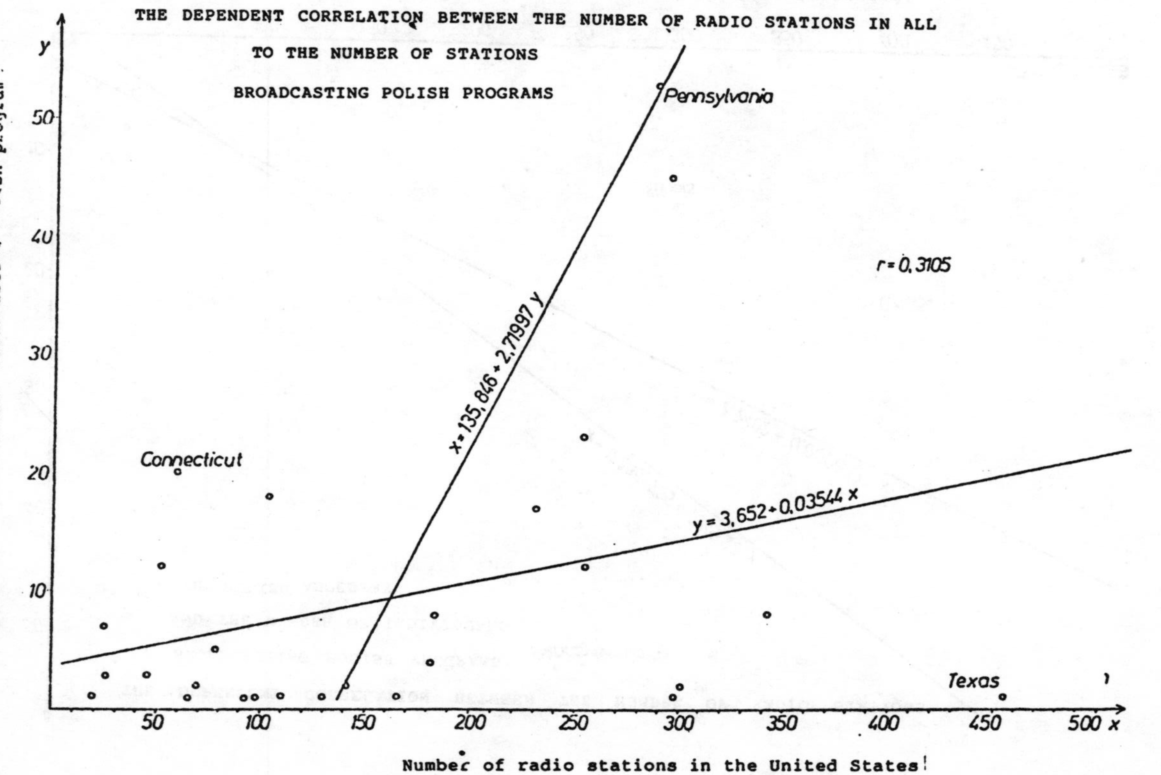
THE DEPENDENT CORRELATION BETWEEN THE NUMBER OF RADIO STATIONS IN ALL
TO THE NUMBER OF STATIONS
BROADCASTING POLISH PROGRAMS
Pennsylvania
r = 0,3105
x = 135,846 + 2,71997 y
Connecticut
y = 3,652 + 0,03544 x
Texas
y
50
40
30
20
10
50
100
150
200
250
300
350
400
450
500 x
Number of radio stations in the United States
Number of radio stations broadcasting Polish programs

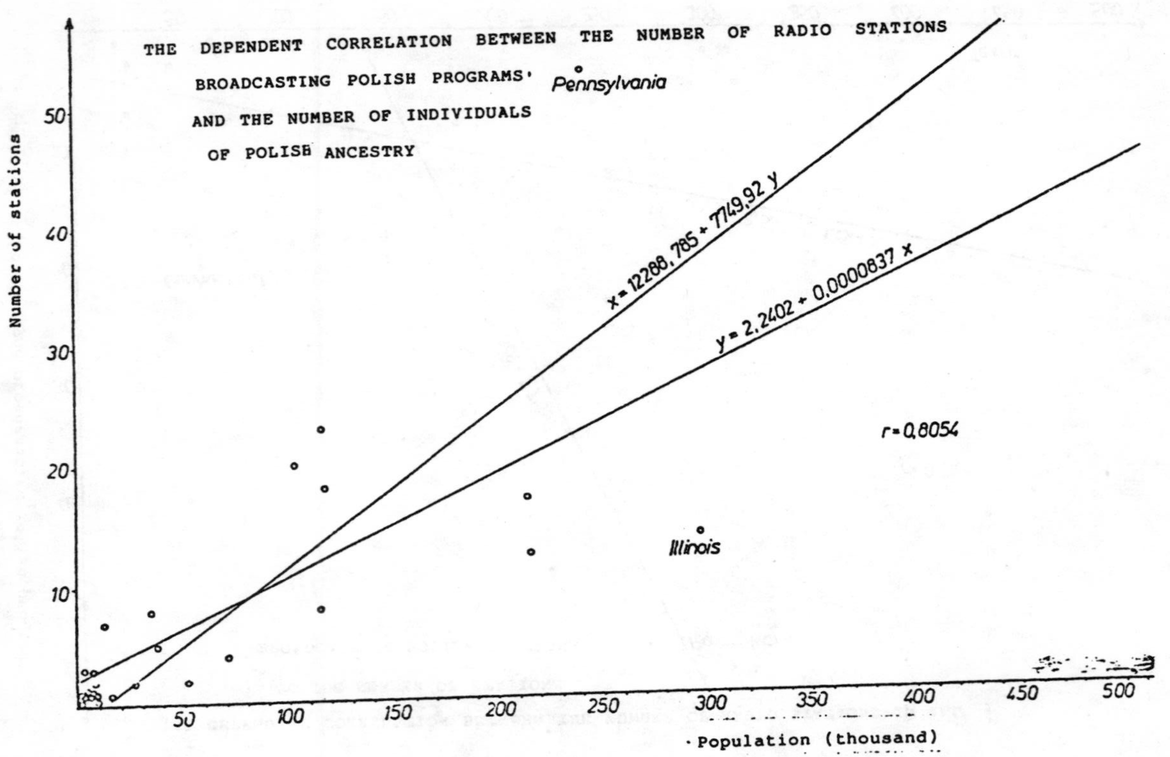
THE DEPENDENT CORRELATION BETWEEN THE NUMBER OF RADIO STATIONS
BROADCASTING POLISH PROGRAMS'
AND THE NUMBER OF INDIVIDUALS
OF POLISH ANCESTRY
Pennsylvania
Illinois
x = 12288,785 + 7749,92 y
y = 2,2402 + 0,0000837 x
r = 0,8054
Number of stations
10
20
30
40
50
Population (thousand)
50
100
150
200
250
300
350
400
450
500

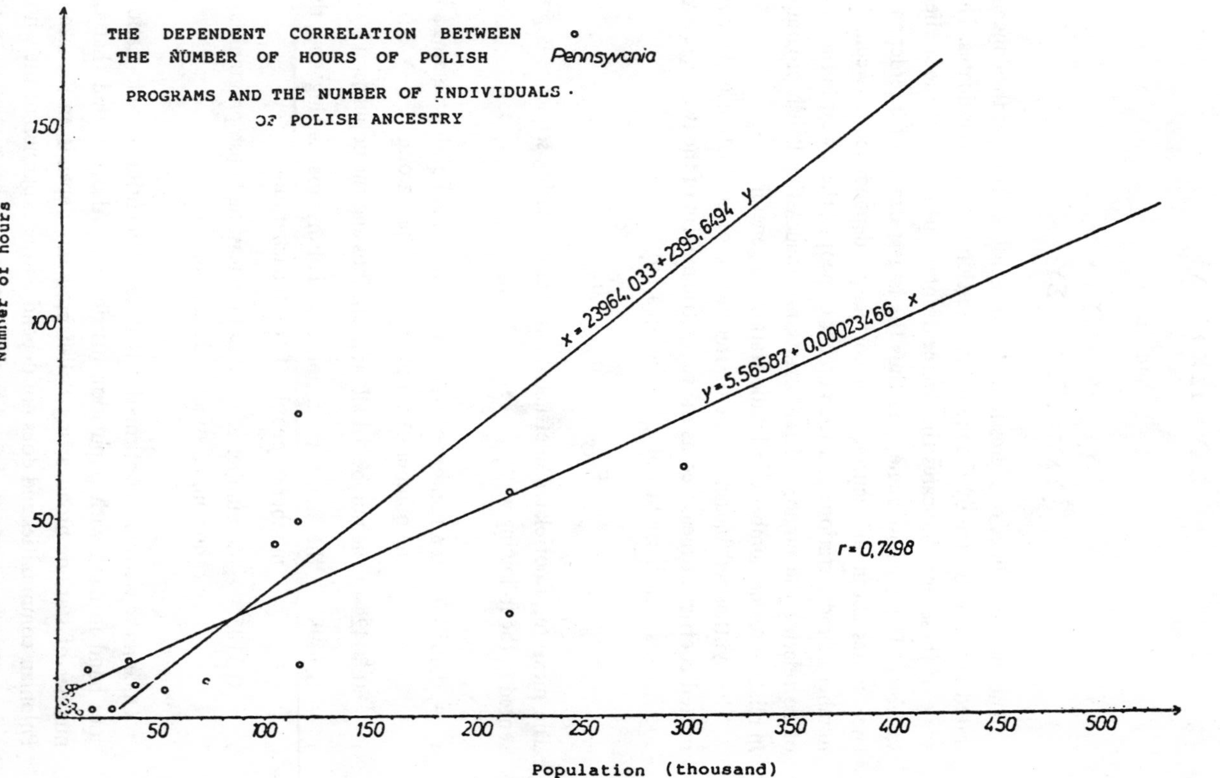
THE DEPENDENT CORRELATION BETWEEN
THE NUMBER OF HOURS OF POLISH
PROGRAMS AND THE NUMBER OF INDIVIDUALS
OF POLISH ANCESTRY
Pennsyvania
x = 23964,033 + 2395,6494 y
y = 5,56587 + 0,00023466 x
r = 0,7498
Number of hours
50
100
150
Population (thousand)
50
100
150
200
250
300
350
400
450
500

$$\Sigma Y = Na + b\Sigma X$$
$$\Sigma XY = a\Sigma X + b\Sigma X^2$$

and

$$\Sigma X = Na' + b'\Sigma Y$$
$$\Sigma XY = a'\Sigma Y + b'\Sigma Y^2$$

The indicated lines of regression cut through the center of the concentrated points indicated by the medial progression of their coordinates. The angle of these lines indicates the degree of interdependence of the studied variables. The smallest angle, and thus the largest degree of interdependence comes about in occurrence of correlative dependence between the number of radio stations and the number of people, the lowest in the case of correlating the number of radio stations broadcasting Polish programs in relation to the number of all radio stations in general.

The synthesized measurement of the degree of correlation is the correlated coefficient measured as the geometric median of the two regressive coefficients, which can be noted by the equation:

$$R_{xy} = \sqrt{} b_{yx} - b'_{xy}$$

The measure of correlated coefficients in ever-decreasing sequence is presented in the following way:

r = 0.8054 – the number of stations broadcasting Polish programs and the number of people of Polish background

r = 0.8042 – the number of all radio stations and the population

r = 0.7498 – the number of hours of Polish broadcasting and the number of people of Polish background

r = 0.3105 – the number of stations broadcasting Polish programs and the number of all radio stations.

Once more we find a confirmation that the augmenting of radio stations goes hand in hand with population distribution. Also, we find that the number of stations broadcasting Polish programs depends on the size of Polonian communities and does not depend on the expansion of the whole radio network in general. To a different degree, this has a relation to the length of radio programs measured by the number of broadcast hours for this circle of listeners. From the charts and diagrams, one can note a deviation from the fixed dependence, which in extreme cases, is described.

In conclusion, an analysis of the developmental tendencies of Polish radio broadcasting is presented along with an interpolation of where they are lacking observations. A linear trend based on an incomplete time series was used. The data along with the calculations are found in Tables 6, 7 and 8.

The figures for the numerical trends were obtained as follows:

– the trend relating to the number of radio stations broadcasting Polish programs

$$x = 64.218 + 4.941\,t$$

– the trend relating to the number of hours that Polish programs are broadcast

$$x = 187.649 + 14.413\,t$$

TABLE 6

Radio Stations in the United States Broadcasting Polish Programs and The Number of Hours Devoted to Polish Radio Programs Per Week[37]

Year	No. of stations	No. of hours
1958	85	281
1959	82	211
1960	82	218
1961-1962	105	330
1963	80	248
1965	94	280
1966	109	300½
1967	88	215
1968	113	252
1969	115	366½
1979	181	505
1980	190	547

TABLE 7

Empirical and Theoretical Values of the Development of the Number of Radio Stations Broadcasting Polish Programs in the United States 1958-1980

Years	Number of radio stations x	t	t^2	t x	Theoret. x′	Difference x − x′
1958	85	1	1	85	69,1	15,9
59	82	2	4	164	74,1	7,9
1960	82	3	9	246	79,0	3,0
61	.	.	.	.	84,0	.
62	105	5	25	525	88,9	16,1
63	80	6	36	480	93,9	−13,9
64	.	.	.	.	98,8	.
65	94	8	64	752	103,7	−9,7
66	109	9	81	981	108,7	0,3
67	88	10	100	880	113,6	−25,6
68	113	11	121	1243	118,6	−5,6
69	115	12	144	1380	123,5	−8,5
1970	.	.	.	.	128,4	.
71	.	.	.	.	133,4	.
72	.	.	.	.	138,3	.
73	.	.	.	.	143,3	.
74	.	.	.	.	148,2	.
75	.	.	.	.	153,2	.
76	.	.	.	.	158,1	.
77	.	.	.	.	163,0	.
78	.	.	.	.	168,0	.
79	181	22	484	3982	172,9	8,1
1980	190	23	529	4370	177,9	12,1
	1324	112	1598	15088		

Source: Broadcasting Yearbook 1958, 1959, 1960, 1962, 1963, 1965, 1966, 1967, 1968, 1969, 1979, 1980 Broadcasting Publications Inc., Washington, D.C.

TABLE 8

Empirical and Theoretical Values of the Increase in the Number of Hours of Polish Programming in the United States 1958-1980

Year	Number of programming hours x	t	t^2	t x	Theoret. x′	Difference x − x′
1958	281,0	1	1	281,0	201,1	79,9
59	211,0	2	4	422,0	214,5	−3,5
1960	218,0	3	9	654,0	227,9	−9,9
61	.	.	.	.	241,3	.
62	330,0	5	25	1650,0	254,7	75,3
63	248,0	6	36	1488,0	268,1	−20,1
64	.	.	.	.	281,5	.
65	280,0	8	64	2240,0	294,9	−14,9
66	300,5	9	81	2704,5	308,4	−7,9
67	215,0	10	100	2150,0	321,8	−106,8
68	252,0	11	121	2772,0	355,2	−83,2
69	366,5	12	144	4398,0	348,6	17,9
1970	.	.	.	.	362,0	.
71	.	.	.	.	375,4	.
72	.	.	.	.	388,8	.
73	.	.	.	.	402,3	.
74	.	.	.	.	415,7	.
75	.	.	.	.	429,1	.
76	.	.	.	.	442,5	.
77	.	.	.	.	455,9	.
78	.	.	.	.	469,3	.
79	505,0	22	484	11110,0	482,7	22,3
1980	547,0	23	529	12581,0	496,1	50,9
	3750,0	112	1598	42450,0		

Source: Broadcasting Yearbook 1958, 1959, 1960, 1962, 1963, 1965, 1966, 1967, 1968, 1969, 1979, 1980 Broadcasting Publications Inc., Washington, D.C.

From examining the trends, the average yearly increase in the number of stations broadcasting Polish programs is 4.9 percent and the average yearly increase in the number of broadcasts is 13.4 percent. These tendencies, however, had different forms in individual states; this will be discussed further in the historical portion of this study.

To compare the development of Polish radio programs with other ethnic programs, a juxtaposition illustrating the growth of the number of radio stations and the number of weekly hours of broadcasting is given below for the Polish and Italian communities in the United States.[38]

USA–in Total

	Polish Programs		Italian Programs	
Year	No. of stations	No. of hours	No. of stations	No. of hours
1958	85	281	117	443
1959	82	211	95	258
1963	80	248	90	300
1968	113	252	97	281
1969	115	366½	98	241

State of Illinois

	Polish Programs		Italian Programs	
Year	No. of stations	No. of hours	No. of stations	No. of hours
1958	6	52	5	30
1959	7	63	3	18
1963	4	40½	3	17
1968	2	36½	2	21
1969	4	46½	3	23

	Number of Listeners	
Year	Polish	Italian
1970	214,863	143,644
1980 (estimated)	800,000	300,000

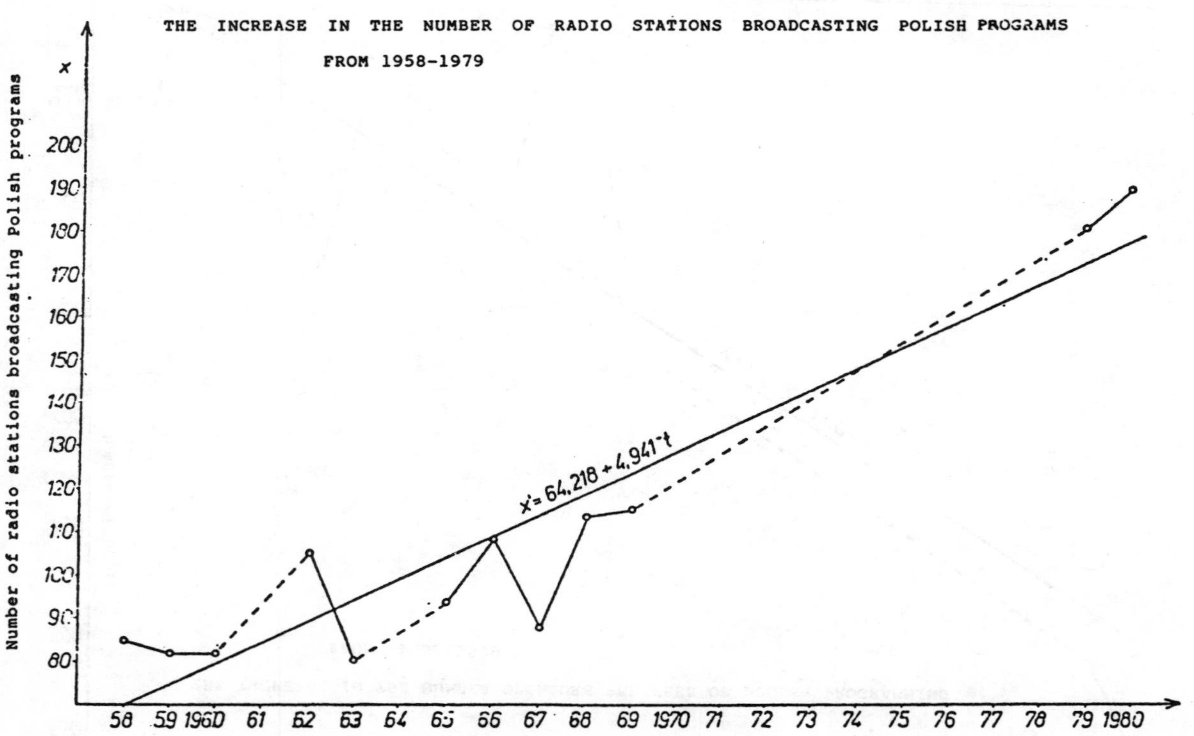
THE INCREASE IN THE NUMBER OF RADIO STATIONS BROADCASTING POLISH PROGRAMS
FROM 1958-1979
Number of radio stations broadcasting Polish programs
x
200
190
180
170
160
150
140
130
120
110
100
90
80
x' = 64.218 + 4.941 t
58
59
1960
61
62
63
64
65
66
67
68
69
1970
71
72
73
74
75
76
77
78
79
1980

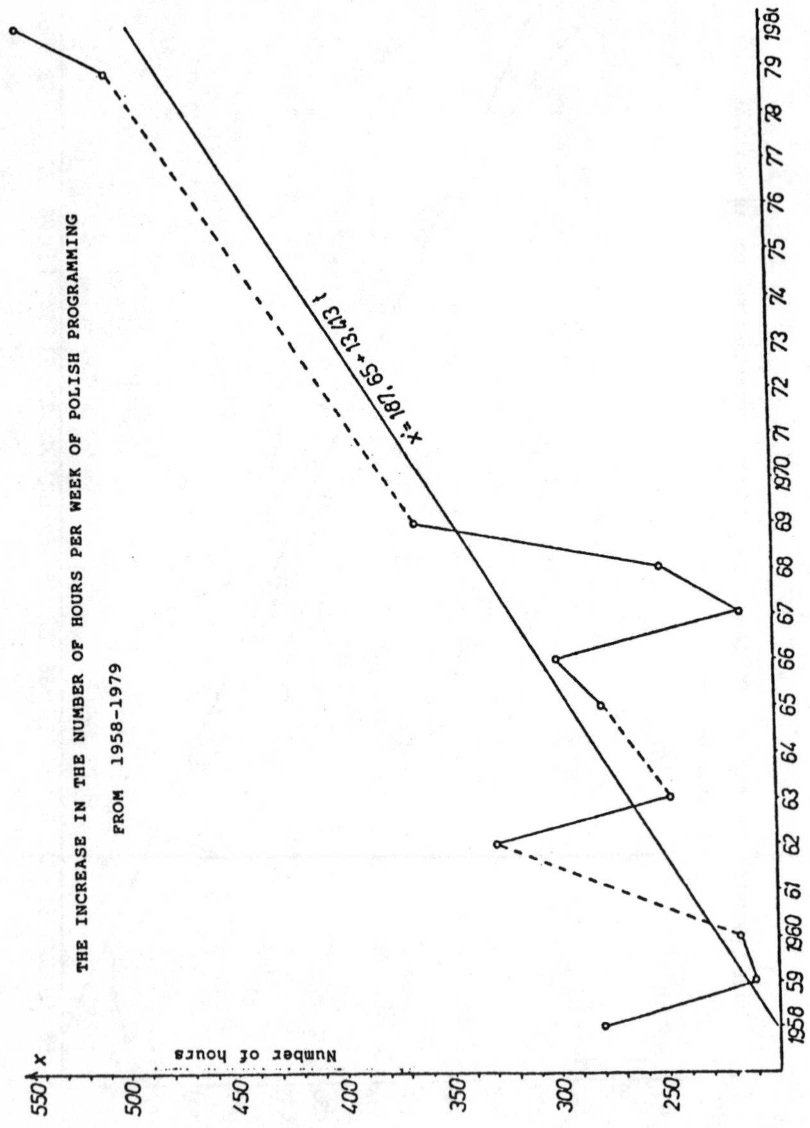
THE INCREASE IN THE NUMBER OF HOURS PER WEEK OF POLISH PROGRAMMING
FROM 1958-1979
Number of hours
x
550
500
450
400
350
300
250
x̂ = 187,65 + 13,413 t
1958
59
1960
61
62
63
64
65
66
67
68
69
1970
71
72
73
74
75
76
77
78
79
1980

PART TWO

Polish Radio Programs in Larger Polish-American Communities

CHAPTER 5

The State of Ohio: The Cradle of Polish Radio Programs in the United States

The first Polish radio program in the United States hit the airwaves in 1926 in Cleveland, Ohio, on radio station WJAY.[1] The management of radio station WJAY asked John M. Lewandowski, who spoke English and Polish equally well, to organize the first program. During this first Polish radio program, Paul Faut, a singer who had come from Poland in 1922, sang Polish songs.

From 1927 on, station WJAY broadcast regularly-scheduled Polish programs under John Lewandowski's direction.[2] These programs were broadcast every Sunday from noon until 1:00 p.m. Every week the orchestra under the baton of conductor John Stavarz and the well-known baritone soloist John Pekanis, as well as various invited guest artists presented Polish songs and music ranging from popular to classical to the Polonia of Cleveland. Lewandowski also broadcast two other weekly programs in 15-minute segments. Each Saturday at 9:00 a.m., a choir which rendered favorite Polish songs was broadcast. The second program, also on Saturdays but at 1:00 p.m., was devoted to children from the ages of four to 14. The program featured children who played various musical instruments or participated in singing lessons. A different group of children performed every week in these special broadcasts organized by John Lewandowski.

As time went on, Paul Faut took part in many of Lewandowski's popular programs. Born in Russia to a Polish family, Faut became a favorite singer with his Polish public. In a short time, he created his own radio program in Cleveland which he and his wife, Maria managed together.

John Lewandowski was born in Cleveland. He became a town council member and represented the 14th Ward. He was also active in veterans organizations since he had participated in World War I in the Euripean Theater of operations. Lewandowski was the pioneer of Polish radio programs in the United States. His radio programs were very popular and listened to universally. He was well-liked; everone knew him and respected him; he enjoyed great popularity. In September 1962, Lewandowski retired and left Cleveland, settling permanently in California where he died five years later. He was buried with great honors in his native Cleveland.[3]

Following in the footsteps of John Lewnadowski was Paul Faut. An excellent singer, composer, film and theater actor, he was also the producer of the most popular Polish records in the United States. Paul began broadcasting his own Polish radio program in 1931 over station WHK.[4]

The programs were aired every Sunday from 11:30 a.m. and lasted 45 minutes. The orchestra of Louis Rich played during Faut's broadcasts. They played light Polish music, such as operettas, folk or popular songs.

Sketches and other materials necessary for the programs were prepared by Faut himself. Faut's broadcasting career was played out over various radio stations such as WHK, WJAY, WCAR, and WTAM. He carried on these programs until the end of 1970. Paul Faut was a multitalented person. While still in Poland, he played the lover's role in a silent film. In the United States he was called the "Polish Rudolph Valentino." During the 1920s he acquired and operated the theater at Broadway and East 71st Street in Cleveland called "The Polonia Theater."

One example of how his entrepreneurial skills linked to his creativity is in a remembrance of the flight of two Polish pilots who flew from Europe to the United States and landed in the Azores. Faut wrote a song in their honor, composing both the words and the music. He then turned this into a gramaphone record. The record titled "Polskie Orły"

(Polish Eagles) was a smash hit, breaking all previous sales records. In the course of two months, 100,000 of these records were sold.[5]

Paul Faut, who also worked using his mother's maiden name of Mirecki, belonged to the ranks of the most distinguished and well-liked actors. He also appeared on the boards of theaters in Buffalo, Detroit and Pittsburg until 1931 when the great economic depression caused the majority of theaters to close, including Faut's own "Polonia Theater" in Cleveland.[6]

From 1931 Faut devoted himself exclusively to his radio career. The radio programs of Paul and Maria Faut which were very popular in Cleveland, were taken over by George and Eugenia Stolarczyk in 1970.[7]

George Stolarczyk was born in Bielica, Poland, newar Wilno on November 27, 1930. He immigrated to the United States in 1952. His wife, Eugenia, was born in Wloszczowa, Poland, on January 2, 1936. George Stolarczyk was a graduate of Western Reserve University in Cleveland. He received his bachelor's degree in 1967, while his wife, Eugenia, studied at Poznan University in Poland. With a special love for Polish music and folklore, the talented, ambitious, hard-working couple began a radio career in 1961. The Stolarczyks broadcast their first radio program from station WJMO and four months later switched their programs to WADC in Akron, which brought them a greater number of Polish listeners. Their show "Melodies from Poland" consisted of Polish popular music, radio plays, radio versions of novels, interviews with people in the field of science and the arts, local news, national and international news, and numerous announcements about life of the local Polonia. For a time, the Stolarczyks were the first to broadcast Polish-language lessons in their programs. In 1962, George and Eugenia Stolarczyk took over the oldest Polish radio program in the United States, established and produced by John Lewandowski.

In 1969, the Stolarczyks began to broadcast their programs from Cleveland station WXEN-FM on Sundays from 10:30 a.m. to 11:30 a.m., and on Wednesdays and Fridays from 7:30 p.m. In 1970, they took over Paul and Maria Faut's program and WERE (broadcast since 1931) and aried it from 9:00 a.m. to 10:30 a.m.

Apart from their radio work, George and Eugenia Stolarczyk devoted much of their time to community work. The organized exhibitions of Polish painters, lectures by Polish professors at the University of Cleveland, performances by Polish and Polish-American artistic groups and solo artists. George Stolarczyk served for four years as vice president of the Ohio division of the Polish Americam Congress in the 1970s; he headed the Copernican Anniversary Year celebrations in Ohio in 1973. Eugenia Stolarczyk devoted herself nearly full time to the popularization of Polish culture. For decades in Cleveland, there was hardly a Polonian event without the participation of George and Eugenia Stolarczyk.

George Stolarczyk died of cancer in December 1983. His wife continues to air Polish programs and continues her active work in the Polish community.

A popular radio polka program in Toledo, Ohio, is broadcast by Chester J. Zablocki from the 5000-Watt station WTOD. "Chet's Polka Party" is broadcast every Sunday for three and a half hours. Besides music, this program includes news and community information. Chester Zablocki has been airing his program since April 13, 1947.[8]

The creator of "Melodies of Poland" a Polish radio program of Toledo was the late Stanley Wos.[9] The program has been broadcast since 1950. This program was taken over in 1968 and run by Michael Rogaski. "Melodies of Poland" is on the air every Sunday from 8:00 a.m. to 9:00 a.m., in Polish and English. The program consists of folk music, hit songs, popular music and community announcements. From 1968 to 1970, this program was aired from station WOWA and from 1970 to now, from WIOT-FM. This extremely popular programs in heard by people in northwest Ohio and southeast Michigan.

Since 1961, Joseph Szulecki has announced the popular radio programs broadcast every Sunday from 7:00 a.m. to 8:00 a.m. from station WZZP in Cleveland. Polish folk music and folk songs make up most of the program.

The "International Polka Parade," a Polish radio program broadcast every Wednesday from 11:00 p.m. to midnight premiered on January 21, 1963, on WXEN-FM, then on WELW, and since 1974 on WZAK in Cleveland. The program is announced in both Polish and English, and provides Polish music, news, and announcements of Polonian activities. The producer and announcer of the program, Frank Swita, also runs his own travel agency and is active in many Polish-American organizations.[10]

A teacher by profession, George P. Lesnanasky (a.k.a. Larry Walk) is producer and announcer of a popular Polish radio program called

"Larry Walk's Happy Polkaland," broadcast on stations WFAR and WTCL for six hours every Sunday and for 45 minutes on Saturdays. Ninety percent of polka shows are hosted in English; the Polish language is used only occasionally.[11]

WZAK radio in Cleveland had daily Polish broadcasts that aired 20 hours weekly and were hosted by A. W. Zebrowski. The programs were broadcast Monday through Friday from 5:30 a.m. to 8:30 a.m.; on Sundays from 5:30 a.m. to 9:00 a.m.; and on Saturdays from 11:00 a.m. to 2:00 p.m. The programs, announced in a casual combination of Polish and English, presented polkas, obereks, waltzes, news and community announcements.

Zebrowski died while broadcasting his program in December 1980, and his program went off the air.[12]

The same station, WZAK, broadcast the Saturday programs of Chris and Bill Dehouske[13] (from 8:00 p.m. to 9:00 p.m.). The programs, announced in English, popularized Polka music. In 1978, WZAK changed its format and now airs ethnic programs only in the early morning hours on Sunday.

The Sunday schedule at WZAK includes Duane Dobies' program from midnight to 1:30 a.m. These are polka programs announced in English.[14]

Dellas Murawski hosts the "Polish Program" from the WAUP radio station in Akron, Ohio, every Sunday for two hours. This program is also announced in English.[15]

Polish athlete and internationally-known weightlifter Stanislaus Radwan aired a Polish program in WXEN-FM on Thursdays at 7:30 p.m., on Fridays at 3:00 p.m., and on Sundays from 6:00 a.m. to 8:00 a.m. Four years ago, Radwan retired from his radio career.[16]

The radio program "It's Polka Time" airs on Sundays at noon from station WYCH in Hamilton, Ohio. Another program, the "Greg Holtz (Polka) Show" was broadcast from WBOE-FM in Cleveland on Sundays starting at noon.

Finally, the "Polka Parade" program hosted by Rob and Joyce Zielinski is broadcast Saturdays from 12:30 p.m. to 2:00 p.m. from station WGOR in Toledo.

In the state of Ohio, Polish radio programs are broadcast on 23 stations.

CHAPTER 6

Dynamic Growth of Polish Radio Programs in Illinois

The birth of Polish radio in the Chicago area in the later 1920s has been documented in the Polish-American press. Mrs. Halina Paluszek-Gawronski, in her "Stories About Polish Programs in Chicago," published by the "Dziennik Zwiazkowy" (Polish Daily Zgoda newspaper) in April 1977, writes the following:

> They claim that old radio programs have not disappeared totally, but are out there somewhere in outer space and some time in the future, improved radio sets will be able to catch them. Let us imagine that our future grandchild is playing with the dial of his set, searching for the latest rock'n'roll, and hears the following greeting: 'Dzien dobry panstwu!' (Hello, ladies and gentlemen!). Who could that be? Maybe it's Przeczkowski beginning his 'White Eagles Hour,' broadcast only several weeks in 1927, which 58 years ago was the beginning of Polish radio in Chicago. Maybe Joseph Kapustka, an organist in the Polish National Church, beginning his first Sunday Polish radio program in 1928? . . .[17]

The list of Polish radio programs broadcast in Chicago is long indeed, as it should be in the nation's largest Polish-American community. The role they played in the life of Polonia is quite varied as well. Some of them reached the Polish-American listener with the living Polish language and reliable information, On March 20, 1937 the "Dziennik Chicagowski" (Polish Daily News) wrote:

> The airwaves can take a lot, and the human ear can endure an unimaginable amount of torture. But everything has its limits. Even radio. Even Polish programs which assert their right to cultivate the Polish language and Polish art through the invincible beauty of the Polish tongue. There must be an aesthetic limit that cannot be crossed . . . . There are good Polish programs that should be lauded for propogating Polish folklore, language, music and songs. But in this multitude of Polish programs, there is certainly too high a percentage of . . . cultural hideousness. There are programs that violate, by far, the limits of aesthetics. There are programs so absurd, so badly hosted, so idiotically planned, that they evoke only pity and a feeling of shame, because they go beyond the limits of common sense . . . .

From the perspective of many years, those harshly criticized programs seem in recollection slightly less horrendous. They belong to history, I will enumerate them among others, for they helped create the colorful picture of Polish life in Chicago.

The Polonian organization "Golden Age Committee" in a note published in the Polish Daily Zgoda on October 27, 1928, invited Chicago Polonia to listen to a Polish radio program broadcast on Sunday, October 28, from 1:00 p.m. to 2:30 p.m. from station WORD on the wavelength 1190kHz. This program featured Polish music, songs and conversation. It was on the air from time to time on an irregular basis. The Golden Age Committee, as part of educational and cultural activities, also organized similar Polish programs in later years devoted to various issues. The committee made great contributions to the development of Polish radio in the early, most difficult years of its existence.

Polish radio broadcasts came to Chicago on a regular basis with the White Eagle drama circle, whose producer and host was Ferdynand Drzewicki.

From a notice in the Polish Daily Zgoda dated April 15, 1929, we learn that on that date between 10:00 p.m. and 11:00 p.m. Casimir Wierzynski, a Polish poet who won the first literary prize at the Ninth

Olympic Games in Amsterdam, would take part in the White Eagle program broadcast from radio station WEDC. Also broadcast on that day were humurous songs and sketches performed by Thaddeus Kanter.

The Polish Bible School began airing its programs on October 20, 1929, from radio station WWAE, between 9:00 a.m. and 10:00 a.m.

The owners of the bigger stores located in Polish neighborhoods created their own Polish radio programs. Among the first to do so was the New Grand Leader Co. department store, which began to broadcast its own Polish program from WEDC on October 29, 1929. The programs reached Polonia every Tuesday at 9:19 a.m. Klara Mallek, a Polish employee of the store, was its announcer.

The Bruno Kujawski Piano Co. in Chicago started airing its own Polish radio program from WHFC between 7:00 p.m. and 8:00 p.m.

The commercials broadcast on Polish programs began to bring good results. No wonder new Polish language programs were started. Various radio stations in Chicago started to introduce Polish into their program schedule.

On December 21, 1930, WSBC began broadcasting a one-hour Polish program from 2:30 p.m. to 3:30 p.m. The show was a comedy titled "The Mayor's Problems" with music and songs for variety. The main roles were played by Valerie Glowacki, Thaddeus Malinowski and Witold Skubikowski.[18]

On April 3, 1930, Karol Syzdak began broadcasting a new Polish program, one a week between 9:00 p.m. and 10:30 p.m. from radio station WKBI.

The same month, Oktaw Orlowski put his one-hour program on the air from 7:00 p.m. to 8:00 p.m. on station WEDC.

Station WEDC also broadcasted the Association of Polish Merchants and Manufacturers radio program every Monday from 10:00 to 11:00. On Tuesdays, WEDC presented the radio program of the White Eagles drama circle from 7:00 to 8:00.

On December 5, 1929, Ritter's Furniture Store[19] began broadcasting its own Polish radio program on WCFL, first from 8:00 a.m. to 9:00 a.m., then from 1:00 p.m. to 2:00 p.m. Alexander Bonczkowski was producer of the program. He was also the conductor of the then-popular Polonian archestra, which performed on numerous Polish radio programs.

In the autumn of 1930, Ludwik Paluszek, who was well-known among American advertising agencies, began his nationwide Sunday afternoon half-hour radio program sponsored by Wonder Cut Bread, from station WBBM, one of the most powerful in Chicago. The artistic part of that program featured Janina Loboda, Marian Marski and Walenty Mossakowski–vocal. Little Halina Paluszek read the "Stachórka Diary" from the children's periodical "Płomyk," published in Warsaw.

On December 11, 1930, a new Polish radio hour was created, thanks to the efforts of the Grunwald Victory Society,[20] group 1104 of the Polish National Alliance. It was aired from station WEDC from 10:00 a.m. to 11:00 a.m. Stanly Stasiak's orchestra took part in the program, playing numerous Polish folk songs, polonaises and waltzes. The producers of the program were Bruno Zielinski, John Marszalek and Casy Kapanowski. In the late 1930s, the program added humorous sketches of the fictitious Siekierka family, presented in an anachronistic Polish dialect by Pelagia and Bruno Mroz, Walter Panek, Ferdinand Drzewicki and Bruno Zielinski.

The Grunwald program has remained on the air up to today. It was broadcast from station WOPA four times a week from 7:00 p.m. to 8:00 p.m. and produced by Bruno Zielinski, a popular Chicago-area personality. In 1984, the program moved to WCEV, in suburban Cicero, Illinois, from 6:30 p.m. to 7:00 p.m. Tuesdays, Thursdays and Fridays. It should be added that Bruno Zielinski was a pioneer of Polonian television. He broadcast the first Polish-American television program in 1957. For two years, Zielinski's "It's Polka Time" was carried the ABC Network in 29 states and was popular among TV audiences.

Still more Polish radio programs were being created in the Chicago area. From April 1, 1930, WCRW[21] radio began to air a Polish program.

On May 21, 1930, tradesmen and businessmen from the Brighton Park area in Chicago began their own radio hour on WSFL[22] between 7:45 a.m. and 8:45 a.m. Such artists as Casey Majewski, Marian Marski and M. Pucinski took part in them.

On June 9, 1930, the Polish-American company Star West Wash Laundry began broadcasting its own hour-long radio program in WEDC.[23] Oktaw Orlowski became its producer..

The Dziennik Zwiazkowy (Polish Daily Zgoda) notes that on Friday, May 4, 1930, between 7:00 p.m. and 8:00 p.m., during the daily "Dziennik Zwiazkowy" radio program, broadcast on station WHFC, Stanislaus Adamkiewicz, a candidate for congress from the eighth district, was to speak.

On the same day, at 9:30 a.m., radio station WCHI also broadcast a Polish program under the management of J. Stephan Zielinski.

Station WSBC broadcast an unusual program of Polish music songs on May 10, 1930, from 8:00 to 9:00. This program was directed also by J. Stefan Zielinski.[24]

On Monday, October 6, 1930, the following Polish radio programs were broadcast:[25]

7 to 8: The Radio Hour of O. Orlowski, station WEDC
8 to 9: Ritter's Radio Hour, station WCFL
9 to 10: The Radio Hour of Karol Syzdak, station WKBI
10 to 11: The Radio Hour of the "Biały Orzeł" (White Eagle) Dramatic Circle and the Association of Merchants and Manufacturers on station WEDC.

Ritter's Polish Radio Program also broadcasting on Mondays over station WCFL presented the following program on Monday, October 6, 1930:[26]

1. "Wiazanka piesni legionowych" (Medley of Legionnaire Songs) –J. Sikorski
2. "Owczarek" (The Shepherd)–oberek (a Polish folk dance) –W. Osmanski
3. "Jaskółka" (The Swallow)–śpiew (song)–F. Drozd
4. "Automobil" (The Automobile)–a polka–Ignacy Podgorski and his orchestra
5. "Amerykański" (American)–śpiew (song)–Walter Ochramowicz
6. "Pieśn podróznych" (The Travelers' Song)–Ignacy Jan Paderewski
7. "Natalia" (Natalie)–polka–S. Szczuszczewicz
8. "Wierna dziewczyna" (The Faithful Girl)–śpiew (song)–W. Zielinski
9. "Po Warszawsku" (In the Warsaw Manner)–mazurka–W. Osmanski in an orchestral rendition
10. "Przygody Walentego Gomuły" (The Adventures of Valentine Gomula)–performed by K. Majewski
11. "Dziarski" (A sprightly Melody)–masurka–orchestral rendition
12. "Polka u Rittera" (A Polka at Ritter's)–rendered by K. Majewski

13. "Marsz dragonów" (The Dragon's March)–J. Trzcieniecki in an orchestral rendition
14. The orchestra directed by Stanislaus Stasiak

The arranger and director of the program was Alexander Bonczkowski and the announcer was Casey Majewski (Kazimierz Majewski). It was a good program in the musical portion and the participation of the best artists and orchestras of the time leads to the conclusion that Ritter's radio programs were on a high artistic level.

Another press not dated October 3 announced the "Polski program radiowy izby handlowej" (The Polish Radio Program of the Chamber of Commerce) on Milwaukee Avenue[27] from radio station WSBC from 8:00 p.m. to 9:00 p.m.

Radio stations with a wide broadcasting range conducted their own Polish programs. WLS, for example, advertised a new program in Polish newspapers, encouraging Polonia to listen to the hour-long program between 12:30 p.m. and 1:30 p.m. on October 5. A male quartet composed of J. Nowicki, W. Malecki, E. Lakome and B. J. Zaleski performed during this program. The radio programs broadcast over WLS in Polish had a large following in several states.

Station WEDC broadcast its first Polish program February 1931. The program was sponsored by the Three Leader Stores and was daily from 10:30 a.m. to 11:00 a.m.

On May 17, 1931, a new Polish radio hour called "Liric"[28] was created at the WEDC radio station, and aired from 7:00 p.m. to 8:00 p.m.

Daily programs in Polish were presented to the Chicago Polish community by station WKBI at 9:00 p.m. The producer and announcer of those programs was a local journalist Boleslaw Czuwara.

In November 1931, a new Polish program owned by the men's clothing store Salk Clothing Co.[29] went on the air on WSBC on Sundays at 3:00 p.m.

Starting in January 1932, station WSBS began broadcasting programs in Polish on Mondays, Wednesdays and Fridays from 8:00 p.m. to 9:00 p.m. and on Sundays from 2:30 p.m. to 3:30 p.m. The programs included folk and classical music and vocal numbers. Universal Broadcasters Inc. managed these Polish programs.

In January 1932, WLS radio informed its listeners that it was starting a Polish program sponsored by Polish tradesmen on Sundays from 12:30

p.m. to 1:30 p.m., while station WGES announced a Polish program from 7:00 p.m. to 8:00 p.m. on Thursdays.

In October 1932, a new porgram was started on WGES which aired from 3:30 p.m. to 4:00 p.m. by General Credit Stores. Anna Turel and Ferdinand Drzewicki were the hosts of these programs. By the end of the month, on October 28, General Credit Stores increased the number of their Polish-language programs to four weekly.[30]

The Golden Age Committee continued to broadcast radio programs in Polish sporadically, announcing the subject of each broadcast in advance.

Ritter's Polish radio hour was then broadcast daily from 2:00 p.m. to 3:00 p.m. from WCFL.

At WGES, Zbigniew Jaworowski aired his own program from 8:00 a.m.

In December 1932, on station WEDC, the Kosciuszko Polish Theater[31] began broadcasting its program every Sunday from 4:00 p.m. to 5:00 p.m., in which it announced, for example, its future plays.

In May 1933, a radio program was created by the scouting movement connected to the Polish National Alliance.[32] It was broadcast every Sunday from 4:00 p.m. to 5:00 p.m. on WEDC.

In 1933, Polish radio programs of the General Credit Stores were broadcast over WGES on Mondays from 8:00 p.m. to 9:00 p.m., on Fridays from 5:00 p.m., and on Sundays from 3:30 p.m. These programs features such artists as Mr. and Mrs. Bednarczyk, who appeared on stage and on the air as "Wojtek" and "Magda." Their specialty were sketches and jokes, with which they entertained radio audiences.

In July of that year, the Evans Fur Co.[33] began broadcasting programs in Polish. The programs were aired on WSFL every Sunday at noon. The producers and announcers of the programs were Adela Raczynski-Walton and Zbigniew Jaworowski.

Aslo in July of 1933, WGES presented its Polish Sunday radio program from 3:30 p.m. with the participation of such artists as John Rafalski, Ewelina Drzewicki and Edmund Terlikowski on violin.

The Z. G. Herbs Co. in May 1933 organized a daily radio program in Polish, [34] on WJJD, which had a large broadcast range. It was on the aire daily from 5:00 p.m. and on Sundays from 5:30 p.m. Such artists as Casey Majewski, Halina Majewski, Anna Pedicini and an orchestra under the direction of Maximillian Olefski appeared in those programs. Waclaw Rzewski hosted the broadcasts.

In April 1934, a Polish variety show sponsored by the Vervena Co.[35] (a cosmetic firm) began broadcasting on station WCES. The programs were given Wednesdays and Fridays at 5:00 p.m. on Saturdays from 6:300 p.m. and on Sundays at 4:30 p.m. The producer and announcer of these broadcasts was the talented young journalist Halina Paluszek.

In October 1934, "Pola and Lola" a new Polish-language program began to be transmitted from station WGES at 11:00 a.m. under the direction of Stach Milewski. Among other things, the novel "Cyganeria" (The Bohemian Life) or the Annals of True Love was broadcast during this program.

Ritter's radio programs was hosted by Zbigniew Jaworowski. Radio sketches were perfomed by Casey Majewski and his daughter Halina, while Adela Walton sang. Political commentaries were presented by a municipal official Szczepan Kolanowski. In 1934, Wlodzimierz Sikora began hosting Ritter's program.

In November 1934, "Rataj's Radio Hour"[36] went on the air. Rataj was the owner of a furniture store in Chicago. The programs were broadcast over WGES on Thursdays from 7:00 p.m. to 8:00 p.m. They featured Maria Gruszczynski and Jadwiga Furmaniak.

Anna Pedicini, a Polish stage artist, who had appeared in various radio programs, began broadcasting her own program from WSBC on Saturdays from 2:00 p.m. to 3:00 p.m. in February 1935.[37]

In June 1935, one more Polish radio program was created at WGES and broadcast on Fridays from 5:00 p.m. to 6:00 p.m. This program featured Stefania Niedzwiecki, one of the best Polish-American vocalists of those times.

The Polish Daily Zgoda printed the following schedule on August 31, 1935:

A Survey of Polish Radio Programs

MONDAY:

The Polish Syndicate's Radio Hour
Station WGES, 7:00 p.m. to 8:00 p.m.
Announcers: W. Sikora and F. Drzewicki

WEDNESDAY:

Rataj's Radio Hour
Station WGES, 7:00 p.m. to 8:00 p.m.
Announcers: Panek and Drzewicki

THURSDAY:

Rataj's Radio Hours
Station WGES, 7:00 p.m. to 8:00 p.m.
Sketches–Humor–Songs
Announcer: F. Drzewicki

FRIDAY:

Mother's Radio Hour
Station WSBS, 10:00 a.m. to 11:00 a.m.
Music–Humor–Satire–Sketches
Announcers: Ferdinand Dzewicki, Bruno Zielinski

SATURDAY:

An Hour of Polish News
Station WSBS, 8:00 p.m. to 9:00 p.m.
Questions from listeners and answers from the announcer
Director and Announcer: Ferdinand Drzewicki

SUNDAY:

Ritter's Radio Hour
Station WCFL, 9:00 p.m. to 10:00 p.m.
Bonczkowski's Orchestra
Announcers: Ritter, Bruno Zielinski, Sikora

In early 1936, the "Dziennik Zjednoczenia" (Alliance Daily) announced a competition for the most popular Polish radio program, radio features and the most popular announcer. The results of this contest were published in its issue dated March 22, 1936. The "Grunwald Hour" took first place with 293 votes; second place went to the "Early Birds" radio program hosted by Zbigniew Jaworowski with 191 votes; third place was won by "Ritter's Hour" produced by Alexander Bonczkowski with 133 votes. The Z. G. Herbs programs followed with 49 votes; the "Sunny Hour" hosted by Lidia Pucinski received 22 votes; and the "Pola-Lola" radio program managed by Halina and Ludwik Paluszek received 20 votes.

In the category of the most interesting radio sketches, the results of the competition were as follows: "The Siekierka Family" featuring the Mrozes and B. Zielinski received 191 votes; "Bartek Bieda" by Thaddeus Kantor recieved 58 votes; "Ogórkowa" with Anna Pedicini received 20 votes; "Dziadek Gaweda" by Antoni Bednarczyk received 17 votes; Ferdinand Drzewicki received 14 votes; Wlodzimierz Sikora received eight votes; Casey Majewski received seven votes; and Waclaw Rzewski received one vote.

In April 1936, the Z. G. Herbs Co. changed its name to the Stanis Co. and began boradcasting daily Polish programs Monday through Saturday from 7:00 p.m. to 8:00 p.m. on radio station WJJD under the management of the known humorist "Bartek Bieda" (Kantor).[38] Stanislawa Dobrosielski, "Kasia". the only Polonian actess of the time who had graduated from drama school in Warsaw, participated in the programs. The humorous sketches presented in those programs won tremendous popularity among listeners. The air times of those programs changed later to the following schedule: Monday through Saturday from 8:00 p.m. to 8:30 p.m. and on Sundays from 8:00 p.m. to 9:00 p.m. In the second part of August 1936, the air times of Ritter's programs were also changed. The daily programs were broadcast in WJJD from 5:00 p.m. to 6:00 p.m., while the Sunday program aired from 7:45 to 8:45.

In October 1936, Lidia Pucinski's programs were given permanent status. "Poranek Sloneczny" (Sunny Morning) was broadcast at that time at 8:30 a.m. from station WSBS every day except Sunday. She often played the role of "Mary Kocurek" in various sketches along with the supporting actresses Maria Gruszczynski and Maria Zdanowicz. Lidia Pucinski read to her listeners Helena Mniszek's popular novel "Trendowata" (The Leper) and often provided recipes for her listeners. These features remained permanent highlights in the program.

The radio programs of Antoni Bednarczyk "Dziadek Gaweda" (The Old Storyteller) were also popular in those days. Broadcast daily at 3:00 p.m. on WSBC, the programs featured the songs of Dziadek Gaweda, vocals by Lola Zdanowicz, radio version of the Polish novel Behind Cloister Walls," as well as folk songs.

Polish-American comedians Thaddeus Kantor and Stanislawa Dobroseilski appeared as "Bartek Bieda" and "Kasia" in the daily broadcasts owned by Gantkowski's herb company, Stanis. The programs aired on WJJD from 5:00 p.m. to 6:00 p.m.

The Polish radio program "Ślubne Dzwony" (Wedding Bells) produced by Zofia and John Jaworski, owners of the Peacock Bridal Ship which made custom-ordered wedding dresses, was distinguished for its presentation of classical music and the recitals of a singing sextet made up of Stefania Niedzwiecki, Wladyslawa Schmidt, Irene Czyzewski, Pola Baranowski, Zofia Jaworski and Maria Sniegocki. Helena Wiatrowski was conductor and accomapnied the singers. The "Wedding Bells" program was hosted by Zofia Jaworski and Aniela Gorny, with recitations by Lonia Rozanski.

In 1937, several new programs were presented to Polish listeners. In January, WGES premiered "Zwierciadło chwili" (Mirror of the Moment),[39] at 2:00 p.m. The education department of the Polish National Alliance honored Thaddeus Kosciuszko with a special program prepared by Francis Zolynski, while Bruno Mroz appeared as "Walerian Wiatrek" in humorist sketches.

In the "Dziadek Gawenda" program, a radio version of the Polish novel "Potega Milości" (The Power of Love) was broadcast in installments.

The Polish program " Pola and Lola" continued to be broadcast from station WGES at 11:00 a.m. under the directorship of Ludwig and Halina Paluszek. This program provided news from around the world.

In October, the "Glos Zycia" (Voice of Life)[40] daily Polish radio program went on the air from WSBS at 8:15 a.m. Also in October 1937, "Glos Polski" (The Polish Voice) was introduced by WGES. This program was broadcast in a Polish mountain dialect on Fridays at 4:00 p.m. Thaddeus Muza was producer and host of this program. "Familia Radiowa" (Radio Family) was the name of a new Polish program of the General Credit Stores, broadcast on WGES every Wednesday at 6:30 p.m.

In November 1937, the radio hour of the Polish National Catholic Church[41] was created and broadcast every Sunday at 3:30 p.m. from station WHIP in Hammond, Indiana. In the first program, Bishop Francis Bonczak of Milwaukee, Wisconsin, addressed listeners. The radio program of the National Church continued to air intermittantly on various stations, including WCEV, until the early 1980s. Bishop Leon Grochowski was a frequent guest on these programs.

In May 1938, station WSBC presented a new Polish radio program "Sanito," and in it there were humorous sketches, Polish songs and music.

There was also an increase in the number of radio programs sponsored by the General Credit Stores in 1938, in which listeners were entertained by "Bertek Bieda" and "Kasia" in their comedy acts. These programs are now broadcast in Sundays at 2:00 p.m., on Mondays, Wednesdays, Thursdays and Fridays at 6:30 p.m., still from the WGES station.

The Polish Radio Syndicate[42] was registered in the state of Illinois on February 20, 1938. Its organizers were: Bruno Zielinski, Antoni Bednarczyk, Lidia Pucinski, Ludwik Paluszek, Ferdinand Drzewicki and Wlodzimierz Sikora. The Syndicate aimed to organize the advertising market to eliminate unhealthy competition among radio broadcasters and to improve the quality of programs. The outbreak of World War II interrupted the activities of the organization.

On December 23, 1938, Lidia Pucinski broadcast a well-produced and enchanting Christmas Eve program on WGES at 6:30 p.m. Listeners heard the "Polish Bethlehem" written by Lucjan Rydel and the vaudeville segment "The Guys from Krowodrze." The best artists of the Polish stage in Chicago took part in this holiday program: Antoni Bednarczyk, Wawrzyniec Czubachowski, Rosalin Dreznion, Thaddeus Kantor, Walter Krasowski, Casey Majewski, and Ludwik and Halina Paluszek, with an orchestra under the direction of Antoni Kawalkowski.

In January 1939, an independent radio hour was created by the Association of Polish Merchants and Manufacturers[43] and broadcast over WGES on Sundays at 1:30 p.m.

"Ratay's Radio Hour" was broadcast in WHIP on Sundays at 1:00 p.m. In Ratay's program of February 11, 1939, listeners were treated to the Polish opera "Halka" performed by local singers.

Lidia Pucinski's program broadcast October 6 from station WGES[44] between 6:00 p.m. and 8:00 p.m. discussed political issues dealing particularly with the cessation of military operations in Poland. Kinga Jarecki, the wife of a district judge in Chicago, talked about Polonia's participation in helping the Polish poeple during the war through the intermediary of the American Red Cross. In a special radio program sponsored by the General Credit Stores, and a broadcast by station WGES on Thursday, November 30, 1939, news about the war was broadcast. Stanislaus Milewicz also talked about a new novel "Chleb i serce" (Bread and Heart).

On October 30, 1939, during Zbigniew Jaworowski's program "Wieczorny Dzwon" (The Evening Bell)[45] on station WCFL at 9:00 p.m., Francis Swietlik, the Censor of the Polish National Alliance delivered a speech about organizing material help for Poles who found themselves in various countries as well as in interment camps and refugee camps because of World War II.

In the first period of the development of Polish radio in Chicago, the directors, producers and announcers of Polish radio programs were mainly Polish theater actors or journalists. Many Polish radio programs were on a high artistic level. Music dominated the broadcasts, predominantly folk music and songs, but popular and classical music was also played. An important part of the Polish programs were the humorous sketches and recitations. Orchestras made up of several musicians played during these broadcasts, but for financial reasons, many programs started using records for music and songs.

Concluding this review of Polish radio programs in Chicago before World War II, let us recall the names of those who were linked with those pioneer years:

SINGERS:

> Rosalia Czubachowski, Maria Data, Jadwiga Fuvmaniak, Thaddeus Lapicki, Janina Loboda, Stanislaus Milewski, Stefania Niedzwiecki, Walter Ochranowicz, Irene Scislowski, Maria Zdanowicz. Violin performances by Antoni Kawalkowski and Edmund Terlikowski should also be noted.

HOSTS of their own radio programs or of the programs owned by sponsors:

> Antoni Bednarczyk, Larry Czubachowski, Boleslaw Czuwara, Ferdinand Drzewicki, Zbigniew and Adela Jaworowski, Joseph Kapustka, Casey Majewski, Klara Mallek, Marian Marski, Paul Miczko, Thaddeus Muza, John Nieminski, Oktaw Orlowski, Ludwik and Halina Paluszek, Walter Panek, Zeb Zarnecki, Anna Pedicini, J. Przeczkowski, Lidia Pucinski, Waclaw Rzewski, Wlodzimierz Sikora, Karol Syzdak, Bruno Zielinski, Stefan Zielinski, Francis Zolynski.

The following artists appeared in radio sketches:

St. Dobrosielski and Thaddeus Kantor as Kasia and Bartek Bieda; Antoni and Helena Bednarczyk; Lidia Pucinski as Marysia Kocurek; Walter Krasowski and Bruno Mroz as Medrkowiak and Glupkowiak; Walter Sikora and his group as the Marek Family; Bruno Zielinski, Pelagia and Bruno Mroz as the Siekierka Family; Boleslaw Czuwara in Gypsy Campfire; and finally, Casey Majewski and his daughter Halina.

CONDUCTORS AND MANAGERS OF MUSIC ENSEMBLES:

Alexander Bonczkowski, Sylvester Klosowski, Frances Linhart, Maximillian Olefski, Oktaw Orlowski, Stanislaus Stasiak, and David Wolkow.

The level of Polish radio programs in the 1920s and 1930s was extremely varied—they ranged from very good to difficult to accept. This is what the "Dziennik Chicagowski" (The Chicago Daily) had to say on the subject:

> The air is patient, and the human ear can bear a huge amount of torture. But, of course, everything has a limit. Even radio. Even Polish programs having the pretention to claim that they are cultivating Polish speech and art by means of the immortally beautiful native word. An aesthetic line that one may not cross must exist .... Good Polish programs exist and they display a praiseworthy activity of propagating Polish speech, folklore, music and songs. But in the crowd of 'Polish hours' a defintely too large percentage of cultural monsters exists. There are programs that go far beyond the line of good taste. There are programs so poorly produced, so idiotically composed, so absurd that they only arouse shame and sorrow, because they go beyond the bounds of the rational ....[46]

Oktaw M. Orlowski in the early 1940s directed from station WSBC in Chicago "Poranny Program" (Early Morning Program) in Polish from 10:00 a.m. to 11:00 a.m. He worked actively in Group 2768—The Society of Polish Theater—of the Polish National Alliance. In 1948, he moved to

Port Isabel, Texas, where he died in 1977 at the age of 87. Mostly he broadcast folk music. The older generation in Chicago still remembers these programs fondly.

The war period was marked by a significant slowdown in the development of Polish radio programs in Chicago. A number of programs were eliminated because American industry was geared to producing war goods. As a consequence, there were shortages of goods in the private sector, even shortages of basic necessities. The demand for goods remained the same, but the supply decreased considerably. In such a situation, there was less need for advertising. The source of financing for Polish programs diminished since the fundamental means of support for Polish radio was advertising.

In the development of Polish radio in the Chicago metropolitan area, Ludwik and Halina Paluszek made a substantial contribution.[47] Ludwik Paluszek, who graduated from the Rzeszow High School (Gymnasium) in Poland, emigrated and in 1916 became the co-founder and co-owner of the first Polish advertising agency in the United States. His firm, "Paluszek Brothers Publishers Representatives," was instrumental in developing the Polish press, as well as Polish radio programs, by gaining advertisements from important American companies for them.

In the fall of 1930, Paluszek was the director and announcer of a radio program sponsored by Wonder Cut Bread which was distributed nationally. The program was broadcast on Sundays at 1:00 p.m. over WBBM. In 1932, he organized on station WGES "Program Radiowy Dziennika Zjednoczenia" (Daily Alliance Radio Program) on Saturdays from 7:00 p.m. to 8:00 p.m. The program consisted of national and international news and lively folk music. For the first time, he also presented a special program on Mother's Day. Also from the same station, at 2 p.m. on Sundays, he broadcast competitions for children. The General Credit Stores, a clothing company, also advertised during these broadcasts.

In 1935, Paluszek L broadcast from WGES "Program wiejski" (The Country Program) in which folk music was played in half-hour segments three times a week. One of the institutions advertising during these programs was the financial firm Local Loan Co.

From 1934 to 1938, Paluszek and his wife, Halina, presented the "Pola-Lola" program daily at 11 o'clock, also from WGES.

From 1937, he broadcast a daily program at 8:15 from station WHFC in Cicero. The Paluszek radio program enjoyed a wide listening audience in the Chicago area.

Halina Paluszek was born in Poland where she completed the School for Girls operated by Professor Jadwiga Kowalczyk in Warsaw on Wiejska Street. She came to Chicago with her mother and other members of the family in 1913. She continued her studies here at evening courses. She worked actively in various Polish organizations. During the first years of her husband's broadcasting activity, she helped him prepare various programs, afterward, she produced radio programs. From 1933 to 1943, on station WSBC, and then on WHES from 11 a.m., she had a 30-minute program five days a week, which was sponsored by General Credit Stores. In 1945 on WGES, she was responsible for the program "Clore Tango Time" broadcast three times a week. She was the co-editor and announcer of the popular program "Pola-Lola" broadcast with her husband on WGES.

After the war, advertisements of companies that had subsidized Polish radio programs before the war reappeared. And of course, new Polish radio programs also reappeared.

In March 1945, the Chicago clothing firm General Credit Stores encouraged Polonia through the colums of the Polish Daily Zgoda to listen to the serialized segments of "Chleb i Serce" (Bread and Heart) on the radio program which they sponsored. Station WHFC in the suburb Cicero presented a daily Polish program from 9 p.m. to 9:15 p.m. W. J. Szepielaski was the director of that program. In September 1945, the Rataj Furniture Co. program returned to the airwaves. Rataj's concert program was broadcast on WGES at 6:20 p.m.

Polish radio programs stabalized in the Chicago area in 1947. On WGES from 7:30 to 8:30, "Ranne Ptaszki" (The Early Birds), an hour-long program was produced and announced by Zbigniew Jaworowski. Local, national and international news were the main components of this program. In addition to Jaworowski, his wife Adela and Paul Miczko also appeared. "Godzina Słoneczna" (The Sunney Hour) directed by Lidia Pucinski was given on WGES at 7 p.m. The same station also broadcast "Porgram Radiowy Polskich Kupców i Przemysłowców" (The Radio Program of Polish Merchants and Manufacturers) under the management of Francis Nurczyk on Saturdays at 1:30 p.m. The Illinois Division of the

Polish-American Congress sporadically preprared programs that were broadcast on WGES.

In 1949, a new Polish radio program presented by District Two of the Polish Sea League on WIEY-FM appeared in Chicago.[48] Francis Jurek and Boleslaw Tyma created the committee for that sea league program. It was their task to search for advertisers for the program. Joseph Migala, the author of this book, was chosen as producer and host of that program.

In this chronological order, I have come to my own person in this report. On October 3, 1950, my wife, Sława, and I inaugurated our own program, which is on the air even today–"Głos Polonii" (The Voice of Polonia). We started with three broadcasts weekly: Tuesdays, Thursdays and Saturdays from 5:30 p.m. to 6:00 p.m. on WLEW. On January 1, 1952, the Voice of Polonia program was moved to station WOPA in suburban Oak Park, but kept the same airtimes. In 1970, the Voice of Polonia was extended to an hour and a half and was broadcast Mondays through Saturdays from 4:30 p.m. to 6:00 p.m.

The content of these programs includes folk music from recordings brought from Poland, popular music, Polish songs, music from operettas and classical music. The first part features Chicago area news. The second part includes 20 minutes of news from and about Poland and Polonia. The third part includes world and international news. In our series "Z ojczystych stron," (From the homeland), we bring Poland closer to Polonia through interviews and reports, both our own and sent in from Poland. In our 10-minute literary corner, we present short stories, radio versions of novels in the form of plays and narrations. Since 1971, each Saturday, we broadcast a 15-minute lesson of conversational Polish for people who want to improve their language.

The Voice of Polonia program now features my son, George, as its principle host, with portions announced by my wife, Sława, and me, as well as George's wife, Grażyna (Grace).

October 1, 1979, the Migala Family put its own radio station into operation in Cicero, Illinois, as Migala Communication Corporation, which received the call letters WCEV and operates on the 1450 kHz frequency. The "Voice of Polonia" program was extended to two hours and was, for a time, the longest daily Polish program in the Chicago area.

I would like to devote slightly more space to one of the initiatives of several Polish programs in this country, including my own "Voice of Polonia"–the teaching of the Polish language over the radio.

How did the Radio School for the Polish Language arise in Chicago? The director of the program "Voice of Polonia" had entertained for a long time the idea of setting into operation lesssons teaching the Polish language within the framework of his broadcasts. The lack of appropriate materials postponed the realization of this idea. When phonograph records were made in Poland to accompany the textbook "Mówimy po polsku" (Beginner's Course of Polish), which appeared in 1970, steps were taken to bring the idea of teaching Polish over the radio to fruition. After consultation with a number of leaders in the Polish-American community, Joseph Migala decided to call together a conference devoted to this matter. "Towarzystwo Przyjaciól Radiol" (Radio Friends Society) and the director of "Voice of Polonia" invited people to participate in the conference by sending them the following letter:

> Gentlemen!
>
> The Radio Friends Society and the director of the 'Voice of Polonia' program, along with the support of the president of the main adminstration of the Polish-American Congress, Mr. Aloysius Mazewski, have the honor to invite you to an important conference to set into motion the first radio school of the Polish language in the United States. The conference, with the participation of President Mazewski. the directors of the Saturday schools of the Polish language and other interested organizations and individuals will take place on Friday, June 4, at 8 p.m. in the meeting room of The Royal Inn, Radio Halls Inc., 3201 N. Long Ave. at the corner of Belmont Avenue. Your participation in this conference is very much desired since the whole subject of teaching Polish via this mass medium carries such important consequences–one result of which will be the considerable enrichment of the life of Polonian organizations. We, the undersigned, respectfully urge you to attend.
>
> Stephen Czarniecki, president of the Radio Friends Society
>
> Evelina Grzybowski, secretary
>
> Joseph Migala, director of the "Voice of Polonia" program

The letter is dated May 27, 1971.

The conference was well-attended. The participants thoroughly discussed the issues and reacted very favorably to the idea of creating a radio school of the Polish language in Chicago.

During the meeting, an advisory-pedogogical committee composed of experienced language teachers and cultural activists of Polonia was chosen.

The secretary of the conference, Halina Bonikowski, presented the following prepared press release, which announced the opening date of the activities of the radio school:

The Radio School of the Polish Language in Chicago

> The first lesson of the Polish language will begin October 18 of this year on the program 'Voice of Polonia' broadcast by Joseph Migala from station WOPA at 1490 Kilocycles on your dial. The lessons will start at 4:15 p.m. Lucyna Migala, an editor at NBC News, will conduct the lessons. The Radio School of the Polish Language in Chicago came about thanks to the initiative of the Migala's for which they deserve a word of appreciation. It will be broadcast on 'Voice of Polonia' and will be sponsored by the Radio Friends Society under the protective wing of the Polish-American Congress. In connection with this, a special advisory-pedagogical committee was established. The committee is composed of experienced Polish-language teachers and social activists of Polonia. The members of the committee are: Anna Czarniecki and Stephen Czarniecki, president of the Radio Friends Society; Maria Neuman, teacher at the K. Pulaski School; Anna Rychlinski, principal of the H. Sienkiewicz School; Casey (Kazimierz) Lorenc, principal of the T. Kosciuszko School; Halina Bonikowski, teacher at the T. Kosciuszko School; Wanda Rozmarek, principal of the St. Jacek School; Walter Pawula, teacher at Lane Technical High School; Joseph, Sława and Lucyna Migala.
>
> During their meetings, the advisory-pedagogic committee has already set forth certain guidelines and directives which will be of help in carrying out the lessons of the Polish language. The study of language with the aid of radio has its own old and beautiful traditions. It is always based on textbooks especially written for this purpose and is also based on acoustic impressions. To be

able to follow the lessons of Polish broadcast on the radio, it will be necessary to have the book 'Mowimy po polsku' (Beginners Course of Polish), which has been purchased in Poland and which will be distributed at various centers of the Polish-American community. Information about this will be given at a later date.

The lessons are being organized for everyone who wishes to study Polish regardless of his age. We would like to encourage anyone who already cherishes the Polish word or all those for whom it raises new emotions and arouses the desire to get to know the language of their forebears to take advantage of these lessons. They will be treated to the pleasant, resonant voice of Lucyna Migala, who will be explaining Polish complexities and at the same time will be studying with you the native language of her parents.

On wishes real satisfaction and the best results to all those who are beginning the radio course of the Polish language on Joseph Migala's 'Voice of Polonia' and one wishes perserverance to the Migala's in conducting this difficult school.

Halina Bonikowski
June 10, 1971

The day before the radio school began (October 17, 1971) another press release about the Radio School of the Polish Language appeared in the Polish Daily Zgoda.

The first Radio School of the Polish Language in the United States is under the sponsorship of the Polish-American Congress. Up until this time, the considerable number of Polish-Americans in the Chicago area have had no mass medium transmitting the study of Polish. We looked enviously when television programs had a series of regular lessons in various languages, but unfortunately, not in Polish.

Everyone will admit that the world has 'contracted' in the sense that people can cross the Atlantic in a few hours, and as one hears more and more about Poland, one is more interested in her culture. Knowledge of various languages brings nations together and facilitates the road to peace in the world for which everyone hopes.

Our generation's children are beginning to be proud of their Polish heritage, to enjoy it and bost of it. But that is not enough.

To be able to know a country, its culture and traditions, it is necessary to know its language. Such a prospect is now a possibility in the Chicago area for children and adults equally. On October 18, 1971, at 4:15 p.m. on station WOPA-1490 kilocycles, the first lessons of the Radio School of the Polish Language in the United States are beginning. The lessons will be broadcast every Saturday at the same time . . . .

The existence of the Radio School of the Polish Language has been brought about through the interest of the entire Chicago Polonia. As Mikolaj Rej wrote in the sixteenth century, 'The Poles are not geese, they also have their own language. The fate of the Radio School of the Polish Language rest in the hands of Chicago Polonia. Enroll your children and grandchildren into the school. When they grow up, they will be grateful they had the opportunity to learn the language of their ancestors. Registration in the Radio School of the Polish Language is daily, except Sunday, in the office of 'Voice of Polonia' at 5356 W.Belmont,Chicago, Illinois, 60641. Phone 282-7745.

Hanka Czarniecki
Corresponding Secretary

The Radio School of the Polish Language became an accomplished fact. Listeners favorably accepted studying Polish via radio. The school still enjoys an unabated popularity. As mentioned before, the "Voice of Polonia" was able to organize a regular course of conversational Polish, based on tapes and books from Poland. The course has aired for 20 years from 4:15 p.m. to 4:30 p.m. on Saturdays under the auspices of the Polish-American Congress. Since the congress is a national organization, there is interest in expanding this initiative to other Polish-American communities. The question of teaching Polish through radio was put on the agenda of the 9th National Convention of the Polish-American Congress, held in Detroit in 1972. The convention created a committee to study the question and passed the following resolutions:

The Committee for Teaching the Polish Language through Radio and Television, established by the Ninth Convention of the Polish-American

Congress, submits to the convention for approval the following conclusions:

1. Acknowledging the importance of using the mass media, such as radio and television, for teaching Polish. It advises the convention to maintain a permanent commission for the teaching of the Polish language as part of the national board to the Polish-American Congress.
2. Drawing on the material already in the possession of the committee, after some two years of existence of the Radio School of the Polish Language in Chicago, within the framework of the 'Voice of Polonia' radio program, the particular state branches of the Polish-American Congress should organize—where conditions exist—schools of the Polish language taught over the radio and television. The state branches of the Polish-American Congress will give moral support to those producers of Polish radio programs who will take up the task of organizing such language courses. Polish-American Congress assistance could be expressed in the form of finding suitable sponsors, approaching active fraternal organizations in a given area, purchasing needed textbooks and distributing them among children of their members.
3. The convention has requested the Committee for the Teaching of the Polish Language Through Radio and Television to establish contact with those television stations that air only educational programs and obtain from them suitable material.
4. The committee found the activities of the Commission for the Teaching of the Polish Language Through Radio and Television of great assistance to existing Saturday schools of the Polish Language, and has recommended closer cooperation.
5. Both the National Board as well as the state boards of the Polish-American Congress are to give full support to the Committe for Teaching the Polish Language Through Radio and Television in the realization of its goals.
6. The committee recommends that Joseph Migala represent the Committee for the Teaching of the Polish Language Through Radio

and Television in the Polish-American Congress. The committee comprises: Joseph Migala, chairman; Eugenia Stolarczyk, secretary; John M. Kreutz, L. Opatkiewicz, S.T. Kubiak, Maria Drewno, E. T. Stajniak, members.

The recommendations of the committee were approved unanimously by the delegates of the Ninth Convention of the Polish-American Congress.

Reports of the sessions of the Ninth Convention of the PAC were discussed in the colums of the Polish Daily Zgoda on November 4, 1972. To what degree, if at all, were the resolutions of the Ninth Convention of the PAC carried out? The chairman of the Committee for the Study of the Polish Language Through Radio and Television corresponded with the administrations of the state branches of the PAC and proposed 15-minute lessons of Polish recorded on tape.

The committe, in carrying out the resolutions of the Ninth Convention of the PAC, addressed letters to all the state branches of the PAC regarding the establishment of schools for the study of Polish in the individual states. The letter is dated January 17, 1972:

> The National Administration and the Directorate of the Polish-American Congress, valuing the importance of using the mass media for teaching Polish to Polish-American youth, called forth a national Commission for the Study of the Polish Language Through Radio and Television, As the chairman of this commission, I am turning to the branches of the Polish-American Congress for cooperation in order to organize a representative commission at the state level which will work out this important subject and will bring to fruition the study of Polish via radio and television in various Polish-American centers. Please call together a meeting of the directors of Polish radio programs and television in your territory to discuss this subject and to choose at lease one representative to the newly formed national commission. Please supply the correct address and telephone number along with the name of the person who is chosen. Our commission utilizing the material already in possession of the Radio School for the Study of the Polish Language in Chicago, organized by the directorship of the radio program "Voice of

Polonia," has prepared and will make available material recorded on tape to those state branches who have the conditions necessary to put radio schools in operation.

From experience gathered to date, it is best to organize this type of radio school to the directors of the most popular radio programs in the area of the state branch and under its aegis. We in the national commission will be most eager to meet with the directors of these radio programs.

The Polish-language lessons consist of 15-minute segments. To profit from them most fully, it is necessary to have the textbook. The commission will have a certain number of textbooks at its disposal for a fee. The state branches of the PAC are not financially obligated to run the radio schools, but they should provide full moral support to the directors of those radio programs who will be organizing this type of school. Branches of the PAC can help by finding sponsors or by turning to other fraternal organizations in the area. For example: Polish National Alliance (Zwiazek Narodowy Polski); Polish Roman-Catholic Union (Zjednoczenie Polsko-Rzymsko Katolickie); Polish Women's Alliance (Zwiazek Plloek) and others. Such groups can be asked to buy necessary quantities of books and distribute them to the children of their members.

It is necessary to keep an accurate file of the students of the radio schools for purposes of eventual reports and also to maintain direct contact with them (a questionnaire sent to the students is enclosed). In some areas it is possible to organize Polish language schools on television. Our commission is attempting to locate suitable material for this purpose. To support our efforts we need certain statistics from you. We need informations whether television stations like Channel 11 in Chicago, which broadcast cultural and educational programs exclusively exist in your branch area.

At such stations it is sometimes possible to obtain free airtime to conduct lessons of Polish. To set a television school into operation, it is necessary to have a 30-minute segment every week. Our aim is for a 15-minute segment of studying Polish and then another 15-minute portion to show cultural films about Poland in English.

If such educational stations do not exist in the branch area, then it is necessary to work out the problem of free airtime at television

> stations which broadcast on ultra-shortwave. Because every PAC branch is organized differently, the radio schools as well as the television schools of Polish must act accordingly with existing possibilities.
>
> The matter which is discussed here is of extreme importance to the whole Polish-American community and therefore, we ask you to give it your special attention. We shall look forward to a reply regarding matters dicussed above.
>
> Very sincerely yours,
> Joseph Migala
> Chairman of the National
> Commission for the Study
> of the Polish Language through
> Radio and Television

Despite early interest, none of the producers of Polish radio programs decided to take up the initiative of organizing a Polish-language course in their broadcasts. Finding 15-minutes for a Polish-language course in an existing program is not easy. Most Polish radio programs last 30 minutes or one hour. Setting aside 15 minutes, even once a week, could cause difficulties. The possibility of receiving an additional 15 minutes for this purpose adjacent to already existing broadcasts is also difficult, as radio stations do not have free time to offer and rather have a tendency to cut or even eliminate Polish radio programs, rather than extend them.

Teaching Polish on television did not progress either, despite serious efforts on the part of the chairman of the commission to prepare necessary material in Poland.

The fate of Polish-language courses in the mass media in the particular Polonia centers in the United State explained in a report on the activities of the Committee for the Teaching of Polish by Radio and Television given to the 10th PAC Convention in Philadelphia on September 27, 1976:

> Since the last PAC convention, regular radio Polish lessons have been broadcast each week within the 'Voice of Polonia' program in the Chicago area. The cost of airing these educational segments is covered by the management of the 'Voice of Polonia.' In answer

to the letter sent to the particular state branches of the PAC, which offered the material for teaching the Polish language over radio, only a few branches replied, giving objective reasons why the creation of such courses was hindered. Those reasons were: lack of suitable funds for this purpose and difficulties in receiving suitable time on the air. The chairman of the committee, however, continues to organize material for a Polish-language course on television.

The lack of action by the PAC state divisions is a very serious matter as the Polish language is clearly endangered in the United States. A noteworthy article on this subject was published in 1979 by the popular 'Nowy Dziennik' printed in New York. Its headline: 'For Bilingualism in the USA' The article states 'We have already raised an alarm several time. Polish is beginning to disappear among Polish-Americans, while knowledge of all foreign languages . . . in the United States is drastically falling. The special presidential commission that has examined the state of and causes for this decline, has called the situation scandalous. The report sent to the president states that (1) only 15 percent of high school student learn foreign languages. In 1965, it was 25 percent; (2) only eight percent of colleges in the United States require some knowledge of a foreign language from applicants; (3) federal scholorships for the study of foreign languages have dropped from 2,557 to 828, while the Fulbright scholarships program has been cut by one-half; (4) only 66 percent of the staff of the Department of State has a sufficient knowledge of a foreign language and only 35 percent have some knowledge of Arabic languages; (5) Americans have difficulties communicating with their allies, when the local language must be used. Deficits of $28.5 billion in American trade abroad are the results, among other things, of difficulties in negotiating contracts; (6) American foreign tourists are considered mute. This is true not only in the case of tourists. When the Second Vatican Council deliberated in which language it was to conduct proceedings, and primarily whether Latin should be used, John Cardinal Krol of Philadelphia stated that if proceedings were conducted in Latin, then the American Church at the Council would be a silent church. This jocular statement contained much truth. Even in the American Catholic Church, which prides itself on being universal, the knowledge of Latin among the top hierarchy is minimal, not to mention the lower echelons.

The commission, established by the president, comprising prominint personalities, recommended 65 various means of solving this problem, among them–higher language requirements at high schools and colleges; subsidies for colleges with effective language teaching methods; more regional linguistic centers and special programs, for example, for business people. The commission recommeded that some $180 million should be spent for this purpose annually, believing that this investment would pay off.

For a country of immigrants, of ethnic revival, a country where the melting pot theory is not longer valid, this state of affairs is sad. At the same time, it seems that there is such a simple solution: the sons and daughters of immigrants should cultivate the language of their parents' origin. It is ever so much easier for an American of Polish descent to maintain his knowledge of Polish, or for an Italian–of the beautiful language of Petrarca and Papini. Meanwhile, fewer and fewer offer Polish language courses.

We applaud the presidential commission. But first of all, let us ask ourselves, as one of the more numerous ethnic groups: What are we doing, at every level, to ensure that there are enough people in the United States with a knowledge of Polish. Recently, in an interview for the 'Nowy Dziennik,' the president of the Kosciuszko Foundation said that each year 400 Americans of Polish origin go to Poland for various courses. After their return, they disappear, no one hears about them. Where are they? What are they doing with the knowledge they have gained?

Does our Polish-American passivity go so far, or has our intellectual level reached such depths, that we do not know how to develop our own talents? The Polish nation is not too numerous. But it is also not all that small. American links with Poland and Poles are close. It is worth knowing about them.

This article appeared in 1979. Since then advances have been made in the teaching of foreign languages in the United States. Still, the decline of the knowledge of Polish in this country continues unchecked.

Back to our chronological review of Polish radio in Illinois. The Polish Daily News in its February 22, 1955 edition, informed listeners that the

Polish radio station WLEY broadcasts the following programs: "The Polish Polka Program" from 7:00 p.m. to 8:00 p.m.; the daily program of the "Chicago Polish Daily News" from 8:00 a.m. to 8:15 a.m.; and "Polish Barn Dance" from 8:15 to 9:00. The producer and host of those programs was Zeb Zarnecki.

On October 1, 1954, the following notice appeared in the Chicago Polish Daily News:

> The Alliance of Polish Clubs radio program on station WOPA. Peter Wiecek, chairman of the committee for the radio hour of the Alliance of Polish Clubs, informs readers that this program will be broadcast from station WOPA on 1490 kilocycles. The programs will air Saturdays from 5 p.m. to 5:30 p.m. The new producer and announcer is Joseph Migala, an active member of the alliance and announcer of his own daily radio program, 'Voice of Polonia.'

This Alliance of Polish Clubs program was established in 1934 and remained on the air until 1972. The 30-minute programs of the Alliance of Polish Clubs were consecutively hosted by Paul Miczko at WGES, Maria Data at WSBC and Joseph Migala at WOPA (from 1954 to 1963). The program was supervised by a committee established by the Chamber of Delegates of the Alliance, which received monthly financial reports. It was the comittee's duty to seek out advertising and to collect information on the activities of the various clubs belonging to the Alliance and other organizational news which was announced on the programs. The cost of broadcasting this program was covered by advertising. The Alliance of Polish Clubs program contributed significantly to the growth of this charitable organization, which in its peak years had more than 200 member clubs, each club consisting of members from a particular village or town in Poland. Each club aided the villages and towns from which its members emigrated, most often by providing funds for the building of schools, fire stations, hospitals, community centers, churches and kindergartens.

Under the directorship of Joseph Migala, the broadcasts of this organization belonged to the most popular in the Chicago metropolitan area. The program content consisted of music and songs, news from Poland, about Poland and Poles, as well as organizational communiques. From 1954 to 1963, these broadcasts brought in considerable profits reaching

$16,440. More detailed information on this subject is contained in the "Pamietnik Zlotego Jubileuszo Zwiazku Klubow Malopolskich" (Memorial From the Fiftieth Jubilee of Clubs from Malopolska) published in Chicago in 1978.

Robert Lewandowski,[49] a graduate of the State Institute of Theatrical Arts in Poland, arrived in the United States from England in 1951 and worked in Detroit on Polish programs run by John Kreutz at station WJLB. Lewandowski moved to Chicago and June 1, 1953, began presenting his own program on station WHFC. These 30-minute programs were expanded to one and a half hours and were broadcast daily Monday through Saturday from 2 p.m. to 3:30 p.m. In 1963, WHFC was sold and changed to a format exclusively serving Black-Americans. Lewandowski moved his program to WSBC, where he broadcasts to this day from 7 a.m. to 8:30 a.m. Monday through Friday and on Sundays from 2 p.m. to 3 p.m.

Lewandowski presents popular music and songs in this broadcasts, featuring also musicals, classical music, radio plays, fairy tales for children, weather forecasts, current new and community announcements. Lewandowski's programs are ranked among the most popular Polish programs in the Chicago area.

Written recollections received from Florence Summers dated June 18, 1980, give a brief history of Polish radio programs broadcast from station WHFC (later WCEV) in Cicero, a near western suburb of Chicago. Florence Summers was office manager at WHFC from its creation up to its liquidation in 1963.

In the early 1930s, daily Polish programs were transmitted by WHFC in the mornings by George Baranowski. For many years, Zeb Zarnecki broadcast his daily "Polish Barn Dances" from this station. His programs presented folk music played by an eight-man orchestra under David Wolkow. The famous Maria Data sang in those programs as well. (Zeb Zarnecki later received a permit from the FCC to build a station operating on FM, and soon to put WLEY-Fm on the air. From its beginnings, the station suffered financial difficulties, as there were few radio sets capable of receiving FM programs at that time. Lacking listeners and sufficient advertising, the station was sold to a transport company and used for business communication purposes.

The morning Polish program at WHFC was taken over and run by John Nieminski. His broadcasts featured the Polish-American singer

Zofia Jurkowski, who also hosted some of the programs. Music was provided by an orchestra under Francis Linhart. Many of the broadcasts were aired live from the Wozniak Cassino, a local Polish-American picnic garden, and sponsored by Canadian Ace Beer.

Maria Data also broadcast her own program on WHFC between 11 a.m. and noon, Monday through Saturday. Those programs were recorded on tape and then broadcast. Maria Data's programs were devoted to folk music and folk songs, as well as religious songs, in Data's own rendition. The quality of Polish used by Maria Data in her programs left much to be desired, but it obviously served her listeners, who spoke a combination of country Polish and street Polish. Her program continued for the next 15 years, up to 1972, Monday through Friday for 15 minutes on WSBC.

Following the sudden death of John Nieminski, the morning Polish programs on WHFC were hosted by John Pszczola, up to the station's liquidation in 1963. Between 1953 and 1963, Robert Lewandowski also broadcast his programs on WHFC.

In December 1955, the Polish Radio Program of Casey (Kazimierz) Iwanicki[50] was created, broadcast over WOPA, Monday through Friday, from 2 p.m. to 3:30 p.m. After a short period, the program was moved to WLEY-FM, where it aired Sunday through Friday between 4:40 p.m. and 5:30 p.m. and on Saturday from 11 p.m. to 2 p.m. Iwanicki's program featured recorded music and community announcements.

Station WLEY-FM began broadcasting Saturday Polish programs prepared by Maria Sadecki[51] at 7:30 p.m. This "Highlander Radio Program," serving immigrants from the Polsih maountains was soon discontinued. As mentioned before, few listeners had FM radio sets to receive the broadcasts.

In January 1956, "Happy Chicago Airwaves"[52] was created. These programs were heard on WOPA Monday through Friday from 6:30 a.m. to 7:30 p.m., on Saturday from 11 a.m. to 11:30 a.m., and on Sunday from 1 p.m. to 2 p.m. Michael Przemyski was the producer and host of those programs.

Also in January of that year, Waclaw Rzewski[53] began broadcasting his one-hour "Polish Variety Program." His programs were heard on Sundays at 6 p.m. on WOPA.

In 1958, the weekly program schedule for Polish radio in Chicago was as follows.[54]

Monday and Tuesday

PROGRAM	STATION	TIME
Hello Missus Adam Grzegorzewski	WOPA	6:30 a.m. to 7:00 a.m.
Early Birds Zbigniew Jaworowski	WGES	7:00 a.m. to 8:30 a.m.
Polish Merry-Go-Round Wlodzimierz Sikora	WOPA	11:00 a.m. to 12:00 p.m.
Hello Missus Adam Grzegorzewski	WOPA	12:00 p.m. to 1:30 p.m.
Polish Program Robert Lewandowski	WHFC	3:00 p.m. to 3:30 p.m.
Radio Program Casey Iwanicki	WLEY-FM	4:30 p.m. to 5:30 p.m.
Voice of Polonia Joseph and Slawa Migala	WOPA	5:30 p.m. to 6:30 p.m.
Sunshine Hour Lidia Pucinski	WGES	6:15 p.m. to 6:30 p.m.
Variety Program Wlodzimierz Sikora	WGES	6:30 p.m. to 7:00 p.m.
Highland Program Maria Sadecki	WOPA	9:30 p.m. to 10:00 p.m.

Wednesday

PROGRAM	STATION	TIME
Happy Chicago Airwaves Michael Przemyski	WOPA	6:30 a.m. to 7:00 a.m.
Polish Early Birds Zbigniew Jaworowski	WGES	7:00 a.m. to 8:30 a.m.
Polish Program Maria Data	WSBC	10:00 a.m. to 10:30 a.m.
Polish Program Robert Lewandowski	WHFC	10:30 a.m. to 11:00 a.m.

Wednesday (cont.)

PROGRAM	STATION	TIME
Polish Merry-Go-Round Wlodzimierz Sikora	WOPA	11:00 a.m. to 12:00 p.m.
Hello Missus Adam Grzegorzewski	WOPA	12:00 p.m. to 12:30 p.m.
Polish Program Robert Lewandowski	WHFC	2:00 p.m. to 2:30 p.m.
Polish Program Casey Iwanicki	WLEY-FM	4:30 p.m. to 5:30 p.m.
Voice of Polonia Joseph and Slawa Migala	WOPA	5:30 p.m. to 6:00 p.m.
Daily News Wlodzimierz Sikora	WGES	6:00 p.m. to 6:15 p.m.
Sunshine Hour Lidia Pucinski	WGES	6:15 p.m. to 6:30 p.m.
Variety Show Wlodzimierz Sikora	WGES	6:30 p.m. to 7:00 p.m.
The Siekierki Family Bruno Zielinski	WGES	7:00 p.m. to 8:00 p.m.
Happy Hour Francis Las	WOPA	9:00 p.m. to 10:00 p.m.

Thursday

PROGRAM	STATION	TIME
Happy Chicago Airwaves Michael Przemyski	WOPA	6:30 a.m. to 7:00 a.m.
Polish Early Birds Zbigniew Jaworowski	WGES	7:00 a.m. to 8:30 a.m.
Polish Hour Maria Data	WSBC	10:00 a.m. to 10:30 a.m.
Polish Merry-Go-Round Wlodzimierz Sikora	WOPA	11:00 a.m. to 11:30 a.m.

Thursday (cont.)

PROGRAM	STATION	TIME
Hello Missus Adam Grzegorzewski	WOPA	12:00 p.m. to 12:30 p.m.
Radio Program Robert Lewandowski	WHFC	2:00 p.m. to 3:30 p.m.
Polish Program Casey Iwanicki	WLEY-FM	4:30 p.m. to 5:30 p.m.
Voice of Polonia Joseph and Slawa Migala	WOPA	5:30 p.m. to 6:00 p.m.
Daily News Wlodzimierz Sikora	WGES	6:00 p.m. to 6:15 p.m.
Sunshine Hour Lidia Pucinski	WGES	6:15 p.m. to 6:30 p.m.
Polish Cavalcade Wlodzimierz Sikora	WGES	6:30 p.m. to 7:00 p.m.

Friday

PROGRAM	STATION	TIME
Happy Chicago Airwaves Michael Przemyski	WOPA	6-30 a.m. to 7:00 a.m.
Polish Early Birds Zbigniew Jaworowski	WGES	7:00 a.m. to 8:30 a.m.
Polish Hour Maria Data	WSBC	10:00 a.m. to 10:30 a.m.
Polish Program Robert Lewandowski	WHFC	10:30 a.m. to 11:00 a.m.
Polish Merry-Go-Round Wlodzimierz Sikora	WOPA	11:00 a.m. to 11:30 a.m.
Hello Missus Adam Grzegorzewski	WOPA	12:00 p.m. to 12:30 p.m.
Polish Program Robert Lewandowski	WHFC	2:00 p.m. to 2:30 p.m.

Friday (cont.)

PROGRAM	STATION	TIME
Polish Program Casey Iwanicki	WLEY-FM	4:30 p.m. to 5:30 p.m.
Voice of Polonia Joseph and Slawa Migala	WOPA	5:30 p.m. to 6:00 p.m.
Daily News Wlodzimierz Sikora	WGES	6:00 p.m. to 6:15 p.m.
Polish Cavalcade Wlodzimierz Sikora	WGES	6:30 p.m. to 7:00 p.m.
Variety Program	WHFC	8:30 p.m. to 9:00 p.m.
Polish Program Robert Lewandowski	WHFC	10:00 p.m. to 11:30 p.m.

Saturday

PROGRAM	STATION	TIME
Polish Hour Maria Data	WSBC	10:00 a.m. to 11:00 a.m.
Polish Program Robert Lewandowski	WHFC	10:30 a.m. to 12:00 p.m.
Happy Chicago Airwaves Michael Przemyski	WOPA	11:00 a.m. to 11:30 a.m.
Polish Program Casey Iwanicki	WLEY-FM	4:30 p.m. to 5:30 p.m.
Voice of Polonia Joseph and Slawa Migala	WOPA	5:30 p.m. to 6:00 p.m.
Happy Hour Francis Las	WOPA	6:00 p.m. to 6:30 p.m.
Daily News Wlodzimierz Sikora	WGES	6:00 p.m. to 6:15 p.m.
Sunshine Hour Lidia Pucinski	WGES	6:15 p.m. to 6:30 p.m.

Saturday (cont.)

PROGRAM	STATION	TIME
At the Fireside Adam Grzegorzewski	WOPA	9:00 p.m. to 10:00 p.m.

Sunday

PROGRAM	STATION	TIME
Happy Hour Francis Las	WOPA	10:00 a.m. to 12:00 p.m.
Happy Chicago Airwaves Michael Przemyski	WOPA	1:00 p.m. to 2:00 p.m.
Polish Program John Caputa	WOPA	4:00 p.m. to 5:00 p.m.
Polish Variety Program Waclaw Rzewski	WOPA	6:00 p.m. to 7:00 p.m.
Daily News Wlodzimierz Sikora	WGES	6:00 p.m. to 6:15 p.m.
Polish Cavalcade Wlodzimierz Sikora	WGES	8:00 p.m. to 9:00 p.m.

The following were producers of Polish radio programs broadcast on WOPA in 1958:[55] Michael Przemyski, Joseph and Slawa Migala, Adam Grzegorzewski, John Pszczola, Waclaw Rzewski, John Caputa.

The following were producers of "polka" shows aired from the same station:[56] Eddie Kuta, Ron Terry, Eddie Korosa, Mickey and Marcie Krupski, Chet Gulinski and Tom Kula, Jimmy and Mario Dub, Leon Kosicki, Jolly and Ray Raducha, Chester Wolski, John Hyzny, Carl Bauman, Stan Noyes, and program director Al Michel.

Nina Czuwara,[57] the wife of Boleslaw, who had made her debut earlier as the Gypsy Nina in the radio program "Gypsy Campfire," in the 1960s presented her own programs to Polona. They were broadcast every Sunday from 11 a.m. to noon from WXRT-FM. In her "Polish Voice" programs, she presented music from around the world in two one-hour segments. Although born and educated in the United States, Nina Czuwara spoke excellent Polish. Her programs were very popular among Chicago area Polonia.

In 1962, station WGES was sold to a firm outside Chicago, which reorganized the station, eliminating all ethnic broadcasts, among them six Polish programs that had been on the air for 30 years. The protests and appeals of the ethnic producers to the Federal Communications Commission were to no avail. After hearing both sides in Chicago, the FCC decided in facor of the owners of WGES. Polish radio programs were forced to move stat to other radio stations. In the process, the popular "Early Birds" program hosted for years by Zbigniew Jaworowski was liquidated.

After her Polish programs at WGES were abolished, Lidia Pucinski aired her programs over WEDC daily at 8:30 a.m. to 9:30 a.m. The program "Poland in Music and Songs," broadcast for years by Adam Grzegorzewski on WGES moved to WOPA in Oak Park, a Chicago suburb.[58] The programs of Wlodzimierz Sikora, also switched to WOPA from WGES as did the "Grunwald Program" hosted by Bronislaw Zielinski.

In October 1964, a new Polish program "Evening and the Microphone"[59] was created, broadcast on WSBC on Tuesdays from 9 p.m. to 10 p.m. The producer and host of this program is Romuald Matuszczak. The program has remained on the air to this day.

Jadwiga and Eugene Rylski[60] started broadcasting their own radio program on station WSBC on Sundays between 3 p.m. and 3:30 p.m.

No significant changes in the schedules of Polish radio programs in the Chicago area were noted up to 1974. In that year the schedule was as follows:[61]

WOPA:	"News from and About Poland" / Marian Czarnecki daily from 6:00 a.m. to 6:30 a.m.
WOPA:	"Morning Bells" / Michael Przemyski daily from 6:30 a.m. to 7:30 a.m. Saturdays from 11:00 a.m. to 11:30 a.m.
WSBS:	"Polish Program" / Robert Lewandowski Mondays through Fridays 7:00 a.m. to 8:00 a.m. Sundays from 2:00 p.m. to 3:00 p.m.

WEDC: "Sunshine Hour" / Lidia Pucinski
daily from 8:30 a.m. to 9:30 a.m.

WTAQ: "Tony Pienkowski Show" / Jadwiga and Tony Pienkowski
daily 9:15 to 10:00 a.m.
"International Hour" / Jadwiga and Tony Pienkowski
Saturdays 6:35 p.m. to 7:00 p.m.

WTAQ: "The Salvatorian Fathers' Hour"
daily 7:00 a.m. to 7:30 a.m.

WOPA: "Poland in Music and Songs" / Adam Grzegorzewski
Mondays through Fridays 12:00 p.m. to 12:30 p.m.

WOPA: "Polish Cavalcade" /Wlodzimierz Sikora
daily 1:00 p.m. to 3:30 p.m.
daily 6:30 p.m. to 8:00 p.m.

WOPA: "Voice of Polonia" / Joseph and Slawa Migala
Mondays through Fridays 4:30 p.m. to 6:00 p.m.
Saturdays 4:00 p.m. to 6:00 p.m.

WOPA: "Program of the Union of New Polonia in American" / Michael Pawelek
Mondays through Thursdays 11:20 a.m. to 12:00 p.m.

WOPA: "The Grunwald Program" / Bronislaw Zielinski
Tuesdays through Fridays 7:00 p.m. to 7:30 p.m.

Polish radio programs in Chicagoland area broadcast once a week:[62]

WXRT-FM: "Red Poppies" / Ref-Ref–Felix Konarski
Sundays 10:00 a.m. to 11:00 a.m.

WTAQ: "International Hour" / Jadwiga and Tony Pienkowski
Saturdays 6:35 p.m. to 7:00 p.m.

WXRT-FM: "Sunday Concert" / Stan Lobodzinski
Sundays 11:00 a.m. to 12:00 p.m.

WJOB: "Religous Program of the Savatorian Fathers"
Sundays 10:00 a.m. to 10:30 a.m.

WTAQ: "Religious Program of the Salvatorian Fathers:
Saturdays 7:00 p.m. to 7:30 p.m.

WJOB: "Polish Program" John Caputa
Sundays 1:30 p.m. to 2:00 p.m. (Hammond, Indiana)

WSBC: "Polish Program" / Jadwiga and Eugene Rylski
Sundays 3:00 p.m. to 3:30 p.m.

WSBC: "Evenings at the Microphone" / Romuald Matuszczak
Tuesdays 9:00 p.m. to 10:00 p.m.

WOPA: "Alliance of Polish Clubs Program"
Saturdays 6:30 p.m. to 7:00 p.m.

WOPA: "Happy Radio Program" / Lil Wally–Walter Jagiello
Sundays 10:30 a.m. to 11:00 a.m.

WTAQ: Various Polka programs
Sundays and Saturdays–9 1/2 hours

For comparison, a list of Polish radio programs in the Chicago area in 1976 and 1979:[63]

1976

WOPA: "News from and About Poland" / Marian Czarnecki
Monday through Friday 6:00 a.m. to 6:30 a.m.

WOPA: "Morning Bells" / Michael Przemyski
Mondays through Fridays 6:30 a.m. to 7:00 a.m.

"Poland in Music and Song" / Adam Grzewgorzewski
Monday through Friday 12:00 p.m. to 12:30 p.m.

"Polish Cavalcade" / Wlodzimierz Sikora
Mondays through Fridays 1:00 p.m. to 3:30 p.m. and 8:00 p.m.

"Voice of Polonia" / Joseph and Slawa and George Migala
Mondays through Fridays 4:30 p.m. to 6:00 p.m.
Saturdays from 4:00 p.m. to 6:30 p.m.

	"Grunwald Program" / Bronislaw Zielinski Tuesdays through Fridays 7:00 p.m. to 7:30 p.m.
	"Chet Gulinski Show" / Chet Gulinski Saturdays 12:00 p.m. to 1:00 p.m. Sundays 10:00 a.m. to 1:00 p.m.
WSBC:	"Polish Radio Program / Robert Lewandowski Mondays through Fridays 7:00 a.m. to 8:30 a.m. Sundays 2:00 p.m. to 3:00 p.m.
WEDC:	"Sunshine Hour" / Lidia Pucinski Mondays through Fridays 8:30 a.m. to 9:30 a.m.
WTAQ:	"Uncle Henry Polka Show" / Henry Sloper Saturdays 8:00 a.m. to 9:00 a.m. and 1:00 p.m. to 2:00 p.m. Sundays 8:00 a.m. to 9:00 a.m. and 2:00 p.m. to 3:00 p.m.
WYLO:	"Helena's Program" / Helena Wantuch (from Milwaukee, WI, but heard in Chicago) Sundays 9:30 a.m. to 10:30 a.m.

1979

WSBS:	"Polish Radio Program" / Robert Lewandowski Monday through Friday 7:00 a.m. to 7:30 a.m. Sunday 2:00 p.m. to 3:00 p.m.
	"Polish Program" / Jadwiga and Eugene Rylski Sunday 3:00 p.m. to 3:30 p.m.
WEDC:	"Sunshine Hour" / Lidia Pucinski Monday through Friday 8:30 a.m. to 9:30 a.m.
WCEV:	"Voice of Polonia" / Joseph, Slawa and George Migala Monday through Saturday 4:00 p.m. to 6:00 p.m.
WOPA:	"News from and about Poland" / Marian Czarnecki Monday through Friday 4:30 p.m. to 5:00 p.m. Saturday 4:30 p.m. to 5:30 p.m.
WCEV:	"Roman Catholic Mass in Polish" live from the Chapel of the Jesuit Fathers in Chicago / Father Zbigniew Gorecki Sundays 7:00 a.m.

"Polish Apostleship of Prayer" / Father Zbigniew Gorecki
Sunday 7:30 a.m. to 8:30 a.m.

"Afternoon with Polonia" / Adam Ocytko
Saturdays 6:00 p.m. to 7:00 p.m.

WOPA: "Poland in Music and Song" / Adam Grzegorzewski
Monday through Friday 5:00 p.m. to 5:30 p.m.

"The Grunwald Program" / Bronislaw Zielinski, Bronislaw and Pelagia Mroz
Tuesdays through Friday 7:00 p.m. to 7:30 p.m.

"Polish Cavalcade"/Wlodzimierz Sikora
Mondays 7:00 p.m. to 8:30 p.m.
Tuesdays through Fridays 7:30 p.m. to 8:30 p.m.

"Polish Panorama" / Stanislaus Lobodzinski
Saturday 5:30 p.m. to 6:30 p.m.

"How are You?" / Zbigniew Motta
Saturday 6:30 p.m. to 7:00 p.m.

"Father Justin's Rosary Hour" / The Rev. Kornelian Dende, OFMC
Saturday 7:30 a.m. to 8: a.m.
Sunday 7:30 p.m. to 8:00 p.m.

"The Pierogi King Radio Polka Show" / Stanely Kowalski
Saturday 1:00 p.m. to 2:00 p.m.

WSBC: "Red Poppies" / Felix Konarski–Ref-Ren
Wednesday 8:30 p.m. to 9:30 p.m.

"Evening at the Microphone" / Romuald Matuszczak
Tuesday 9:00 p.m. to 10:00 p.m.

WUIC-FM: "Student Radio-Zak" / University of Illinois Chicago Circle Campus Maryna Polak, Andrew Szczesniewski, Mark Wasilewski
Saturday 4:30 p.m. to 6:00 p.m.

WIVQ: "Cousin Ed's Polka Party" / Ed Nowotarski (Peru, Illinois)
Saturday 9:00 a.m. to 12:00 p.m.

WTAQ: "International Hour" / Jadwiga and Anthony Pienkowski
Saturday 4:30 p.m. to 5:30 p.m.

"On the Road to Emaus" / Salvatorian Fathers
Sundays 5:00 p.m. to 6:00 p.m.

"Bel Aire Polka Party" / Ed Blazonczyk
Sunday 12:00 p.m. to 12:45 p.m.

"Johnny Hyzny Show" / John Hyzny
Sunday 3:00 p.m. to 4:00 p.m.

"Polkarama" / Don Jodlowski
Saturday 2:00 p.m. to 3:00 p.m.

WTAQ: "Polka Merry-Go-Round" / Ann Pszczola
Sunday 4:00 p.m. to 5:00 p.m.

"Polka Hit Parade" and "Chet Schafer Show" / Chet Schafer
Saturday 12:35 p.m. to 1:00 p.m.
Sunday 10:00 a.m. to 11:00 a.m.

"Uncle Henry Polka Show" / Henry Sloper
Sunday 8:00 a.m. to 9:00 a.m. and 2:00 p.m. to 3:00 p.m.

"Li'l Richard Show" / Richard Towelski
Saturday 12:00 p.m. to 12:30 p.m. and 3:00 p.m. to 3:30 p.m.

"The Pierogoi King Radio Polka Show" / Stanley Kowalski
Saturday 3:00 p.m. to 4:00 p.m.

WONX: "The Pierogi King Radio Polka Show" / Sunday 8:00 a.m. to 9:00 a.m.
Stanley Kowalski

The number of Polish radio programs broadcast daily in 1980 did not change compared to 1979 and amounted to 30 hours. In 1980, weekly Polish radio programs in the Chicago area increased by two:[64]

WOPA: "Happy Chicago Airwaves" / Joseph Zielinski
Sunday 1:00 p.m. to 2:00 p.m.

WCEV: "Radio Variete" / Stan Borys
Sunday 3:05 p.m. to 4:00 p.m.

"Happy Chicago Airwaves" is a continuation of the program of the same name founded by Michael Przemyski who died in 1979. The program was taken over by Joseph Zielinski and John Wojewóka, an impresario well-known for presenting Polish talent in the United States.

In 1980, 12 radio stations in the state of Illinois broadcast Polish programs. Polish airtime amounted to 60.5 hours per week.

CHAPTER 7

Polish Radio in the State of Indiana: Among the Oldest Polish Programs in the United States

From a press notice in the Polish Daily Zgoda dated November 29, 1929, and from written information from station WSBT in South Bend, Indiana,[65] we know that the first Polish radio program in the state of Indiana was broadcast from 8:30 to 9:30 p.m. in August 1929 on WSBT on South Bend.

This program was owned by The South Bend Tribune, and its producer and host was Francis Kalikst Czyzewski (1904-1976). The press release informed readers that Father Osadnik, gave a 15-minute speech on Francis Czyzewski's radio program. The notice stated that this was the first time that a priest took part in a Polish radio program in the United States. A six-man orchestra under Professor Waclaw Hayach also appeared in Francis Czyzewski's programs.

The South Bend Tribune added the Polish programs to its schedule and asked listeners to send in their opinions of the broadcasts which were in Polish and English. At first, these programs with Francis Czyzewski were broadcast every two weeks. By April 4, 1930, they were aired every Sunday from 8:30 to 9:30 p.m. on WSBT.

The positive reaction of listeners who had flooded the station with congratulatory letters influenced the development of Polish programs in South Bend. On April 24, WSBT began broadcasting daily informational programs in Polish from 4:45 p.m. to 5:00 p.m., in addition to the Sunday programs. The Polish community in South Bend then numbered 35,000-40,000 people.

Francis Czyzewski's programs included a seven-piece orchestra under Stodolny and Pajakowski, an orchestra of high artistic quality. These Polish music programs were also listened to by Americans who enjoyed good music. For this reason, the program was announced in English and Polish. That "Polish hour" founded by Francis Czyzewski in August 1929, still airs today, produced by his wife and Dr. E. W. Sobol and is the third oldest Polish radio program in the United States. These programs are broadcast on Sunday from 1p.m. to 1:55 p.m. over station WSBT.

The fourth oldest radio program in the United States was inaugurated by Edward Oskierko in December 1929. The "Polish Variety Program" was first broadcast from the WJKS station–now WIND in Gary, Indiana, which is powered by 5000 watts. At first, his one-hour broadcasts aired on Fridays from 8 p.m. Since 1930, they air daily. Several years later they were switched to station WWAE. Today, the air on WJOB in Hammond, Indiana (1000 watt power) on Sundays from noon to 2 p.m.

The dean of Polish radio producers, Edward Oskierko, presents his programs for the first 50 minutes in Polish, the remaining 70 minutes in English. The broadcasts consist of folk and popular music, concerts, interviews, local, national and international news, weather, amateur contest, and community announcements. The programs include religious segments by the Salvatorian Fathers, a Catholoc order active in the northwest part of Indiana. Oskierko's "Polish Variety Program" is the oldest and longest (half a century) Polish radio program in the United States, continually produced and announced by the same man.

Walter Skibinski has for years cooperated with the "Polish Variety Program" as a co-producer. He is active in Polish- American organizations and enjoys popularity in his community.

On April 10, 1930, the Polish Daily Zgoda reported that a new radio program had been created, broadcast from station WJKS (which is now WIND) in Gary on Sundays from 10:45 p.m. to midnight. Boleslaw Menczynski was producer and host of this program.

From WJVA in South Bend, Cas Dzikowski broadcasts his "Polish-American Hour" every Sunday from noon to 1p.m. in both Polish and English.

In December 1949, a program called "Polish Radio" was organized in Gary. The first program went on the air on January 7, 1950, from station WWCA. the producer and host of the broadcast was T. S. Kubiak; the musical director was his wife, Helena M. Kubiak; and their assistant was Lottie Wawrzyniak. The first program featured speeches by the mayor of Gary, by Father Zygmunt Wojciechowski, as well as by many representatives of Polish-American organizations.

By 1958, the "Polish Radio" programs of Gary were broadcast from three stations: On Sundays from 10 a.m. to 11 a.m. over WGRY in Gary—this edition of the program often included live masses trasmitted directly from various Polish-American Catholic churches; on Saturday, T. Kubiak aired his programs on WLOI in La Porte from 8 p.m. to 9 p.m. and from 2 p.m. to 3 p.m.; and on Saturdays on WWCA in Gary.

After the death of T. Kubiak, the "Polish Radio" broadcasts of Gary have been in the hands of his wife, Helena M. Kubiak, who now produces and is hostess of the program; Lottie S. Kubiak, his daughter-in-law, (former secretary general of the Polish National Alliance); and Kubiak's son, Chester L. Kubiak. The broadcasts contain Polish music, historical segments, interviews and community announcements. "Polish Radio" of Gary, now broadcast on WLTH in Glen Park-Gary, Indiana, and continues to enjoy great popularity.

Indiana is one of the states where Polish broadcasting developed early and continues to this day as an important element of the Polish-American community.

At present, eight radio stations in Indiana carry Polish broadcasts. Their airtime is 14.5 hours weekly.

CHAPTER 8

Polish Radio Programs in Connecticut

A large percentage of the Polish radio programs in Connecticut are polka shows.

One of the oldest still on the air is the "Polonia Program" broadcast at present from station WRYM in Newington. The "Polonia Program" premiered on May 3, 1939, when it was beamed from station WTHT in Hartford.[66] Edmund Liszka was the founder of this program, who for many years had worked with Edward Brominski, an actor of the Polish and American stage. In the early 1930s, Brominski hosted a popular radio hour in Hartford. The "Polonia Program" with Edmund Liszka is a continuation of the broadcast tradition begun by Brominski.

Edmund Liszka's radio programs were aired first on WTHT in Hartford, then WKNB in New Britian (1955), WEXT in West Hartford, WYTM in Springfield, and now in WRYM. Initially, the programs were broadcast daily, later three times a week, and now on Saturdays from 10 a.m. to 10:30 a.m., and on Sundays from 7:45 a.m. to 9 a.m. Ninety-nine percent of the program is in Polish. It contains folk and popular music, operetta and classical music, local, national and international news, radio plays, interviews, lectures, wather forecasts and community announcements of Polonia organizations, such as the Polish-American Congress, the Polish scouts, veterans groups, various clubs and associations.

Like many other Polish-American broadcasters, Edmund Liszka the founder of the program, as well as its producer and host enjoys tremendous popularity in his community, and has been engaged in Polish community work for years.

Born in the United States, he spent his childhood years in Poland with his mother. He completed secondary school in Poland. After returning to the United States in 1938, he graduated from the Progressive School of Photography at Yale in New Haven. During World War II, he served in the Air Force, received the Gold Cross of Merit and a medal for participation in the liberation of France. After the war, he returned to his Polish radio program, and opened a travel agency, Liszka Travel, which he runs to this day.

He also found time to work for various organizations, such as the Polish-American Congress, the Center of United Societies (of which he was president for many years), the local Democratic Club. He is also a member of the Polish National Alliance, the Kosciuszko Foundation and numerous other Polish-American organizations. Edmund Liszka used his radio program to organize aid for war immigrants, to collect money for victims of floods in Poland, for the reconstruction of the Royal Castle in Warsaw, for the purchase of books for public libraries. He was active in the committee collecting funds for the Pulaski monument, which Polonia donated to the city of Hartford.

Virginia Seretny broadcast her first "Polka Time" program in September 1960 from station WILI in Willimantic, Connecticut.[67] Her programs were aired on station WINY on Saturdays from noon to 1 p.m. after they were moved from WILI. Their producer and hostess, Virginia Serethy, works actively in Polish-American organizations: She was president of the Junior Women's Club, the PTA Ladies Auxiliary, the Pulaski American Club and the National Polka Association.

The "Sunday Polka Program" in Norwich appeared on February 14, 1949, initiated by Jospeh Ladzinski, manager of a men's clothing store, who broadcasts 90 percent of this program in English, and 10 percent in Polish.[68] The musical portion of the program is devoted to polkas, obereks, waltzes. It broadcasts for one hour on Sundays.

For 10 years now, radio polka shows have been aired by Dick Ident and Casey Staran from WRYM in New Britian.[69] Mondays through Fridays, the program broadcasts from 6:45 a.m. to 7:15 a.m. and on Saturdays from 6:45 a.m. to 9 a.m. The Sunday programs, from 11 a.m. to 2:30 p.m. are live from the Polish community House in Hartford.

In 1948, the "Polish-American Radio Program" was created at station WCNX in Middleton. The founder, producer and host of the program from its inception to the present day is Ed Henry.[70] His programs, devoted to folk music and news, are aired on Sunday from 11 a.m. to noon.

The "Charley and Fred Witek Polka Party"[71] is the name of a Polish radio program broadcast on station WGCH in Greenwich, Connecticut. The Witek brotkers' program has been on the air for thepast 10 years every Sunday from 1:30 p.m. to 2 p.m.

Station WVOF in Fairfield, Connecticut, began airing a Polish program in 1978. It was founded by Saul Nowitz, director of ethnic programming. Casey Majewski contributed to the development of the program. Through the Polish-American Educations Society, he assured the high level of the broadcasts. The program has an editorial board consisting of five people: Saul Nowitz, (producer); Casey Majewski (information branch); Margaret Ozaist, Wieslaw Ozaist and John Kostyszyn (announcers). The program airs on a noncommercial station, owned by a public college. It airs as a public service from 8 a.m. to 10:30 a.m., and is announced in two languages–Polish and English, presenting news from and about Poland, as well as local Polonia news from the greater Bridgeport area. The number of its listeners is estimated at 4,000.

Other interesting Polish programs in Connecticut are:

"Pillar Polkabration" broadcast on WSUB-AM and FM on Sundays from 10 a.m. to 12:30 p.m. It serves Polish-Americans in Groton and New London.

"Polka Time with Dick Yash" broadcast every Sunday from 8 a.m. to 9 a.m. on WNHC, New Haven. The program consists of Polish folk music, polkas and waltzes. It is aired in English.

"Bristol Polka Party" broadcast every Sunday from 10 a.m. to noon from WBIS in Bristol.

"Polka Variety Show" hosted by Walt Solek, aired on WMMW in Meriden every Sunday from 12:05 p.m. to 2 p.m.

"The Jon Jaski Show" broadcast every Sunday from 10:05 a.m. to 10:30 a.m. over WEXT in West Hartford, which feature Polish folk music and news.

Also, Stanley A. Ozimek broadcasts Polish radio programs from station WRYM in Newington; John Zawaski from WSOR in Windsor; Ed Sitnik from WHAY in New Britain; Stan Zaleski from station WMMW Meriden.

The "Polish-American Hour" is broadcast every Sunday from 10 a.m. to 11 a.m. from stations WCCC-AM and FM. It serves residents in Newington and its vicinity. Stanislaus Jasinski's program is also popular and broadcast on Saturdays from 1 p.m. to 2 p.m. and on Sundays from 12:35 p.m. to 4 p.m.

In Connecticut, 20 radio stations broadcast Polish programs. The total airtime is 43.5 hours weekly.

CHAPTER 9

Polish Radio Programs in Massachusetts

The beginnings of Polish radio im Massacusetts date back to the 1930s.

In 1936, Karol J. Mackiewicz, an engineer who graduated from Northeastern University in Boston, organized a "Polish American Radio Program:" at station WUNR in Boston.

This is one of the oldest Polish programs, continually on the air, even to this day. The half-hour program, broadcast Mondays through Fridays is presented half in Polish and half in English. The programs consist of polka music, popular music and songs from Poland, community news, etc.

The "Berkshire Polish-American Program," established in 1939, is also among the oldest Polish radio programs continually on the air in the United States. The founder of this program at WBRK was Karol B. Nowobilski from West Stockbridge, Mass. His programs, broadcast on Sunday mornings, were among the most popular in western Massachusetts. Irene Stryjewski was an assistance to Karol Nowobilski, and after his death in 1970, she took over the program. At present, the broadcasts are aired in both Polish and English, also on Sunday morning, from 10:10 a.m. to noon. Irene Stryjewski's programs include polkas, obereks, mazurkas, krakowiaks, news from the life of the Polish community, local information. Bob Burke, who for years has been connected with American broadcasting, is a co-worker on this program.

The "White Eagle Music Hour," founded in 1949, is broadcast from station WHAI in Greenfield. Its founder and present producer and host is Andrew Wiernasz, a graduate of a two-year radio school. His programs air Sundays from 11:15 a.m. to 1 p.m. on Wednesday from 5:15 a.m. to 5:55 a.m. and on Saturdays from 12:15 p.m. to 12:55 p.m. The program is presented in English and features Polish folk music.

In August 1949, station WACE in Chicopee began airing the "Polish Melody Time." Its producer and host was Andrew Szuberla, who had worked for 10 years as an announcer at WSPR in Springfield on the Polish program run by furniture store owner John Kasko. For the first 15 years of its existence, "Polish Melody Time" was broadcast four hours daily and aimed at Polonia living in the western and eastern parts of New England. Besides folk music, the broadcast carried news from the life of the Polish-American community, national and international news, discussions of old Polish customs and traditions. Special programs were aired on Polish anniversaries and holidays. Since 1962, "Polish Melody Time" is broadcast on Sundays from 2 p.m. to 5 p.m. on WACE in Springfield. Andrew Szuberal, supports community casues on the air, helps collect funds for the reconstruction of churches in Poland, the rebuilding of the Royal Castle in Warsaw, for the Polish-American Congress and others.

He has received an award from the state of Massachusetts in recognition of his many years in the service of Polish radio and the Polish-American community.

On March 16, 1953, a Polish radio program was started over station WBVD in Beverly by Stefan J. Czarnecki and Constanty "Kay" Solodiuk. The program, called "Your Polka Revue," is broadcast in Polish and English on Sundays from 12:05 p.m. to 2 p.m. It airs folk and popular music, information on Polonian organizations and news.

On Sunday, August 15, 1955, at 6 p.m., station WVOM broadcast the first edition (since the reorganization of the "Polish Echo program) of the "Polish Variety Hour."[72] Its producer was Karol Jaskolski, editor of the Boston-based Polish daily "Kurier Codzienny" (Daily Courier).

"Frank Litwin's Polka Varieties" is a Polish radio program broadcast on WESX in Salem in Polish and English.[73] The same programs are aired Saturdays from 11 a.m. to noon, on Sundays from 11 a.m. to noon and from 12:15 p.m. to 2:15 p.m. They feature exclusive polka.

Karol J. Mackiewicz broadcasts Polish music and sons in his "Polish-American Program" aired on station WUNR in Boston on Mondays, Thursdays and Fridays from 7 p.m. to 8 p.m.

The Jehova's Witnesses religious sect presents its own radio program in Polish every Sunday from 7:15 p.m. to 7:30 p.m. over station WMYS in Bedford.[74]

"Your Sunday Morning Polka Parade" is broadcast by Chet and Mary Lou Dragon from station WREB in Holyoke on Sundays from 9 a.m. to 11 a.m.[75] Their program has been on the air since July 4, 1970. Chet Dragon is director of an orchestra. His programs feature mostly music, mainly polkas, obereks and waltzes.

In October 1977, the "Polish Happy Time" program premiered at WMYS-FM.[76] Thanks to the strong power of the station, this program can be heard in a large part of Massachusetts, part of New Hampshire, all of Rhode Island, one-fourth of Connecticut, and part of Long Island, New York, The producer and host of this program, which is almost entirely in English, is Edward L. Piwowarczyk. Edward and John Piwowarczyk's programs air on Sundays from 8 a.m. to 10 a.m. They are in the form of a magazine with Polish music, interviews, news from Polish-American organizations as well as Polish recipes and humor.

Stanislaus Kadziewicz is producer and announcer of a Polish radio program called "The Other Side of Europe."[77] This one-hour program, which was created in September of 1974, is broadcast on station WHRB-FM in Cambridge from 8 p.m. to 9 p.m. The program, presented exclusively in English, acquaints listeners with Polish classical music.

Bill Czuptas presents folk music in his program "Polka Jam Session" from station WLDM in Westfield on Sundays from 9:30 a.m. to 11 a.m.

The Polish radio program "The Marion Wrobel Show" is broadcast on Sundays from 12:15 p.m. to 2 p.m. on WBET in Brockton, and features polka music and information on the life of the Polish-American community.

Johnny Libera broadcasts Polish programs from station WESO in Southbridge on Saturdays from 11 a.m. to 1 p.m. and on Sundays from 11:30 a.m. to 1 p.m. These are programs of Polish music and community announcements.

In Massachusetts, Polish radio programs—mostly Polka shows—are broadcast by 18 radio stations. Their total airtime amounts to 49.5 weekly.

CHAPTER 10

Polish Radio in Michigan: The Longest Polish Programs in the Nation

One of the most dynamic Polonia centers in the United States is around Detroit, Michigan, which has a large Polish-American community. Numerous Polish-American organizations grew there early on and created good conditions for establishing Polish radio service.

The first to organize such service were Polish journalists and Polish stage artists. A local Polish paper, "Rekord Codzienny" (Daily Record) as early as 1930 aired a Polish program on station WMBC on Saturdays from 3:45 p.m. to 4:30 p.m. and on Sundays from 2 p.m. to 3:30 p.m. A press notice in the Daily Record dated May 13, 1933, notes that those programs featured an orchestra under a Mr. Szyszko, while the latest news was presented by editor Kindybala. the article continues as follows:

> In the Sunday program on May 14, 1933, Detroit's biggest parochial choir, namely the choir of St. Stansilaus Parish under Professor Walter Kierszulis, is to make an appearance, singing A. Batycki's polonaise, 'Love of the Fatherland,' the 'Longing Heart' waltz by W. Kierszulis, 'Rejoice, Land of Poland' by W. Bonek, and 'Ave Maria' will be sung by Michael Pierce. Next the orchestra conducted by Walter Kierszulis will play several Polish compositions and Keler Bela's beautiful 'Son of the Jungle.' Stanislaus Wachtel, a prominent dramatic arts artist, well known in Polonia,

> and his group will begin a series of sketches titled 'Flower of the Marshland,' the radio version of a novel by A. Trojanowski. Mr. Wachtel, in his previous series 'The Adventures of Bonek the Reporter,' demonstrated that he can hold the attention of listeners. The new series, based on a story by Mr. Trojanowski allows for creative possibilities since it is written and touches on the sad but unfortunately true phenomena of everyday life. The series is of special interest to parents and teenagers. It contains many valuable and useful pieces of advice for them.

The "Daily Record Radio Hour" had many co-workers in addition to Stanislaus Wachtel; Actors were heard in sketches, radio versions of short stories and novels, and the shows also featured Polish singers.

At the same time, the "Thaddeus Zajac Radio Program" went on the air at WEXL Monday through Fridays from 8:30 p.m. to 9 p.m., and sometimes to 9:30 p.m.[78] Thaddeus Zajac was a comic actor of the Polish stage. His broadcasts featured the latest news and commentaries, recorded music and his own sketches. His wife Maria took an active part in the programs from their inception and wrote some of her own segments. Numerous Polish artists appeared in Thaddeus Zajac's programs, among them the well-known Stanislaus Wachtel.

In 1931, station WMBS (now WJLB) introduced the "Golden Thoughts Program," in Polish which was produced and announced by businessman Walenty Jarosz.[79] The program aired for one hour in the morning and two hours in the evening, Monday through Fridays. It included news and commentaries, Polish music and songs, comic sketches and satire, as well as radio versions of short stories and novels performed by stage and radio actors.

Also in 1931, the "Antek Cwaniak" (Clever Tony") Polish program began its run, produced by Polish stage actor and businessman Walter Golanski.[80] The program was broadcast from station WEXL Mondays through Fridays from 6:30 p.m. to 7:30 p.m. and featured news, commentaries, as well as music and songs from records, Edmund Krutkiewicz, worked with Walter Golinski selling advertising for the program.

In 1931, Walter Leskiewicz began broadcasting his "Variety Program" on WEXL.[81] He arrived in Detroit in 1929, and began a stage career in the local Polish theater. He also wrote satirical sketches making light of current events for the theater and radio. Walter Leskiewicz had his own touring company of actors. His co-workers were his wife, Stanislawa and her son from a previous marriage. The "Variety Program" aired Mondays through Saturdays from 9 a.m. to 10 a.m. presenting national and international news, radio versions of short stories and novels performed by Polish actors, music and satirical sketches. Walter Keskiewicz hosted the show and played character roles in such sketches as "Dziadek Psia Pora" (Bad Weather Grandpa) and "Wloczega" (The Tramp). The latter sketch ran as a series in the Sunday program between noon and 1 p.m. From 1932 to 1938, the "Variety Program" was broadcast evenings on WJBK. In 1938, the programs were suspended for six months because Leskiewicz was ill. In 1939, he resumed his broadcasts on WEXL between 8 p.m. and 9 p.m., and continued them until his death on May 21, 1939. His wife and her son Bronislaw Stawinski continued airing the "Polish Variety Program" until 1947.

Leon Wyszatynski, a businessman from Detroit, began his radio career in 1933 by organizing the "Sunshine Program."[82] It was aired on station WEXL, later on WJBK and others. The "Sunshine Program" was heard Mondays through Fridays from 7 p.m. to 8 p.m., as well as on Sundays. It's announcers were stage and radio actors. Leon Wyszatynski was an amateur tenor and occasionally sang on his programs. News, commentaries, music and songs were the main items on the agenda of the broadcasts. In 1940, Leon Wyszatynski left Detroit for Buffalo, N. Y., where he bought his own radio station.

In 1936, Stanislaus Wachtel, the prominent actor who appeared on the stages of theaters in the bigger Polish-American communities, such as the Alexander Fredro Theater in Detroit, created his own program called the "Morning Polish Program." Since 1932, he had appeared on three Polish programs in Detroit: the "Taduesz Zajac Radio Program," Walenty Jarosz's "Golden Thoughts Program" and the "Variety Program," run by Walter Leskiewicz.

Stanislaus Wachtel's "Morning Polish Program" was broadcast six days a week from 9:30 a.m. to 10:30 a.m. from station WJBK, later from WMBC (now called WJLB).[83] The programs featured the latest news, concerts of Polish orchestras performing music of Polish composers, recorded music and songs, and a "Radio Theater" with radio versions of short stories and novels. His Sunday programs were aired from 1 p.m. to 2 p.m.

Stanislaus Wachtel's wife, Gertruda, began appearing with her husband in 1933 and had her own segments called "Woman's Comment," in which she discussed matters of interest to women. Stanislaus and Gertruda Wachtel did not work on their own; they received a percentage of profits from advertising on their programs.

In 1937, The Wachtel's daughter, Stanislawa, a student of medicine, begn appearing in her own program.[84] Earlier, she had appeared from time to time in the Saturday "Radio Theater" aired by her parents. Her programs were heard on station WMBC on Saturday mornings. Sanislawa's program–'Przyjaciolka Stasia" (Your Friend Stasia) was meant for children's audiences. It aired until 1940, when Stanislawa Wachtel completed her studies and devoted herself to the medical profession.

The "Morning Polish Program" came to an end in 1948 on account of the worsening state of Stanislaus Wachtel's health. He died in Detroit in 1950.

In the 1930s and 1940s, numerous stage artists cooperated with Polish radio programs broadcast in the Detroit area. They appeared in radio versions of short stories and novels, or were engaged as announcers and commentators. Here are some of them:[85]

–Mieczyslaw Jachinski, "Mietek," an actor and announcer; he was also director of a municipal department in Detroit.

–Alexander Drozdz, author.

–Zygmunt Rybak, actor who was connected for years with Polish programs broadcast on WMBC.

–Emilia Pohorecka, actress.

–Anna Ruchlicka, singer.

–Jadwiga Furmaniak, soprano; for many years she appeared on Wladyslaw (Walter) Leskiewicz's "Variety Program".

–Marian Mossakowski, singer.

–Stanislaus Miewicz, tenor-baritone; appeared often in radio theaters.

–Ignacy Ulatowski, actor and comedian.

–Maria Grabowski, character actress known for radio appearances as a Polish housewife.

–Herbert Mertz (of German origin), director of an orchestra, which often played on Polish programs; he was also musical director of station WGBK.

–Stanislaus Olejniczak, actor and announcer.

–Stanislaus Jasinski, singer and announcer; he was connected with Walter Leskiewicz's program, where he also sold advertising.

–Antoni Krysiak ("Redo"), actor; from 1933 anchored news programs; his wife Stefania worked with him; the Krysiak's were owners of the State Roofing Co.

–Irene Kochanowski-Bandrowski, actrss and singer.

–Jakob Kmiec, actor.

–Zofia Nalec, actress.

–Carolina Kajkowski, actress.

–Halina Smarski, singer.

The popular musical group "Musical Players" often appeared back then in Polish programs. This group was made up of Benjamin Stawinski. Thaddeus Lapacki, Mieczyslaw Jachimski, Stanislaus Jasinski and Walter Leskiewicz.

World War II was not a good time for Polish radio programs; many of them went off the air, others shortened their airtime. A resurgence toward the end of the 1940s took place when many new Polish radio programs were created.

The first postwar Polish program was founded in Detroit in 1949, at station WJLB. Its founders, producers and hosts were Eugene Kanstantynowicz and Marian Kreutz.[86] This was the longest daily Polish radio program in the United States. It aired five time a week for four hours daily, on Saturdays for five hours, and on Sundays, two hours. The programs contained local, national and international news, political commentaries, information on various Polonian organizations and their activities, radio plays, talks and interviews. This varied program, run by experienced radio journalists was very popular in the '50s and '60s among Polish-Americans in Detroit. It shaped opinions, influenced political attitudes as well as the cultural and social preferences of Polonia in the state of Michigan.

In the 1960s, the situation in Detroit began to change. While awareness and commitments to Polish heritage was greater than ever, there was a lack of interest in both Polish radio and the Polish language press. This phenomenon could be then observed in all Polish-American centers in the United States. Many Polish radio programs ceased to exist; Polish papers suffered a serious decline. Toward the end of the 1960s, Eugene Konstantynowicz died, and in 1976, John Marian Kreutz died. Their program, shortened and tailored to suit the changing needs of Polonia in Detroit, continued to be aired by John Marian Kreutz's wife, Celia, who gained radio experience working with her husband.

Since 1969, the Kreutz program has been carried by WMZK-FM, which is powerful enough to be heard in Toledo, Ohio, and in northern Michigan and even in Canada.

Celia Kreutz's program, cut down to one hour daily, was rich in content. Its musical segments included folk and popular pieces as weel as classical music. Famous artists such as Marian Owczarski presented talks on the history of Polish art. Talsk on social and political subjects were prepared by journalist Olgierd Szczeniowski and Professor Vincent Chrypinski. Segments for young people and Polish scouts were included in the broadcasts as well as segments for the Polish American Congress and various charities. The Polish chronicle of sports events was very popular among listeners and was prepared by George Rozalski, a graduate of the Warsaw Academy of Physical Culture.

The Kreutz program was taken over by George Rozalski[87] on August 1, 1978, after Celia Kreutz moved to Washington. He reorganized it and renamed it. The new show included features for women, children, sports fans, art and music lovers as well as science fans. There is a society segment, interviews, religious and literary talks, special commemorations for Polish national anniversaries and holidays, as well as national, international and local news, and weather forecasts. As a fule, George Rozalski never comments on the news; he leaves that to his listeners. "Polish Variety" broadcasts daily Mondya through Friday from 7 p.m. to 8 p.m.; on Saturday from 10 a.m. to noon and on Sundays from 1 p.m. to 5 p.m.

Station WJLB, which had carried Polish programs for decades, stopped airing ethnic programs. Appeals to the Federal Communications Commission in Waschington D.C. urging the maintenance of Polish broadcasts at this station were made by Polish organizations led by Michigan division of the Polish-American Congress–spearheaded by its president Casey Olejarczyk. These petitions brought no results.

In Garden City, Danuta Sworski runs a distinguished Polish program broadcast in WIID Mondays through Sundays from 2 p.m. to 3 p.m. and on Mondyas through Fridays from 6 p.m. to 7 p.m. The program carries music, newscasts, Polish-American organizational information and community news.

A welcome and popular radio program in Detroit, "Polish-American Matinee" is broadcast by John Sadrack from station WMZK-FM, Mondays through Fridays from 2 p.m. to 4 p.m.

Another Polish program worth noting is the Polish program "Happy Polka Time" hosted by John Ludwig on Sundays from 1 p.m. to 2 p.m. on WDJD.

Mark Ksiazek broadcasts the "Good Time Polka" programs, Mondays through Fridays from 6 p.m. to 8 p.m. on WIID in Garden City.

Gene Szymanski presents his music program "Polka Party Time" on Saturdays from 2 p.m. to 3 p.m. on station in Detroit.

The "Evening Polka Show" on WKCQ in Saginaw is presented by Martin Herzog, Mondays through Fridays from 5 p.m. to 6 p.m.; on Saturdays from 9 a.m. to 1 p.m., featuring polkas, waltzes and obereks.

While in Jackson, Adam Jankowski initiated the "Polka Show" in 1934 on station WIBM.[88] Jankowski's program didn't last long, but in 1936 Eddie Klucz started broadcasting his "Polka Show" on WIBM. Unlike Jankowski's program, Klucz's one-hour Sunday program lasted for 23 years.

Klucz's only sponsor was a Polish-American firm, Jerry Rowe's Furniture Store. Eddie Klucz aired his last program July 13, 1959. He died four days later. Polish radio programs also of the polska show type were then presented by Eddie Fryt.

On July 13, 1965, station WIBM introduced a Polish radio program called "Polka Time with Joe and Lil" hosted by the married couple Joe and Lil Pancerz.[89] During the 19 years of existence, the program was very popular.

"Polka House" is the name of the program hosted by Klement Misiak in Rogers City since October 10, 1968, on station WHAK.[90] His show, 20 percent in Polish and 80 percent in English, is heard every Saturday for two hours.

Don Parteka broadcasts his "Saturday and Sunday in Poland" from WATZ-AM and FM in Alpena.[91] The programs premiered in 1947 and returned to the air in 1968. They are broadcast in English and Polish and offer polkas, waltzes and obereks.

Since 1952, Diane Gorkowski has broadcast her "Polka Party" from WLEW in Bad Axe on Saturdays and Sundays. The 55-minute program is announced in English.[92]

For the past 13 years in Saginaw, Tommy Radar and Harold Mitas have aired their "Saturday; Sunday Polka Show" on WKCQ.[93] Mostly in English, the programs are broadcast Saturdays for four hours, and two hours on Sunday mornings. Folk music makes up the musical part of the broadcasts.

In 1977, the "Polish Religious Program" was created in Detroit at station WMUZ-FM.[94] Its director is the Rev. Boleslaw Krol, a catholic priest from St. Jyacinth's Parish. The half-hour religious broadcasts are heard every Saturday at 6:30 p.m. They include talks on religion and morals, news about Polish parishes in Detroit, a liturgical calendar, information on church events, etc.

In the state of Michigan, 17 stations broadcast Polish radio programs. Their total weekly airtime amounts to 57 hours.

CHAPTER 11

The History of Polish Radio in New York State

The president of the executive board of the Association of Polish Journalists in America, the oldest active Polish hournalist in the world, Ignacy Morawski, at the request of the author, gave the following report of the early history of Polish radio in New York:[95]

> Probably the first producer of a regular Polish radio program after World War I was Ludwick Cieciuch, brother of the chief of police of Jersey City, New Jersey. He had a several hour-long program on station WHOM. Driving home once after broadcasting his program, he fell asleep and was killed when his car hit a pole one Pulaski Skyline Drive, linking Jersey City with Newark.
>
> At the same time, for a number of years, K. Jarzembowski and his wife, Florentyna had a very popular program. Jarzembowski distinguished himself in World War I in the U. S. Army.
>
> A better quality program, first under the management of Jarzemboewski, was the 'Two Edwards' program, broadcast for many years and up to today.[96]
>
> Edward Witanowski, who is a city commissioner on Long Island, in a suburb of New York, and Edward Katowicz who lived in neighboring New Jersey, run the program. Good Polish language, a broad viewpoint, good commentaries and music are features of the programs aired by the 'Two Edwards.'

A former linotypist for the 'Nowy Swiat' (New World) daily, Michael Kecki, the son of a former Russian government official, presented his two-hour radio program, the 'Voice of Polonia' on WLIB for many years. For two seasons, the editor-in-chief of the New World, Ignacy Morawski, was a political commentator on this program. Kecki's program was and remains popular even after his death when it was produced by his wife Natalia from Greenpoint, a Polish neigborhood in Brooklyn.

In the '60s, editor Henry Landowski ran a Polish radio program which appeared and disappeared like meteors.

Metropolitan New York had numerous other smallet stations which broadcast Polish radio programs. In neighboring New Jersey and Connecticut, popular 'Polish Polka Hours,' are run usually by bandleaders.

Thomas Deren, a longtime correspondent of the New World in Philadelphia, who resided in the southern part of New Jersey, produced a Polish radio program together with his wife, a former musical comedy actress from Warsaw.

In the nearby New Jersey cities of Jersey City, Newark, Passaic, Paterson—there were various Polish programs. Maximillian F. Wegrzynek, publisher and editor-in- chief of New World, appeared very often (and for some time, on a regular basis) on these programs. He even had his own program, which he paid for and in which his co-editors appeared.

To these recollections of Ignacy Morawski, "a living history of American Polonia," we should add several details:

As late at 1970, the "Polish Voice of the New World" was heard on station WHBI-FM on Saturdays from 10 a.m. to 10:30 a.m.

"Two Edwards" program created on November 15, 1945, in 1970 was broadcast Mondays through Fridays from WPOW at 6 p.m. for an hour, and on Sundays from 10 a.m. to 11 a.m., from WHBI-FM. At present, it is broadcast only from WPOW Mondays through Fridays from 8 a.m. to 9 a.m.

Natalia Kecki's "Voice of Polonia" is aired on WHBI-FM on Saturdays from 3:30 p.m. to 4:30 p.m., and on Sundays from 11 p.m. to 11:30 p.m.

The Polish broadcasts of B. Rosalaka[97] were aired in the 1940s daily, from noon to 1 p.m., from WBNX in the Bronx, New York. Besides

Polish music, organizational and community news, Polish novels were read in those program, including such classics as "The Teutonic Knights" by Henry Sienkiewicz.

The oldest daily Polish radio program broadcast to this day in Buffalo is "Polonia Varieties."[98] It was established by Mieczyslaw Korpanty in 1940. The program aired on WHLD daily from noon to 2 p.m. It consists of news and commentaries, a radio theater, community announcements, as well as music–mainly of the folk type.

Since 1940, Polish programs on WKNY in Kingston have been hosted by Bronislaw Hudela.[99] Since their creation, these programs have been on the air from 9:30 a.m. to 10 a.m.

Stanley Jasinski, who as early as 1934 produced Polish programs in Detroit, in aired them in Buffalo in 1940.[100] At present, they are on station WXRL, which Jasinski built himself in 1964. The program airs on Saturdays from noon to 2 p.m. and on Sundays from noon to 3 p.m.

His program is called "The Voice if Buffalo Polonia," and consists of 15-minute segments of news, commentaries, interviews and Polish music–from folk to classical. The programs are done in Polish and English. For the past 30 years, Stanley Jasinski has transmitted Mass every Sunday live from St. Stanislaus Catholic Church in Buffalo.

Since April 10, 1948, Michael Bubniak has broadcast his "Polka Party" show on WCSS in Amsterdam, New York.[101] The program is heard on Sundays from 11 a.m. to 1 p.m. amd ,ost of it is in English.

George Wantuch, graduate of the College of Commerce in Krakow, founded a Polish program called "Concert of Popular Music" in 1948.[102] The program was heard on station WHLD in Niagra Falls on Sundays from 10 a.m. to 11:30 a.m. The broadcasts contained popular songs, operatta music, interviews, radio plays, poetry, community announcements and news. The program was discontinued in 1976.

The WKOP station in Binghamptin broadcasts two Polish radio programs.[103] On Sundays from noon to 2 p.m. WKOP airs "Bill and Barbie Mack's Sunday Polka Program," with polka music, news and community announcements. The program was created in 1969 and continues to serve the local Polish-American community.

WKOP also carried five-minute programs called "Bill Flynn's Polka Capsule" at 9:25 a.m., 12:25 p.m. and 6:25 p.m., Mondays through Fridays. Besides polka music, the "capsules" feature Polish carols at Christmas time and Easter songs during the Easter holidays. Occasionally, station WKOP transmits Mass in Polish.

"Polish Polka Jamboree; The Best Co Jest" (The Best There Is) is the name of a program broadcast for years on station WSOQ in North Syracuse by Bob Pietruch. Folk music dominates the program, along with the news and community announcements. The jamboree can be heard Saturdays at 10 a.m. and Sundays at 1:30 p.m.

The Hupaj-Siupaj" program is broadcast by Richard Rudolph from WRIV Mondays through Saturdays for 30 minutes and on Sundays for 90 minutes.[104] The programs are announced primarily in English and feature Polish music, news and community announcements.

"Polish Memories" has been produced by Bernie Witkowski since 1970 every Sunday for 30 minutes from station WEVD.[105] The broadcasts are in Polish and English. The spotlight is played by Bernie Witkowski's orchestra. Witkowski is a multi-instrument musician, composer and singer. Bernie Witkowski is sometimes called "The King of the Polka Kings."

Ron Kurowski has hosted Polish programs since 1970.[106] From March of 1970 to October of 1976, he aired them on WTBQ in Warwick, New York; from February to October 1977 on WEOK-AM and FM in Poughseepsie and presently only in WEOK-AM. His programs are heard Sundays from 10:05 a.m. to 11 a.m. Ron Kurowski's daughters also appear on the shows: 13 year-old Donna and 11 year-old Debbie. Kurowski's "Polka American Hour" is done mainly in English and stresses polka music.

The "Polka Party" program went on the air over station WGGO in Salamanca in 1974.[107] The programs, 30 minutes every Sunday, are aired in two languages–Polish and English.

Gus Kosior began broadcasting his "Polka Party" program in October 1978.[108] the programs are heard on WTBQ in Warwick, in English. The "Polka Party" programs are devoted to music, polka band music, obereks and waltzes, performed by polka bands from around the country.

The "Polish Bells" program of Halina de Rocha is heard on WHBI Sundays from 1 p.m. to 2:30 p.m. "Poland Sings" is hosted by Halina Kaminski at WHBI-FM station in New York. Her music programs are heard Tuesdays and Wendesdays from 7:05 p.m. to 7:30 p.m. Swede Olsen has polka programs Sundays at noon on station WVHC Sundays at 1 p.m. on WTHE and Tuesdays at 7:05 a.m. on WVHC. "Big Stash's Polka Program," hosted by Stanislaus Kowalski, is heard Sundays at 11 a.m. to noon on WVCR-FM on Londonville. "john Firlit's Polka Carousel" is broadcast in WLFH in Little Falls, Sundays at 12:30 p.m.

Ed Godlewski airs his "Polka Country Show" on Sundays from 9 a.m. to 10 a.m. on WKOL in Amsterdam, New York.

"Polka Party" with host Bernie Wyta airs every Sunday at 11 a.m. in WEVD in New York.

Don Kielbasa and Margie Pisarski broadcast their own "Polka Party" program on Sundays from 11 a.m. to 1 p.m. from WCSS in Amsterdam, as well as the "Polka Power" program on Sundays at 10:30 a.m. from WOKO in Albany.

Don Nikolski's and John Polka's "Polka Party" is broadcast Sundays from 10 a.m. to 11 a.m. on station WWWD in Schenectady. Ed Czernecki calls his program "Jedzie Boat Polka Varieties" (The Polka Varieties Boat is Coming) every Sunday at 9 a.m. on WALY in Herkimer. The Polish program "Jimmy Sturr Polka Sessions" is broadcast from WALL in Middletown every Sunday from 1 p.m. to 3 p.m.

Janek Godlewski presents his "Polish Hit Parade" every Sunday at 9:30 a.m. from station WBRV in Booneville. "Polish Melodies" is a program produced by Michael M. Dziedzic and broadcast Sundays from 9 a.m. to 1 p.m. on WBVM in Utica. "Gussie Kosior's Polka Party" is broadcast on Sunday from noon to 1 p.m. on WTBQ in Warwick.

The "Wednesday Morning Polka Party with Jolly Rich and Polka Randy" is presented appropriately on Wednesdays from 7 a.m. to 8 a.m. on WHBI-FM in New York City. Styczynski-Diette-Bogus broadcast their "Hey Polka Show" on Sunday from 1 p.m. to 2 p.m. on WABY in Albany.

The "Bob Petrowsky Polka Bandstand" is heard Tuesdays fro, 10:30 a.m. and Fridays from 5 p.m. to 6 p.m. on station WBAU on Long Island, while "John and Ann Marszalek's Contemporary Polish Music and Polka Happy Hour" aires Sundays from 10 a.m. to noon on WWWG in Rochester.

Bill Skibilski presents his programs Saturdays at 6:10 p.m. on WFUV, Sundays at 10 a.m. on WVOX in New Rochelle and Wednesdays from WHBI in New York City. "Bill Mack's Sunday Polka Show" is heard on WKOP in Binghamton Sundays at noon.

In the state of New York, Polish radio programs are broadcast by 45 stations. Their total airtime amounts to 100 hours weekly.

CHAPTER 12

Pennsylvania: The State with the Most Stations Broadcasting Polish Programs

One of the oldest Polish broadcasts in Pennsylvania is the "Polish Radio Program" in Erie, established in 1933 by Joseph Zdunski. It aired on station WWGO, which later changed its name to WEYZ.

In 1968, this program was taken over by Peter Garnowski, who produced it until 1979.[109] At present, this program is run by his wife, Kazimiera Garnowski, and her daugher, Bozena; the mother speaks on the air in Polish; the daughter in English. The program is heard every Sunday morning for two hours and consists of Polish music, from folk through classical, poetry and literature, interviews, announcements of Polish-American activities as well as 15-minute religious features from the American Shrine of Our Lady of Czestochowa.

The entire Garnowski family takes an active part in the community like of local Polonia. Their "Polish Radio Program: serves the Polonian community in Erie well and deserved its popularity.

The "WCED Sunday Morning Polka Party," created in the 1940s, is now produced by Michael Rudzinski and goes on the air Sundays from 9 a.m. to 11 a.m.[110] The programs are aired on station WCED in Du Bois, mostly in English, and feature mostly polkas, obereks, and waltzes.

WCED also carries the "Mike and Frank Polka Party" broadcast Sundays from 9 a.m. to 11 a.m.

Since 1953, a Polish radio show has been on station WPME in Punxsutawny. The producer of this program, which airs Monday through

The producer and announcer of the "Paul Oles Polka Show,"[111] which has been broadcast since October 3, 1953, on station WCDL in Carbondale, is Paul Oles, a graduate of Scranton College. His programs present onehour of Polka music daily as well as news and weather forecasts. The program is announced in English.

Since 1953, Polish radio programs have been produced in Philadelphia by Theodor Przybyla. The "Gwiazda Polarna" (North Star) weekly Polish newspapter of October 15, 1979, informed its readers that the "White Eagle sports club had presented a memorial plaque to the producer of the Polish radio program in Philadelphia, Mr. Theodor Przybyla, for presenting Polish sports reports on the air for more than 25 years."

Johnny Kotrick had for 12 years worked in a coal mine. On October 1, 1961, he began to broadcast Polish radio programs on station WNCC in Pennsylvania. The program is heard only on Sundays, but for for a full seven hours. It is called "Johnny Kotrick's Sunday Sound of Polka Music."[112] The program is announced in Polish; the music is predominantly polkas, obereks, waltzes, with local, national and world news each 30 minutes. Johnny Kotrick has been nicknamed the "Polka Giant of the Coal Mines."

Since August 2, 1962, Polish programs have been heard on station WTKL in Philadelphia on Sundays at 3:45 p.m.

The Polish part of the program, which is announced by Genia Gunther, lasts 45 minutes, while the English runs for 15 minutes.[113] WTKL is a 10,000 watt station, so Genia Gunther's popular program can be heard by about half a million people. The program called "Genia Gunther's Show" presents music, interviews, announcements of Polonian organization, religious segments from American Czestochowa and the news. Genia Gunther is president of district 205 of the Polish National Alliance and secretary of Group 3131 of the Alliance. She has received the Gold Cross Merit of the Polish National Alliance and "Haller's Sword" Merit, an award of the Association of Polish Army Veterans.

"Frank's Polka Party" is a Polish program broadcast since 1968 on station WBCW in Jeannette.[114] The founder of the program, producer and host is Frank Powloski, who is a draftsman and works for the Westinghouse Co. His programs air for three hours on Sunday, half in Polish and half in English. They consist of Polish music and songs, polkas, waltzes and obereks.

Ronald F. Slomski, founder of the "Ron Slomski's Polka Time" program, has been on the air since 1969 on WHYP-AM and FM, every Sunday for three hours.[115] Ronald Slomski presents 90 percent of his program in English and 10 percent in Polish. By profession, his is manager of the stations. Ron Slomski is also producer of a Polish cultural program called "Polish American Spotlight," broadcast in English by 100 radio stations across the United States.

"Jo-Jo's Polka Swing" is a radio program broadcast on WIYQ-FM, a 50,000 watt station in Johnstown.[116]

Its founder, producer and host is Joseph V. Vesnesky, who holds a bachelor's degree from Lockhaven State College and is a history teacher. His three-hour programs are aired every Sunday, in English and Polish with Polish folk music, news and community announcements.

Doran Richardson,[117] producer of the "Polka Party" program airs his broadcast on Sundays for three and a half hours. Eighty percent of his programs is in English and 20 percent in Polish. It airs on station WWBE in Winber. Doran Richardson is a steel worker.

"Polka Joy Show,"[118] on WYZZ-FM, a 50,000 watt station in Wilkes-Barre can be heard in six states. The producer and host is Bobby "Z," a graduate of a musical college who works professionally as a music teacher. The "Polka Joy Show" is aired three hours on Sunday in English.

Eva Tumiel-Kozak,[119] a graduate of the Poznan Music College in Poland, is the producer of programs called "Musica Polonica" on station WQED-FM since 1976. Her programs can be heard in three states: Pennsylvania, Ohio and West Virginia. "Musica Polonica" is announced in English, but the annual Christmas program is 40 percent in Polish and 60 percent in English. This is exclusively a music program with preference shown for classical music. Special programs are devoted to specific composers and the program also features interviews with musical artists.

The "K and K Polka Show" goes on the air on WICK in Scranton on Sundays from 11 a.m. to 1 p.m. It presents polka folk music and announcements of Polish-American organizations.

The "Gil Yurus Polka Review" is broadcast in English every Saturday and Sunday from 10 a.m. to noon on WKEG in Washington, Pennsylvania. It presents folk music and announcements.

"Jolly St. Nick's Polka Revolution" is the name of a program broadcast on WPHB in Philipsburg every Saturday from 2 p.m. to 5 p.m.

"John Koza's Polka Varieties" is on the air Sundays from 9:30 a.m. to 10:30 a.m. fna from 11 a.m. to 6 p.m. from WVAM-AM and FM in Altoona. John Koza presents polka music, news and community announcements.

Gary Loncki broadcasts his program of Polka music every Sunday from noon to 3 p.m. at WERG in Erie.

The "Lil John Polka Show" reaches listeners over station WTRA in Latriber every Sunday from 3 p.m. to 5 p.m.

"Alicia's Polka Show" is broadcast in English on WOCS in Central City, daily from 11 a.m. to noon and on Sundays from 9:15 a.m. to 1 p.m. The program features polka music, the news and Polish-American community announcements.

Johnny Haas airs Polish programs on WPAZ on Pottstown on Saturdays at 12:45 p.m.

"Happy Polka Jean" is on the air Sundays from 11:30 a.m. to 1:30 p.m. on WQIQ in Aston.

In Hazleton, station WAZL airs program called "Carl's Polka Show" every Sunday from 12:15 p.m. to 2 p.m.

Polish radio programs are aired by 53 stations in the state of Pennsylvania. Their total weekly airtime amounts to 173 hours.

CHAPTER 13

Significant Polish Radio Programs in Other States

"Arizona Chet's Polka Parade" is a Polish radio program that has been on the air since 1958, first on KFMN-FM station and then on KTUC-AM in Tuscon, Arizona.[120] the program is hosted by Chet Czerniak. The "Sitarz" orchestra under the direction of Sitarzewski, has cooperated with this program since its inception. Polkas, waltzes, obereks make up the musical part of this very popular broadcast.

In San Francisco, California, the "Polish American Variety Hour"[121] has many listeners on station KBRD Sundays from 10 a.m. to 11 a.m. The "Polish Cultural Hour" is broadcast on KQED-FM in San Francisco Sundays from 7 p.m. to 8 p.m. In Los Angeles, Polish programs are heard on KTYM Sundays from 2:30 p.m. to 3:00 p.m.

In Wilmington, Delaware, station WJBR airs popular Polish broadcasts hosted by Joseph Kowalewski.[122]

Since 1967, station WJBR in Wilmington has aired the "International Radio Show."[123] Its producer and host is Zygmunt Gordon, a Polish Jew, born in Lodz, who survived six years in the Auschwitz Nazi concentration camp. Ziggy Gordon entertains his numerous audience with good music and humor every Sunday at 8 a.m.

Leon Widawski, a graduate of the Detroit Institute of Music Arts, in 1947 organized the "Polish Radio Hour" in Miami, Florida.[124] The consecutive hosts of this broadcast after Widawski were: a retired editor, founder and first president of the Polish American Club in Miami, Walter

Zymalski; John Niedzialek (from 1955 to 1965); Maria Damski (from 1966 to 1980). The program is run by the Polish-American Club of Miami. It has been aired by various AM stations with stron power and now is on WGLY-FM with rather small coverage. The 30-minute program can be heard on Saturdays at 9:30 p.m. It consists of Polish music, news and reports on the life of Polonia in the Miami area. The costs of airing the program are covered by advertising and voluntary donations, with any deficit picked up by the Polish-American Club of Miami.

In the early '50s, the "Polish Radio Program" of Group 3036 of the Polish National Alliance (PNA) was broadcast in Miami.[125] The producers of this program were a married couple, Francis and Stanislawa Synowiec. After her husband's death, Stanislawa continued the program herself. The "Polish Radio Program" of the PNA was aired once a week for an hour on WEDR.

In Baltimore, Maryland, "Echoes From Poland"[126] was heard Sunday mornings as early as 1936. Its founder, producer and announcer was Mieczyslaw Kniejski. Barbara Miegon had worked on the program with him, since 1967. In 1972, after Mieczyslaw Kniejski's death, "Echoes From Poland" was taken over by Barbara Miegon and her husband George. In April 1972, the Miegons created a second 30-minute program, "Polish Melodies," broadcast every Sunday afternoon. The program began with the traditional, old Polish hunting tune, "A hunting we will go . . . ." In their new program, the producers put a greater stress on cultural affairs. Unfortunately, because of financial difficulties, this program was liquidated. The Miegons were fortunate enough to add an additional 30 minutes to their morning program in early 1976 and thus created a 60-minute "Echoes From Poland" broadcast, which included cultural and entertainment elements such as classical music, folk music and the most popular Polish songs.

The announcers still broadcast some advertisements in English to hold on to listeners who do not know Polish very well. Letters from listeners come from Baltimore as well as all over the state of Maryland. Letters also come from the neighboring states of Delaware, New Jersey, Virginia, Pennsylvania and Washington, D. C.

The station range is quite large, since it can be heard within a 100-mile radius. The producers and announcers of the only Polish radio program in Baltimore, "Echa z Polski" (Echoes From Poland) George and Barbara

Miegon carry on their broadcasts on a very high level and they are very popular. Their undoubted merit is that they have revived what was a dying Polonian culture in Baltimore.

The Rev. Zbigniew Kaszubski, a Catholic priest, broadcasts his "Polish Radio Hour"[127] every Sunday from 2:30 p.m. to 3 p.m. on station KUXL in Minneapolis, Minnesota. His broadcasts feature religious commentaries, reports on Polish-American events, national news and Polish news, as well as Polish music.

In the state of New Hampshire, the popular radio program "Polka Radio Program" is run by Robert (Bob) Opal, who is very proud of the fact that in the years 1934 to 1938, he attended the gymnasium (high school) in Wadowice with Karol Wojtyla, the present Pope.[128]

The popular "Polka Radio Program" created in 1969, has been aired by various stations. Now the "Polka Radio Program" is heard on station WKVT in Battleboro daily from 6 a.m. to 7 a.m.; Sundays on WKNE in Keene from 7 a.m. to 8 a.m. and on WTSV and WECM in Claremont from 11 a.m. to 12:20 p.m. Bob Opal presents his programs in Polish and English.

The "Ed and Chet Polka Show,"[129] one of the better Polish radio programs, is broadcast every Sunday from 9:05 a.m. to noon on station WYDM in Elij, New Jersey. The producers and hosts of these programs are Edward and Chester Slomkowski.

Bernard Goydish broadcasts his musical program "Happy Bernie's Polka Party" on station WCTC in New Brunswick, New Jersey, every Sunday for 90 minutes.[130] The program first went on the air in 1967.

A popular radio show is the "Polka Parade" presented by Max Smulewicz every Sunday from 10 a.m. to noon on WSUS in Franklin, New Jersey.[131]

Ted Chmura has aired his program, "Ted's Polka Show," since 1953 on station WWON in Woodsocket, Rhonde Island, exclusively in English.[132] The program includes polka music, entertainment features and news.

In the early 1930s, Stanislaus Nastal founded "Our Polish Radio Hour" in Milwaukee, Wisconsin at WEMP, later at WFOX.[133]

After his death, the program was continued by his son, Stanislaus Nastal. In 1954, station WFOX passed into the hands of new owners, who eliminated all foreign language programs. The young producer of "Our Polish Radio Hour" did not try to move the broadcast to another station, stating that the Polish language was used less and less by young people and for that reason, a Polish radio program cannot have sufficient advertising support in Milwaukee.

Another pioneer of Polish radio programs in Milwaukee was J. Szymczak, who broadcast his programs on station WRJN in the 1940s. Since 1952, the "Radio Corner of the Polish Veterans' Association in Milwaukee" was a part of that program. In January 1953, this segment was expanded into a full program called "Echoes From Polan." The veterans' group in Milwaukee also aired a cultural and musical program in 1955 to 1956, in addition to the "Echoes From Poland." The show was produced by Professor W. Drzewieniecki, with the participation of A. Bartosz, an editor of the "Gwiazda Polarna" (North Star) Polish newspaper of Sevens Point, Wisconsin.[134] Ten radio stations in Wisconsin carried it.

After Professor Drzewieniecki, the producers of the "Echoes From Poland" program were: Janusz Kaminski, Zbigniew Jaskorzynski, Alexander Romanski, Henry Gontarek, and since 1979, Halina Jaskorzynski. The program is aired on WYLO-AM in Jackson, Wisonsin, every Sunday from 10:30 a.m. to 11:30 a.m. The prorgram is made up of Polish music, featuring folk and classical pieces, interviews, community announcements, poetry recitations and the news.

As mentioned earlier in the Illinois chapter, a 30-minute program, "Helena's Polish Radio Show" is broadcast every Sunday from 10 a.m. to 10:30 a.m. by Helena Wantuch in Milwaukee.

Richard E. Mech presents his "Polish Varieties Program" every Sunday from 9 a.m. to 10 a.m. on WRKR-FM in Racine, Wisconsin.

CHAPTER 14

The Polka Show Phenomenon and the International Polka Association

The history of Polish language radio in the United States would not be complete without dwelling a bit on one cultural phenomenon–namely, the popularity of polka music and polka programs. This is a relatively new Phenomenon as the first radio program of this type was broadcast in 1950 and soon found dozens of imitators. At present, for very many listeners, Polish radio is synonymous with those polka programs.

The producers of polka shows are usually leaders of orchestras which play music based on Polish and other European folk motifs, but created in the United States. The American polka is a lively dance in 2/4 time, usually performed by a couple. It originated in the 1800s in Czechoslovakia, but is now a uniquely American musical form. The quality of the art form varies, often shocking listeners from Poland as too loud and not aesthetic. Its quality depends on the talen and good tast of those who play this music. Polka music fans can be found not only among Polonia, but also among many other european ethnic groups and Americans with no ethnic ties. American pola music has both its ardent opponents and faithful fans. Some believe that the American polka is ephemeral and will pass without trace; others see a bright future for it and good growth prospects. What matters is that this music is winning over opposition, breaking barriers, and finding more and more new fans.

Among the first to start radio polka show programs in the United States was Walter Jagiello–Lil Wally. He aired his first program as a 22-year-old youth in 1950 from station WCRW in Chicago on Monday from 5 p.m. to 5:30 p.m. Next he expanded the show to a 60-minute program at 10 a.m. on Sundays from station WOPA in Oak Park, Illinois. After barely a few weeks, his tremendous popularity allowed him to extend the program to three hours on Sunday, while Monday through Fridau, he aired it from 7:30 a.m. to 8 a.m. and 4 p.m. to 5 p.m., and on Saturdays at 2 p.m.

Li'l Wally moved his programs from WOPA to WLS, a much stronger station, which can be heard in several states. Walter Jagiello owes his great popularity to his polka band which he created himself. They say that Jagiallo is a man of many talents; He sings, writes songs. arranges music and plays various instruments. He began singing when he was eight years old. He learned to sing by himself, listening to his parents and their friends sing at social gatherings. He created his own orchestra, criss-crossed the United States with it and also played in Europe, including Poland, where he is well-known. In 1949, he recorded eight of this own compositions for Columbia Records. By 1951, he had established Jay Jay Records, the biggest company producing polka records. In 1959, he built his own recording studio.

His Polish and English song "Wish I Was Single Again" was recorded in 1954 and became a fantastic hit. In Chicago alone, 150,000 copies were sold in two weeks time, while the total sale of these recordings and cassettes surpassed six million.

Li'l Wally became the indisputable "Polka King." At present he lives in Miami, Florida, where he has a studio and record company.

In the early 1960s, the idea of creating an association for polka lovers of the United States and Canda surfaced in Chicago. Annual polka moonlight dances had been organized in Chicago since 1960 and had attracted thousands of people. By 1963, the first polka convention was held in Chicago, followed by conventions each succeeding year in Chicago, Detroit and Buffalo, New York.

In January 1968, an organizational committee made up of Johnny Hyzny, Leon Kozicki, Joe and Jean Salomon, Edward Blazonczyk and Don Jodlowski, met in Chicago to plan the next convention. Their discussions developed the idea of forming the International Polka Association, which would organize the annual conventions. The International Polka Association was chartered by the state of Illinois as a not-for-profit corporation and was registered in Cook County (the Chicago area) in August 1968.

Its charter described the purposes and goals of the organization: "An educational and social organization for the preservation, promulgation and advancement of polka music; and to promote, maintain and advance public interest in polka entertainment; to advance the mutual interests and encourage greater cooperation among its members who are engaged in polka entertainment; and to encourage and pursue the study of polka music, dancing and traditional folklore."

Leon Kozicki served as the first elected president of the association from 1968 to 1973. Edward Blazonczyk was the first elected secretary and Don Jodlowski was the first elected treasurer. In 1969, the association's first information bulletin appeared which was edited by Eddie Arenz.

Since 1968, the association has organized an annual International Polka Festival and Convention each January—a month which was dubbed by the association as National Polka Month.

Delegates at the first convention in 1968 voted to present annual Polka Music Awards and to establish a Polka Music Hall of Fame as a way to honor deserving polka personalities. The Association decided to bestow membership in the Polka Hall of Fame to performers, radio announcers, producers, and others who have rendered faithful service to the polka entertainment industry.

The Polka Music Hall of Fame is administered by a seven member board of trustees. The IPA created an academy of more than 100 persons who elect the honorees to be added to the Hall of Fame. Each year two prominent living personalities are to be elected and one deceased personality. Candidates must have been actively engaged in the polka field for a minimum of 20 years. They are selected from all regions of the United States and Canada, regardless of ethnic origin, locality, or style preference of polka music. The IPA has retained the Institute of Industrial Relations of Loyola University in Chicago to conduc the elections and certify the winners. Those elected to the Hall of Fame are honored with a banquet and installation ceremony. The first members of the Hall of Fame were elected in 1969. They were Li'l Wally Jagiello and Frank Yankovic. Names were added in subsequent years.

In 1972, a deceased category was added to honor contributors to the "Polka Movement" who had passed away. In 1983, a "pioneer" category was added to recognize forgotten old-timers who were still living, but no longer active in Polka music.

A list of all members of the Polka Music Hall of Fame is given below:

Polka Music Hall of Fame

Frank Yankovic	1969
Li'l Wally Jagiello	1969
Frank Wojnarowski	1970
Eddie Blazonczyk	1970
Walter Dana	1971
Bernie Wyte Witkowski	1971
Marion Lush	1972
Ray Henry	1972
Eddie Zima (Deceased)	1972
Gene Wisniewski	1973
Ray Budzilek	1973
Mattie Madura (Deceased)	1973
Walt Solek	1974
Dick Pillar	1974
Marisha Data (Deceased)	1974
Harold Loeffelmacher	1975
Steve Adamczyk	1975
Johnny Pecon (Deceased)	1975
Dick Rodgers	1976
Chet Schafer	1976
"Whoopee John" Wilfhart (Deceased)	1976
Leon Kozicki	1977
Joe Lazarz	1977
Brunon Kryger (Deceased)	1977
Alvin Sajewski	1978
"Joe Pat" Paterek	1978
Ignacy Podgorski (Deceased)	1978
Marv Herzog	1979
Al Soyka	1979
Romy Gosz (Deceased)	1979
Johnnie Bomba	1980
Stan E. Saleski	1980
Ted Maksymowicz (Deceased)	1980

Polka Music Hall of Fame (cont.)

Casey Siewierski	1981
Ray Stolzenberg	1981
Lou Prohut (Deceased)	1981
Happy Louie Dusseault	1982
Johnny Libera	1982
Joe Fiedor (Deceased)	1982
Walter Ostanek	1983
Johnny Hyzny	1983
Lawrence Duchow (Deceased)	1983
Eddie Oskierko (Pioneer)	1983
Bernie Goydish	1984
Jimmy Sturr	1984
Fez Fritsche (Deceased)	1984
Charlie Hicks (Pioneer)	1984
Joe Wojkiewicz	1985
Larry Chesky	1985
Earl McNellis (Deceased) (Cousin Fuzzie)	1985
Stan Jasinski (Pioneer)	1985

The announcement of the first Polka Hall of Fame members in 1969 propelled the International Polka Association into even higher gear.

Chicago was chosen as the site of Polka Festival again in 1970. Again, the great January festival coincided with the Polka Association's birthday celevration. All proceeds were earmarked for the fund to acquire a building for the Polka Music Hall of Fame, as were proceeds from other association parties. In 1970, the Rev. Walter Szczypula, a Catholic priest, was appointed chaplain of the Association. The new editors of the association's bulletin were Ed Sterczek and Richie Gomulka, followed by John Jaworski and John Poloko. Besides dances and occasional concerts, the Association organized numerous sports events to benefit the Music Hall of Fame fund. Those events received enthusiastic reviews, however, there was also criticism of the artists or athletes who received awards.

In 1971, the popularity of the Polka Festival reached its zenith. People walked in the streets with huge signs reading "January–National Polka

Month," "The Polka For Everyone in 19171," etc. But there was also bad publicity. Association co-founder Leon Kozicki sent a letter to the *Wall Street Journal* protesting the newspaper's negative and even slanderous remarks about polka music. Starczek and Gomulka resigned their posts as editors and their places were taken by John Jaworski and John Poloko.

The Association applied to the Internal Revenue Service for relief from paying taxes and received tax exempt status. In January 1972, the next festival was held, at which polka bands from the state of Michigan were a great success.

Association activities began to grow very intensively. A fashion show was organized as well as new dances and sports events, a dancing course, street parades, and youth competitions. An annual membership fee of $5 was set.

In January 1973, the executive committee decided to move the site of the festival to Milwaukee. At the group's January banquet in Chicago, Leon Kozicki received a silk American flag and the banner of the Association as an award. These prizes were made possible through the efforts of Joe Paterek and congressman John Fary of Illinois. The Music Hall of Fame fund continued to grow. Hardly any of the association's events ended in deficit, while the number of members was constantly on the rise.

Milwaukee remained the site of the festival for the next two years. Throughout January, the capital city of the polka–Chicago–was alight with neon signs popularizing polka music. This was probably the first time such a broad propaganda effort was undertaken. Blance Stanislawski became the next editor of the Associatin News. Thanks to her initiative, the convention for the first time took part in the parade honoring the Polish 3rd of May Constitution, and in the Girl Scouts Parade in Chicago. Numerous picnics were organized. Representatives of the state of Michigan adopted a resolution addressed to the president of the United States asking that January be named "National Polka Month."

In January 1975, singer Bobby Vinton appeared at the Arie Crown Theater in Chicago. After his concert, he received special recognition from the association for his Polka-ballad "Melody of Love," which included words sung in Polish and was one of the hits of the year.

More than 1200 people took part in the Association's annual banquet and ball in 1976 in Chicago. At this event, Lucy Partoszewski received an award for popularizing polka music in the United States. Balls were also held in Dover, Delaware, New Jersey and Massachusetts. Proceeds from them went to the Polka Music Hall of Fame.

January 16, 1977–the coldest day of the past century–more than 800 people took part in the association's banquet and ball. President Fred Rudy responded to a request made by association member Henry Broze and sent a letter to the U.S. Congress protesting the liquidation of polka radio programs in Cleveland. The letter received a positive response and ultimately the programs returned to the airwaves.

In 1974, Lorraine Lincoski, who won a "Miss Polka" contest, also won the title of Miss Pennsylvania and competed for the title of Miss America. The Ninth International Polka Festival was held that year, at which it was decided that the next festival would again be held in Chicago. The committee decided that the site of the 10th festival would be Milwaukee.

In 1979, the Polka Association purchased a former Steelworkers Union Hall at 4145 S. Kedzie Ave. in Chicago and renovated it into their Polka Hall of Fame and Museum. Association meetings are now held in the Hall of Fame Room, while the small Museum Room contains Polka memorabilia. The building also holds the administrative offices of the Association.

Among the most recent initiatives of the Polka Association was their own weekly radio polka program, "The IPA Polka Show," aired Saturdays from 12:05 p.m. to 1 p.m. on WTAQ in La Grange, Illinois, from 1979 through August 1985. The program was produced and hosted by members of the Polka Association's board of directors.

Since 1984, the Association had distributed awards for the most popular polka music of the year, in various categories. Polka Music Awards for 1984 and 1985 are as follows:

1984

Favorite Song:	"Mountaineer Music" by Eddie Blazonczyk
Favorite Album:	"Polka Medley" by Eddie Blazonczyk
Favorite Male Vocalist:	Eddie Blazonczyk
Favorite Femal Vocalist:	Renata Romanik
Favorite Instrumental Group:	Eddie Blazonczyk's Versationes

1985

Favorite Song:	"No Problem Polka" by Dick Pillar
Favorite Album:	"Simply Polkamentary" by Lennie Gomulka

Favorite Male Vocalist:	Eddie Blazonczyk
Favorite Female Vocalist:	Renata Romanik
Favorite Instrumental Group:	Eddie Blazonczyk's Versatones

About 343 polka program directors have already joined the International Polka Association. Probably there are many more who are not yet members. In recent years, there has been a significant increase in the number of radio stations broadcasting Polish programs, and an increase in the number of hours devoted weekly to Polish radio programs. This has been possible to a large extent thanks to the popularity of the Polka Phenomenon.

CHAPTER 15

Profiles of Polish Radio Pioneers in the United States

JOHN M. LEWANDOWSKI
The Father of Polish Radio in the United States

John M. Lewandowski was born May 29, 1890, in Cleveland, Ohio. His parents were natives of the Congress Kingdom section of Poland and having emigrated from Poland to the United States around 1880, settled in Cleveland. John Lewandowski studied at St. Mary's School at Broadway and Mound avenues. After his studies, he worked at the Peerless Motor Car Co. as an automobile mechanic and then as an administrative inspector. In 1915, he entered the Cleveland police force.

At that time the American Polonia, under the leadership of Ignacy Jan Paderewski, was making an intensive effort and propoganda in the matter of Polish independence. The Polish patriotic activity must have found a keen response in the heart of the young Lewandowski, who had been raised in the Polish spirit. This fact is attested to, since Lewandowski was among the 100,000 volunteers who answered President Wilson's call in 1917. The patriotism of the Polish-Americans of that time is clearly visible as they comprised 50 percent of all the volunteers. The American Polonia tried to convince the U.S. government to form an army of 100,000 composed exclusively of Polish-Americans and requesting that the army be named "The Kisciuszko Army." Unfortunately, this proposal was ignored. The initiators of this idea had intended to bring 500 officers from the Polish army in Russia headed by Joseph Dowbor Musnicki. These officers were to organize the Kosciuszko Army and were to train the volunteers. Arming Polish-Americans as a unit became a reality only when the French President Raymond Poincare issued a decree concerning the formation of an autonomous Polish Army in France. About 40,000 Polish-Americans were to be found in that unit.

Lewandowski served in France in the 83rd Division, ammunition train #308 after completing basic training. After the victorious end of World War I, he was sent to serve in the American Army of Occupation in Germany. In 1919, he was honorably discharged with the rank of staff Sergeant.

Returning to civilian life after his return from Europe, Lewandowski engaged in organizing the Polish Legion of American Veterans. His efforts were crowned with success, for John Lewandowski became the organization's co-founder. Evidently, his effort was properly appreciated since for two terms he held the highly honored position of National Commandent of the Polish Legion of American Veterans. Lewandowski was also an active member and founder of the American Legion Veteran of Foreign Wars for the state of Ohio.

He also participated in the veterans organization Army and Navy Union.

After having passed the necessary training and state examinations, Lewandowski set up a real estate office in 1920, which he successfully operated for many years.

In the 1920s a "radio craze" swept over American society. In 1926 WJAY, the pioneer radio station in Cleveland asked Lewandowski, who knew Polish well, to prepare and present a trial radio program in Polish. The trial test program turned out superbly. Polish organizations and individual listeners bombarded the station with thank you notes. During this first Polish radio program, the soloist Paul Faut, a Polish stage artist, performed along with several others.

Lewandowski was bewitched by the possibilities of radio as a result of this initial experience. He was determined to present radio programs to the Polish ethnic groups in and around Cleveland in its native language. He did this skillfully and soon garnered a large group of listeners which allowed him to stabalize his new undertaking. From 1927 on, Lewandowski broadcast Polish radio programs in Cleveland, thus inaugurating Polish radio in the United States.

Lewandowski was also a pioneer in the financial manner in which those programs were set up. Lewandowski ran those programs at his own cost. The programs neither belonged to a sponsoring firm nor to the broadcasting radio station as was customary at the time. In relation to the radio station, Lewandowski was an independent "broker" who worked for himself. He paid the radio station a certain designated sum of money, found advertisers himself, paid the orchestra and any performing artists who appeared on his show and also paid for any recorded music used during the programs.

Lewandowski's daughter Yvonne says that her father had an orchestra consisting of 13 musicians and that he ordered his records from Poland. In this way, not only was his audience treated to good folk music, but they heard classical music and the latest hits from Poland as well.

His programs had a wide audience and many advertisers who remained with him for years, which indicates that the advertisers had good results. Organizing Saturday broadcasts on which children performed testifies both to his entrepreneurial skills and to his knowledge of human psychology. It was quickly apparent that the most eager supporters of these broadcasts were the parents, or perhaps to an even greater degree, the grandparents of the youthful radio artists who were performing as members of choruses.

Lewandowski, director and announcer of these first Polish radio programs, was an extremely popular person in and around Cleveland. He was the toastmaster at numerous banquets, ceremonies and celebrations of Polonian ogranizations such as the "Zwiazek Narodowy Polski" (Polish National Alliance), "Zjednoczenie Polakow" (Polish Union), "Zwiazek Polakow" (Alliance of Poles), "Sokolstwo" (Falcons) and others.

He promoted numerous social welfare initiatives through his radio broadcasts and in cooperation with Polonia. In company, he was always the center of attention. He amused people with his story-telling and his wit. He was always smiling and cheerful and his presence brought with it pleasant surroundings and a good-humored spirit.

He constantly perfected the Polish he had learned at home by associa--ing with Poles who knew the language well. He read a great deal, both Polish books and Polish newspapers. Lewandowski attributed his mastery of Polish to the influence of his friend Lucyan Adamczyk, a Polish officer who had been a captain in the cavalry, and who he saw a great deal.

Lewandowski married Helena Brzuszkiewicz, who was born on July 16, 1901, in Cleveland. Her parents came from the Bialystok area of Poland and had immigrated to the United States before 1880. John and Helena reared two children: a son who died prematurely and a daughter, Yvonne, who lives in California with her mother.

In 1931, the mayor of Cleveland named Lewandowski as the chairman to the Commission for the Aid of Soldiers and Sailors, a position he filled until 1932, when he was chosen to be a member of the city council. From 1939 on, he remained a city council member by election. From 1941, he was vice chairman of the Parks Committee and the Security Council.

In the early 1930s, Lewandowski was host to members and pilots of the Polish delegates who attended the National Airplane Ride in Cleveland, and served as a translator.

Station WJAY, on which Lewandowski started, changed its call letters to WHK and later the WERE. In time, the ethnic programs were transferred to station WGAR, where a multimember orchestra played for Polish, Slovakian, Czeck and Slovenian listeners from the same studio and only the announcers of the above named languagues alternated at the microphone. During World War II, members of the orchestra were drafted to military service and recorded music and took the place of the orchestra. As president of the National Broadcasting Association, Inc., Lewandowski was intrumental in the development of radio programs in Hungarian, Italian and Croatin. For several years as president of the Music of Nations, he directed three Sunday radio programs: "The Polish Program" from WDOK from 11 a.m. to noon; "Polish Melodies" from WJW from 10 a.m. to 11 a.m.; and "The Polish Program" from WJNO from noon to 1 p.m.

Lewandowski owned a serious collection of Polish recordings performed on the Odeon label and others in Poland as well as Polish music and songs recorded in the United States.

He loved music; his fondness for music is expressed even by the fact that in addition to his Polish language programs, he conducted broadcasts of light music twice weekly from station WDOK in the 1950s. When he was retiring, he received a certificate of recognition from the Kiwanis Club of Garfield Heights, a Cleveland suburb.

In 1962, Lewandowski moved to San Diego, California, with his family. He died there January 19, 1967. He was buried in his native Cleveland. His funeral was a magnificent manifestation of the outpouring of sentiment by the people of the town he had faithfully served for many years.

The mayor and the town council of Cleveland as well as the mayor and town council of Garfield Heights sent condolences to the family. They paid tribute to John Lewandowski as a great citizen for his meritorious service as an activist for social welfare; as the long-time director and announcer of the oldest Polish radio programs; as a veteran of World War I; as a past Commandent of Lincoln Post L13 and of the Polish Legion of American Veterans; and as a citizen whose memory will live forever among the residents of these two towns.

This information is based on interviews and written material supplied by Lewandowski's daughter, Yvonne, from California.

Paul Faut

Among the pioneers of ethnic radio programs in the United States, Paul Faut, the owner and producer of the second Polish radio program in Cleveland, is a colorful character.

He was born in 1898 in Kazan, Russia, the son of Czeslaw and Katarzyna nee Mirecki. Before moving to Russia, the parents had been owners of a furniture store in Warsaw. The store was taken over by Czeslaw's brother and he ran it successfully until the time of Hitler's occupation of the city. A family conviction exists that this store was the cause of the tragedy for the Fauts of Warsaw. The Germans wishing to take ownership of the store, arrested and deported the whole family to concentration camps.

Paul Faut was the youngest child in a family of 13 children. After completing his studies, he attended the Moscow Theater School which he completed with honors–one of few to do so. He made his debut appearance at the Imperial Theater in Moscow. His repertoire included roles in Chekov's "The Three Sister" and "The Cherry Orchard" and Gorky's "The Lower Depths."

In 1921, Paul Faut's family members, who had continually maintained their Polish passports, left Russia and moved again to Warsaw. Back in Warsaw, Faut acted in newly formed film studios. He appeared in five silent films. He used his mother's maiden name, Mirecki, as his stage name.

In the films "Az trzy spojrzenia" (Three Glances) and "Ludzie mroku" (The Twilight People), he played the leading roles.

Fascinated by the development of motion pictures in the United States and armed with letters of recommendation from Polish film producers to their Hollywood counterparts, Faut left Poland with his mother in 1922 and came to the United States. He did not use the letters of recommendation, since he preferred a career in theater rather than film. The 24-year-old Faut lost no time in starting his theatrical career in the United States.

On the second day after his arrival in Cleveland, he performed at a local theater.

He performed also at theaters in Cleveland, Detroit, Pittsburgh, Buffalo and New York among others. He performed in Polish, taking his audiences back to their native land and giving them the chance to forget their own worries.

In New York City, Paul Faut met the young and beautiful Maria Krepski. Krepski's parents emigrated from Krasnik in the Poznan province of Poland, and settled in St. Louis, Missouri, where she was born. Maria and Paul met in a clothing store in New York where she worked as a clerk. The young man was so smitten when he went their to buy his wardrobe that he stretched out his purchases by coming every day. They married in 1928.

In 1929, Faut bought the Polonia Theater for himself. The Fauts were totally absorbed with the theater. Maria acted, sewed costumes, made scenery, sold tickets and ran the refreshment stand. After three years of theatrical activity, the economic depression forced them to close the theater.

Faut, lively and full of initiative, did not allow himself to fall into a lethargic inactivity. He sought new possibilities to devote his talent to others. He chose radio. In 1931, the Fauts established the Cosmopolitan Broadcasting Co. which ran several ethnic programs from station WAOC in Akron, Ohio. Faut recalls that the beginning was extremely difficult. The Depression continued and it was not easy to persuade advertisers that commercials on ethnic programs would bring them business. For these reasons, Faut's first radio program only lasted fifteen minutes, but later it was extended to an hour.

Faut established a number of ethnic programs in Hungarian, Rumanian, Italian, German and Lithuanian. Each of these programs popularized the national culture, its music, traditions and language. Of course, these programs carried commercials, since that was the source of income. Faut was something of an innovator in the field of advertisements, as he introduced the singing commercial into his programs. During the time of his radio activity, he produced about 6,000 hours of ethnic broadcasting. Eighteen to 25 ethnic programs reached Cleveland residents and were all produced by Faut.

Faut led a varied, interesting and very hard working life. In addition to being a theater, film and radio actor, he also occupied himself with writing songs, poetry, recording and painting. During his radio career, he found time to act in Christopher Fry's "Ring Around the Moon," a role for which he received much acclaim from theater critics. He also acted in the play, "Stalag 17." Faut also participated in American cinematography, as he played a part in the first Polish color film produced in Buffalo, New York, titled, "Wiejskie Wesele" (Country Wedding).

To Faut's great successes belong the songs written and recorded in Polish for the old firm Victor Talking Machine Co. He recorded about 100 records. "Polskie Orły" (The Polish Eagles) broke the record for foreign language recordings in this country. The song celebrated the attempted flight of two Polish pilots who tried to make a trans-Atlantic flight, but who were forced to land in the Azores, where one of the pilots perished. In a two-month period, 100,000 records were sold.

Faut received many honors and awards for his professional and social activist work. He was extremely popular not only among the Polonia but with other ethnic groups as well.

After 43 years of radio work, Paul and Maria Faut went into a well-merited retirement. The radio programs which they created continue to carry on bringing their listeners the pure, uncorrupted mother tongue, and bringing the culture and art of the homeland to them.

Paul Faut's Polish program was taken over in 1970 by new, young enthusiasts of Polish culture–Eugenia and George Stolarczyk.

This section was based on written and oral information supplied by Paul and Maria Faut.

FRANCIS KALIST CZYZEWSKI

Francis K. Czyzewski, who was the first one in Indiana to organize a Polish radio program, was born June 30, 1904, in South Bend, Indiana. His parents were Francis and Marianna nee Smucinski. His father, who had been born in the Litwa section of Poland, was a carpenter in the building trade and came to the United States around 1900. Francis Czyzewski Sr.'s uncle, the Rev. Walenty Czyzewski C.S.C., organized four Polish parishes and brought many Poles to these parishes in Indiana. Francis was the oldest of the children and had five brothers. His brother Stanislaus was in the building trade; Joseph was a journalist; Boleslaw worked at the Studebaker automobile plant in South Bend. They are no longer living. Still living are his brother Casey, who is a union official in California, and his brother Clement, who is a postal official.

Francis intended to be a priest. For three years, he studied in the seminary of the Fathers of the Holy Cross at Notre Dame University, but he developed lung problems and was forced to leave. After his recovery, he returned to Notre Dame University as a jounalism student. In 1920, he completed his studies and became the editor of the daily "Goniec Polski" (The Polish Courier) published in Polish.

In 1921, the newspaper was changed into a weekly. At about this time, Francis organized a Polish amateur theater in South Bend. He directed, wrote plays for the company and also performed as an actor.

The Francis continued his journalistic work on the South Bend Tribune as a member of the editorial staff. The South Bend Tribune was also the owner of the radio station WSBT in South Bend. At that time, the Polonia in South Bend numbered about 40,000. The management of WSBT determined to organize a Polish radio program and entrusted the program operations to Francis Czyzewski who spoke both Polish and English fluently.

In August 1929, the first broadcast of The Polish Hour took place in South Bend at station WSBT from 8:30 p.m. to 9:30 p.m. This is the third oldest Polish radio program in the United States, and the oldest to broadcast national and international news in Polish (apart from live music and songs). "The Polish Hour" was broadcast in Polish and English since American listeners of the station were interested in Polish music.

At first, the Polish language broadcasts were aired only every two weeks, but starting with May 4, 1930, they were given every Sunday from

8:30 p.m. to 9:30 p.m. In addition, WSBT began broadcasting a daily news program in Polish from 4:45 p.m. to 5 p.m. on May 24, 1930. The new program was inaugurated in response to the favorable letters to the original and continuing "Polish Hour."

On June 25, 1930, Francis married Irene Frantczak, who was born October 2, 1913 in South Bend. Irene's parents emigrated from the Kalisz area of Poland and for the money they received from their holidays in Poland, they built a home in South Bend. Irene was only 6 years old when her father died. She learned Polish from her parents and refined that knowledge by reading Polish books and newspapers and also by attending the parochial school of St. Wojiech's in South Bend where Polish was taught and where Polish was used to teach other subjects.

Francis and Irene had four sons. Bernard is a graphic artist. Francis, born in 1933, has a Ph.D. in Russian and works as a translator for the federal government in Washington D. C. and also knows Polish equally well. Eugene does not work professionally for health reasons. Paul, born in 1937, works at the Institute of Fine Arts at the University of South Florida.

Francis Czyzewski worked as a journalist at the South Bend Tribune until his retirements in 1974. In 1929, during a world's fair, he was a correspondent for his newspaper during his three-month stay in Poland.

He worked actively in many Polish organizations. He was the co-founder of the Central Civic Committee of South Bend, in other words, the headquarters of the Polish social activist organizations. He was the co-founder of the Chopin Cultural Club, and he belonged to the Polish National Alliance. Czyzewski wrote plays for Polish amateur theatrical parish groups and wrote the lyrics to the music composed by Vincent Baluta. He was a good journalistic photographer, pursued the study of astronomy, painted and played the piano. Multitalented, he was a leader of his generation and a shining example for others in his patriotic and social activist work.

In 1936, he received the Silver Cross of Merit from the Polish government for disseminating Polish culture among the "American Poles."

In 1962, the Polonia of South Bend honored his work and meritorious service with a banquet.

Francis K. Czyzewski died December 6, 1976, in South Bend.

The preceeding remarks were based on oral interviews with Irene Czyzewski in South Bend.

EDWARD D. OSKIERKO

Edward D. Oskierki was born in Chicago, Illinois, on May 9, 1893. Edward's parents emigrated from Poland to the United States around 1880. Having completed primary school, he began working. Edward learned correct Polish from his parents and developed a love for Poland. This was translated into his close ties with Polish organizations in Chicago and also in Calumet City, Illinois, to which he eventually moved permanently.

Although he worked hard at a steel plant in South Chicago, he was full of initiative and was attracted to working in radio. His love for music and singing were an additional stimulus in his aspirations. He recalled stepping in front of a microphone for the first time on radio station WCFL in 1927 as a member of the chorus. That was the start of his long radio career. But even earlier, he was already involved radio by selling advertisements for a radio program of merchants and manufacturers.

By the time he decided to have his own radio program, he was 37 years old, a man in full development of his powers. By that time, he already had a considerable achievement in social activist work in various Polish organizations, and he knew the needs and tastes of his countrymen and knew how to promote them.

In December 1929, he began to air "The Polish Variety Program" from radio station WJKS (presently WIND) in Gary, Indiana, with a 5,000 kilowatt transformer. The program was broadcast from 8 p.m.to 9 p.m.

The financial situation of Polish radio programs in the United States was never easy, but for Edward Oskierki it was exceptionally difficult. The United States during the 1930s was experiencing an extremely difficult economic depression. Finding firms wishing to advertise on Polish radio programs was unusually difficult. Oskierki learned this very soon, but the obstacles which he met did not cool his ardor. With determination he worked double hard. He only made enough money to pay for the radio time, while he had to continue working at the steel plant to make his living. He managed to hang on through the bad times and lived to enjoy better ones.

The satisfaction from his radio work gace him the strength for continued work and for seeking better circumstances. After 17 months work at station WJKS, he transferred his program to station WWAE, which is now know as WJOB. "Polish Variety Program" continues to be broadcast to this day.

In 1936, Oskierko enriched his broadcasts with news in Polish, translated from the teletype machine by his co-worker Felix Manclewicz. In 1940, under the direction of Oskierko, the "pasterka," the Christmas Eve service, was broadcast from the church of St. Casimir in Hammond, Indiana. At that time, such a broadcast was a great occurance. In the following years, under his direction, masses were broadcast from St. Joseph's in Hammond. Oskierko transmitted the solemn High Mass celbrated at St. Stanislaus Church in East Chicago, Indiana, on the occasion of the 15th anniversary of the Rev. Julian Skrzypinski ordination and also on the occasion of the 75th anniversary of the founding of the parish of the Blessed Virgin Mary in South Chicago, where Rev. Stanislaus Cyla was the pastor.

Oskierko in his radio broadcasts devoted a lot of time to Polish organizations, advertising their various events organized to contribute to community welfare. He informed the throngs of his listeners about the achievements of these organizations and encouraged them to join these Polish groups. There was hardly any patriotic drive in which Oskierko did not take part, either personally or through his radio programs.

Singing has not lost its attraction for him, and he continues to sing with the Millenium Chorus in Munster, Indiana, where he holds the prestigious position of Chairman of the Lyricists' Council. He is also a member of the Chopin Chorus, and actively works in the Youth Camp (Oboz Mlodziezy) of the Polish National Alliance in Crown Point, Indiana. He has been a member of Group #94 of the Polish National Alliance since 1910. His radio and community welfare work has found an echo in the Polish and American press in the form of articles and interviews with him. The South Bend Radio Program proclaimed Edward Oskierki as "Man of the Year." His radio and community welfare work has been publically acknowledged and rewarded with numerous honors. His radio work has also attained recognition by the management of radio station WJOB; since in 1954 they named Oskierko director of all ethnic programs on that station.

After the second world war, Oskierko visited Poland six times; four times, he was the leader of a group excursion. He recalls when he was twice received by Stefan Cardinal Wyszynski with whom he conducted an interview. He was well-received in Poland every time he visited. He affirms that he never met more polite and more hospitable people than in Poland. He always speaks about Poland with enthusiasm and extreme affection. Although he was born in the United States, he maintained his Polish spirit.

In 1940, as a result of a public opinion poll in Calumet City, Oskierko's Sunday programs (aired from noon to 1 p.m. over WJOB) received the highest evaluation and were acknowledged as the most popular.

Edward Oskierko was honored at a ceremony observing the 50th jubilee of his radio work. He received numerous congratulations from his radio colleagues at station WJOB, from Polish organizations, and from friends all over the United States and Poland.

Although he is 92 years old, Oskierko is still not contemplating retirement. He confesses that should he one day bid farewll to radio, he would move in with his son in Arizona–since his son has a large garden and Oskierko loves to work in the garden.

In addition to his radio work, he will regret leaving his friends at the Retiree's Club with whom he now meets once a week at dinner.

The above information was based on materials supplied by Edward Oskierko and Walter Skibinski. These materials are: The Memorial Program on the occasion of the 50th anniversary of Eddie Oskierko and the 25th anniversary of Wally Skibinski, published on the occasion of the banquet which took place on October 19, 1980, in East Chicago, Indiana.
Information was also provided by an article by Karen Fiasco titled "Calumet City Resident, Polish Broadcaster Feted for 50 years on the Air," which appeared in the "Sun Journal," Calumet City on November 6, 1980.

HALINA PALUSZEK-GAWRONSKI

Halina Paluszek-Gawronski was born November 7, 1896, on the estate called "Piaski" (The Sands) in what is currently Kutno province in Poland. She was the daughter of Maurycy and Jadwiga nee Szmigielski Wolff. The Sands had belonged to her grandfather Zielinski. Her father was an official of the Warsaw-Vienna Railroad; her mother, educated at the patriotically-oriented pension of Jadwiga Sikorski, was an alumna of a music conservatory, who taught music and was an official on the Warsaw Fire Protection Society.

Halina was the youngest in the family which included her sister, Jadwiga, and two brothers, Richard and Maurycy John. The family lived in Warsaw. In 1902, her father died in Sosnowiec, where he had been transferred earlier. The duty of rearing the children fell onto the mother. In order to bring up the children and educate them, the mother drew on funds from the children's trust fund which had been established in the will of their paternal aunt Zofia Wolff.

From her earliest years, Halina studied at Jadwiga Kowalczykowa's "Szkola dla Dziewczat" (School for Girls). Both at home and at school, an atmosphere of Polish patriotism reigns and penetrated Halina's mind and heart.

Her mother remarried and the stepfather who was immigrating to the United States decided to bring over the whole family. Consequently, on November 26, 1913, along with her mother and siblings, landed in Hoboken, New Jersey.

This is Halina's description of this important event in her life:

> During the trip to American with my mother and siblings, I did not experience the Gehenna felt by immigrants who had to travel steerage or in third class who were subject to medical qaurantine on famous Ellis Island, or as it was also called "The Island of Tears." We sailed in a second class cabin where the passengers underwent immigration formalities on the boat before they landed on American soil.
>
> During the voyage we tried to imagine what America looked like. We knew the country from our geography lessons, but we knew it better still from the novels of Karl May (1842-1912), translated from German. I daydreamed that I would meet the red-skinned gentleman Winnetou, the hero of May's novel, or that we would see horses on the prairie like on the postage stamps "American with Ponies," which my brother and I collected in Warsaw. After nine days, our ship got to the shores of America. The panorama of New York's skyscrapers sketched before us. The goddess with a star on her head and a torch in her hand–The Statue of Liberty–seemed gigantic.
>
> We landed at Hoboken, New Jersey, where our stepfather was waiting for us. The next day was Sunday. We took a ferry boat to

New York and then had an excursion on a double-decker bus along Fifth Avenue. We didn't see any Indians or horses, but we were amazed at the Sunday promenading after Mass at St. Patrick's Cathedral. The men were wearing Prince Albert jackets; the women were dressed in the latest fashions. It was just like the English novels for young ladies that we had been engrossed in reading in Polish translation in Warsaw.

The richness of America expressed in fiction quickly paled in our eyes when we got to know the country first hand, so different from the Fifth Avenue elegance. That very Sunday, we went to Chicago. Our first American apartment was in a pretty section near the small, nicely wooded Wicker Park on the Northwest Side of town.

The surroundings in which we lived differed from our Warsaw surroundings through the language which was used here and the acquantanceship with the conditions which prevailed back home. No one believed that our clothing had come with us from Warsaw. Every chat ended with the declaration: 'I'm from the old country, too, and there is no such clothing there.'

In the fall, I enrolled in an evening school for immigrants, for free lessons in English. Except for me, there were only two young Poles in that numerous class. Afterward, I completed evening business courses. During the day, even though I had no experience, I worked in a tailor shop to help my parents get set up in this country.

The first Sunday in Chicago passed among the kind of emotion which only those people could experience who had 'left Warsaw celebrating' the 300 the anniversary of the ruling Russian house of the Romanovs who also ruled 'so graciously' in Poland. It was the 3rd of May, the Polish Constitution Day of 1791. The weather was beautiful. Milwaukee Avenue was hung with American and Polish banners. The colorful parade set off in front of the Polish National Alliance building at Division and Noble streets and ended at the Thaddeus Kosciuszko monument in Humboldt Park, surrounding it with a forest of banners and flags.

Let us recall the time frame in which the future editor of "Glos Polek" (Voice of Polish Women) came to the United States. We know that the

Polish emigration always tied their hopes for an independent Poland to any war in which any one of the partitioning country's took part. Such hopes arose among the Poles in Poland and in the emigration during the Russo-Japanese War in 1904. In Chicago, the "Komitet Narodowy" (National Committee) arose with Marian B. Steczynski as chairman; at that time he was Censor, the top position, of the Polish National Alliance; and the secretary of this group was Karol Wachtel, the editor of "Narod Polski" the newspaper of the Polish Roman Catholic Union. Even greater expectations arose among the Polonia from the news about the outbreak of revolution in Russia and the Polish Congress Kingdon in 1905. Gatherings, meetings took place, resolutions were passed and as a result, a new organization emerged—"Polski Komitet Rewolucyjny" (Polish Revolutionary Committee), founded by socialist activists.

In 1910, within the framework of the Grunwald celebrations, the unveiling of the monuments to the heroes of the War of Independence—Thaddeus Kosciuszko and Casimir Pulaski—takes place in Washington, D. C., and is tied in with a congress devoted to emigration in America by the Polish American Congress. In a ratified resolution of the Congress, it was affirmed:

> We Poles have the right to national independence and consider it our sacred obligation to try to achieve the political freedom of our country.

On December 16, 1912, the "Komitet Obrony Narodowej" (The Committee for the National Defense) arose under the auspices of the centralized organizations of the Polonia and inspired by the establishment of "Komisja Tymczasowyck Skonfederowanych Stronnictw Politycznych" (The Commission for a Temporary Confederation of Political Parties) set up on Polish territories. This commission sided politically with the Central Power. Opponents of this political trend called together the "Polska Rada Narodowa" (The Polish National Counsel) on January 8, 1913, which saw greater possibilities for Poland's independence by working on behalf of the Great Coalition. On July 7 and 8, 1914, in Chicago, the First Congress of the Polish National Counsel took place and on October 2, 1914, the "Centralny Komitet Polski" (The Polish Central Committee), which was later called "Polski Centralny Komitet Ratunkowy"

(The Polish Central Defense Committee) in which all the central Polonia organizations took part and which they also fostored work for Polish independence by the Polonia.

The outbreak of World War I on September 1, 1914, made the American Polonia even more actively involved in helping the work and the struggle for the cherished idea of a free and independent Poland.

The arrival of Ignacy J. Paderewski to America on April 15, 1915, played a crucial role for the "Polish questions" here. Paderewski soon became the unquestioned leader of the American Polonia in its efforts for the freedom of its motherland. Under his leadership, the "Czyn Zbrojny Polonii Amerykanskiej" (The Act of Arming Polish Americans) was established as a result of which a 100,000-member Polish army arose in France under the command of General Joseph Haller and in which some 30,000 Polish-American fought valiantly.

During that period of the greatest blossoming of the Polonia organizations, in 1915 Halina Wolff, young and full of enthusiasm for socially beneficial work, joined the "Zwiazek Polek w Ameryce" (The Alliance of Polish Women in America), a leading and generous organization. She recalled that "the grey-haired Zofia Jandiewicz, who was from the generation of those who were building this organization, signed her up."

During World War I, the headquarters of the Alliance of Polish Women, located on Ashland Avenue near Milwaukee Avenue, was the meeting place of the Polish National Central Committee. Halina took active part in the work of this very meritorious women's organization. She was the secretary of one of its groups and of the charitable "Kolko Dziewczat im. Helena Paderewski" (The Helena Paderewski Circle of Young Ladies). She was also the secretary of the "Centrum Rekrutacyjnego" (The Recruiting Center) which signed up volunteers for the Polish Army in France. Her younger broether Richard Wolff registered at this bureau as a volunteer to the Polish Army and participated in the "Armia Blekitna" (The Blue Army) in the successful battle of the defense of Warsaw in 1920, which was led by Gen. Joseph Haller.

In 1919, Halina married Ludwig Paluszek, the co-owner of the Paluszek Brothers Advertising Agency, the first Polish advertising agency for the non-English press. The young wife occupied herself with raising her daughter, Halina, and her son Andrew. The family moved to New York, where the main office of the firm was located. After the agency was liquidated, Halina worked in the editorial office of the daily "Nowy Swiat" (New

World), where her husband became the head of the advertising department. Under the direction of the managing editor, Peter Yolles, she got to know the complicated matters relating to Polonia journalism.

In 1929, Halina returned permanently to Chicago with her family in order to be occupied with the newly created Polish-American radio.

This important and interesting period of her life is related by Halina in the following:

> For the Paluszek's, the year 1929 took place under the sign of Polish radio. We returned to Chicago permanently. Ludwig assumed the advertising department at the 'Dziennik Zjednoczenia' (The Alliance Daily) and in one fell swoop, he linked the Polish paper with Polish radio. Near the end of 1932, he even persuaded me to become a radio announcer. He directed the first Polish radio program from the powerful WBBM station for a national company as well as the radio program of the Alliance Daily from station WGES, advertising Polish and other merchants, both in the daily newpaper and over the radio. I began on the Sunday afternoon program from WGES, sponsored by the Generl Credit Stores. Soon I was offered the morning program, 'Kukulki' (The Cuckoo Clocks) of the same company and broadcast at 8 a.m. from station WSBC, which at that time was located in the Crillon Hotel at 13th Street and Michigan Avenue. I read the advertising announcements while the actors of the polish staff in Chicago–Antoni and Helena Bednarczyk–presented wity sketches which amused the radio listeners. In the evening, radio program from the General Credit Stores (station WGES), I inaugurated a program for children, in which young people successfully performed declamations and sang in Polish. For station WGES, I announced a 15-minute program for Clorox three times a week. The station manager wanted to introduce something new, so I joined part music and part workds of the Syrena record with the tango of the romantic ballad 'There's a Small Cafe.' In general, the program, 'Clorox Tango Time' was liked and had many imitators.
>
> In 1934, Ludwig began his own program, broadcast daily except for Saturdays, called 'Pola-Lola' in WGES. These were beginnings of Polish radio broadcasting. From a lack of any long-term models,

it was necessary to depend on one's own capabilities, one's own inventiveness and imagination, taking care that the program would be liked by the listeners. The broadcasts at 11 a.m. began with news from the first page of the Alliance Daily. A taxi driver would rush us the still wet copy from the printer in Division Street and Milwaukee Avenue. After that, we would run short and tersely formulated advertisements interspersed with three-minute recordings of music, usually on the Syrena label. I advertised Vervena Cream, which had been introduced to the radio market during the functioning of the advertising agency of the Paluszek brothers. The cream had been made according to the specifications of the oldest brother, Adam, who had also been interested in Chemistry. The soloist on the program was Stefania Niedzwiecki, one of the best Polish-American singers of those times with a large repertoire of Polish songs and tangos. As 'Medrkowiak' (Wiseacre) and 'Glupkowiak' (Dumbbell) played by Walter Krasowski and Bronislaw Mroz entertained the listeners with their sketches, which were printed on the pages of the weekly American Ehco, published in Toledo, Ohio (editor Czeslaw Lukaszkiewicz). For national holiday commemorations, both Polish and American, as well as Christmas and Easter, we presented appropriate texts from Polish literature in poetry and prose.

In 1938, Mira Grelichowski, an announcer of Polish radio in Warsaw, during her stay in Chicago, visited the program 'Pola-Lola' and made her American debut in front of our microphone. After her return to Poland, she described her impressions of Chicago in the Warsaw radio periodical 'Antena,' adding some very courteous words about me.

Our programs served the Polonia in Chicago. Various events of organizations were broadcast free, when they were held for charitable purposes. We urged cooperation with the American Red Cross and buying United States bonds. We also lived through a sad period of appeasement of the Soviets when we were forbidden to broadcast special programs on the occasion of national anniversaries or to play the Polish national anthem. In 1943, we said farwell to Polish radio forever.

In 1944, Halina Paluszek was chosen by the Alliance of Polish Women in America to organize a library for the organizations. From a small basement room, the books were transported to the third floor to two large rooms. In one room, many valuable works of Polish literature and works about Poland in English were stored, while the second room contained memorials of the organization.

At the Diet of the Alliance of the Polish Women in 1951, Halina Paluszek was chosen as the editor of the two-language newspaper of the organization–"The Voice of Polish Women." She improved this periodical with new features: "Poland–What Do You Know About It?" in which she included short information about Poland from history, literature, music and art. Young people were able to use this information about Poland in their school compositions. In addition to information about the organization, the paper also included reviews of new books in English about Poland and news about women's organizations and their activities worldwide.

Since 1952, editor Halina Paluszek was a member of the Illinois Newspaper Women's Association. In 1977, she was honored with a diploma during its annual meeting and celebration of its 25th anniversary. Since 1929, she has been an active member of "Polski Klub Artystyczny" (The Polish Arts Club) where she did the advertising for the Club's programs in the Polish press. She headed the annual bazaars, from which the profits were designated for scholoraships for talented young Polish-Americans. She worked in close cooperation with the founder of the Club, Thaddeus Sledzinski, in organizing the "Rada Klubow Artystycznych" (The Council of the Arts Clubs), which gathered together similar cultural groups working in other Polish-American communities in the United States.

Her long-time work in this sector was rewarded when she was given the honorary diploma of director of the Polish Arts Club in 1978.

Ludwig Paluszek died in 1952. After many years of widowhood, Halina married Waclaw Gawronski, a doctor of law in political science from the King John Casimir University in Lwow, a former Polish diplomat. Dr. Gawronski died in 1979, and earlier her mother and two brothers died.

In September 1981, her daughter, Halina Larson, first a teacher in the Chicago public schools and then for 18 years a teacher in a Catholic school in Springfield, Illinois, died. She too demonstrated great accomplishments as a teacher, having been brought up in an atmoshpere of Polish culture and American culture at home and school. In recognition of her accomplishment, the principal of the school in Springfield set up a scholarship in her name. Halina's youngest sister, Jadwiga zwolski, the closest member of her immediate family, is still living in Poland. Her son and guardian, Andrew Paluszek, resides in Chicago.

Despite her 85 years, Halina lives in a large apartment by herself in Chicago. She feels well and is able to relate events from the life of the American Polonia from prior to World War I. To preserve some of her memories, Halina began writing in 1966 about the events and the people encountered during her long life. These recollections were printed in the former "Dziennik Chcagowski" (The Chicago Daily), the weekly "Gwiazda Polarna" (The Polar Star) published in Stevens Point, Wisconsin, and in the now defunct weekly, "Polonia" of Chicago.

Writing about the past, she recalls people who are no longer with us, about events which were more or less important, and attainments in various sectors of Polish life in the United States. She wrote with the faith that her narration would be used as a source of information for those writing a history of Polonia, a history which she herself was creating for more than 70 years.

She is a wonderful example of a "Polish mother," always faithfully serving the ideals of freedom and democracy as written on the banners of the United States, Poland and American Polonia.

The information was based on written and oral narration of Halina Paluszek-Gawronski.

LIDIA PUCINSKI
Artist of the Theater and Radio

The vitality of Lidia Pucinski was astounding.

Radio was not the only sector of her work. She served as the manager and director of her own theater "Scena Polska" (The Polish Stage), where she continued to mount different plays in which she played the leading roles.

She was born in Cracow in a peasant-bourgeois family. Walter Jedrzejowski, the owner of a restaurant at No. 3 Mariacki Plac (Mariacki Sqare), married Rozalia Biskupowna from the village of Bialki Podhalanskiej near Makowa. From this marriage two daughters were born: Aniela Kazimir and Stanislawa Lidia. In 1907, the father died, and the mother immigrated with her oldest daughter to the United States, leaving Lidia under the care of her family in Cracow where she was studying at the Konarski School. She entered the "Kolka Dramatyczne Gwiazda" (The Drama Circle Star), where she excercised her talent for future profession as a theater actress.

Lidia arrived in the United States in December 1912. She was introduced into the circle of the numerous Polish actors by her mother. At that time, three serious Polish theaters existed in Chicago. Lidia was hired by the "Lola" theater, whose director was Norbert Wicki.

She married Michael Pucinski and together they moved to Detroit. She appeared at the "Union" and Canfield Theaters there. In 1913, the Pucinski's became co-owners of the Lincoln Theater. She played in the Kosciuszko Theater in Buffalo, and just about every town where there was a Polish community, such as Chicago, Detroit, Toledo, Cleveland, Erie and New York. Futhermore, during every break in her engagements, she appeared in plays in parochial halls.

In 1932, Lidia returned to Chicago permanently. In that year, she inaugurated her own radio program. When Lidia began her radio program, the United States was in an economic depression.

During that time, it was very difficult to make a success of foreign language broadcasting. Those first difficult years did not discourage her from expanding her radio broadcasts–on the contrary, they hardened her resolve for a further struggle with the vagaries of fate.

Lidia Pucinski's first radio program was broadcast at 11:30 p.m, but not long afterward, the program was transferred to the 11:30 a.m. slot to make the time for the housewife in the kitchen pass more pleasantly. The radio program, made up of Polish music, practical culinary housekeeping advice, was favorably acepted by the listeners and that, of course, helped in its futher expansion and continuation.

Lidia Pucinski received the sobriquet of "The Sunny Lady" since happiness, courage, and faith in a better tomorrow flowed from her broadcasts. Often she linked advice with her radio theater broadcasts, theater with the microphone, popularizing drama, and acquainting the listeners at large with Polish literary achievement.

From a lack of appropriate material, she herself wrote scenes for various programs. She wrote radio plays based on Polish classics such as *The Knights of the Cross, With Fire and Sword, Mazeppa, The Defense of Czestochowa, The Old Wives' Tale* and many other novels, dramas and comedies.

She also introduced the comic figure of the immigrant girl "Marysia Kocurek," putting into her mouth words of sharp criticsm of the Chicago Polonia. Lidia devoted and still a lot of radio time to the celebration of national holidays and collections for charitable and social welfare causes.

During World War II, she also devoted a lot of radio time to Polish defense and gathered money for the American Red Cross. In the post-war period, she worked actively with the "Rada Polonii Amerykanskiej" (The Polish American Counsel), she organized drives for emigres, veterans and in invalids. She cooperated with the Polish American Congress and with a number of other Polish-American organizations.

Helena Moll, the editor of the Women's section of the "Daily Union" in the Jubilee Memoire, published on the 50th anniversary of Lidia Pucinski's work of social significance, characterized her as follows:

> Writing about the contributions of the person celebrating this jubilee–Lidia Pucinski–in the humanitarian and social fields, one could say in the words of Konrad in the improvisation section of 'The ForeFathers' Eve' that 'I love the whole nation.' That love for the Polish nation from her earliest years, she manifested by extending her care to the poor and the unhappy. Soldiers, veterans, orphans, invalids, the blind, the hungry and the sick turned to her for help and were not disappointed. With vitually a superhuman effort, she intervened to extend help to them and to everyone she invited to work with her, seeing her sincerity and sensing that profound love of humanity, gave in to his own instincts and joined in the humanitarian action. How many tears she wiped away by her deeds only the Creator knows, and it is He who will record in the Good Book the unnumerable good deeds of today's honored guest.

Based on *Lidia Pucinski w pracy dla sprawy polskiej, Lidia Pucinski in Her Work for the Polish Cause*, Chicago, 1963.

BRONISLAW ZIELINSKI

Bronislaw Zielinski was born July 1, 1907, in the village of Jaslo in Poland, the son of Zyomut and Anna nee Marszalek. The Zielinski Family came from the village of Osobnica, which is in the province of Jaslo. Bronek, the youngest in the family, had an older brother, Joseph and a sister, Jadwiga. Bronek's father came to Chicago in 1907 and settled in the Bridgeport section of the city. A year later, Anna and the children followed. Bronek finished the St. Barbara parochial school and then attented Harrison High School from which he graduated in 1926.

From his earliest years, he was fascinated with radio, which in those days was a fashionable mass medium. In 1930, he organized a radio program "Godzina Grunwaldzka" (The Grunwald Hour). Inaugurated on station WEDC, it has lasted to the present day, but is currently broadcast on station WCEV. For decades, the most interesting segment of Zielinski's programs were the humorous sketches called "The Troubles of the Siekierak Family." The texts for these sketches were written by Bronislaw Mroz. The contents of the serial were the everyday troubles of a Polish family of immigrants who tried to solve the problems of their new life while comparing it to their mode of like in the "old country" Pelagia Mroz played the role of the mother; Bronislaw Mroz appeared as the father; Bronislaw Zielinski played their son, Juniorek. Among other actors who appeared in Zielinski's broadcasts were: Antoni Bednarczyk, Casimir Kasperek, Stanislaus Kajkowski, Felicja Lichocka-Kulakowski, Thaddues Krauze and Walter Panka. The humorous sketches amused vast throngs of listeners, and when they were repeated on the stage, they were received with thunderous applause.

Zielinski is also the pioneer of Polish television programs. He started the first Polish-American television program in 1957. The television program, "It's Polka Time," was televised for two years on the ABC network over 29 stations and enjoyed a great opportunity.

In 1935, Bronislaw Zielinski married Anna Synal. They have two children, Nina and James.

From his early years, Zielinski always took and active part in the life of the Polonian organizations in Chicago. He is a member of the Polish National Alliance, Group #1104, of the Grunwald Society, which had been founded by his father, Zygmunt Zielinski, who had also been the co-founder of the Polish company called the Washington Savings and Loan Association located in Bridgeport. Bronislaw continues to be an active member of the Chicago Society, the Polish-American Businessmen's Association, the Polish Roman Catholic Union and a number of other organizations. In 1979, at the heritage banquet, he was presented with the "Heritage Award" by the state Division of the Polish American Congress in Chicago.

During his free time, Zielinski plays a very good game of golf and has received 13 awards at various golf tournaments. His also a member of the Lincoln Park Gun Club where he has set something of a record in shooting competitions by hitting 99 times out of a possible 100.

In 1980, Zielinski visited Poland and was also in Osobnica near Jaslo. On the land where at one time the Zielinski house stood, is now the new home of his maternal cousin, Eurelia Kapanowski, by whon he was cordially received and hospitably treated in the Polish manner. Apparently, the visit to the ancestral Zielinski holdings heartily touched Bronislaw, since in relating this experience, his voice quavered oddly.

Despite his years, Bronislaw Zielinski is young in spirit, always smiling and warm. In Chicago, he is a sociable and pleasant person who is known and liked.

Based on oral interviews with Bronislaw Zielinski.

EUZEBIUSZ ZARNECKI

Euzebiusz Zarnecki was born in Kalisz, Poland, on May 13, 1894, in the family of Michael and Julia, nee Blasejewski, Zarnecki. Euzebiusz' father was a shopkeeper who ran a dairy store. His mother came from a wealthy family from Zyrardow, and her uncle was a canon in the Kujawy-Kalisz diocese. Maria Konopnicka mentions the family in her book *Night and Day*. Euzebiusz was the oldest child in the family and had three younger brothers–Sygmunt, Heliodor and Eugene. His mother also had a daughter by a previous marriage. The father was a 40-year-old bachelor when he married the young widow. The Zarnecki's, living under Russian rule, were a Polish patriotic family. The parents tried to give all their children as good an education as possible. After the birth of her youngest son, the mother remained ill for the rest of her life. To improve her health, the father bought a summer house in Kraszewicy, where the children and the mother spent vacations and holidays. The family continued to live in Kalisz'

Euzebiusz attended a trade school in Kalisz. He grew up surrounded by patriotic teachers and family members who were Polish patriots who rebelled against the Tsarist oppression. He belonged, as did the majority of the Polish youth at that time, to a secret student organization and witnessed the persecution and arrests of his colleagues. His mother tried to persuade him to emigrate. Euzebiusz, with strong emotional ties to his mother, could not bring himself to leave his sick mother and the rest of his family.

When his mother died in 1910, he was determined to heed her advice and along with a group of his closest friends, decided to immigrate to the United States, the country of freedom and great possibilities for advancement. Generally, he assumed that he would only stay temporarily and vowed that he would return. His father, however, had a presentiment that he would never see his son again.

The young men about to leave for the United States tried to get a hold of and read every king of information about the country to which they were going. What enticed Euzebiusz and his friends was the possibility of living in a country of freedom, equality before the law and civil freedoms. The stories about the Wild West and the Indians also enflamed their imaginations.

When Euzebiusz arrived at Staten Island in the United States in 1910, he was 16 years old. He did not have any friends or family on whom he could count on and the situation was made more desperate because he knew no English. Some of the friends he had come with, thirsting for impressions, set off for the Wild West.

Euzebiusz stayed behind and tried various work trying to learn English and to find the possibility of a better existence.

After a time, he learned that a cousin of his mother's Ksawera Witanowski, a widow, had settled in the South Side of Chicago, where along with her three sons, she was running a small shop. He was determined to visit them, and after having seen the possibilities of work which the quickly expanding city of Chicago offered, decided to settle there permanently. He soon found work as a steel plant worker in South Chicago. Euzebiusz understood that only further education and mastering correct English would allow him to atain a better position in this country. When his cousin entered Loyola University to study medicine, Euzebiusz enrolled in Crane College to study English. Soon he began participating in the civic life of the Polonia.

When the United States entered World War I in 1917, Euzebiusz volunteered to the student army cadet corps, hoping to be sent to the field of battle in Europe after basic training. This did not happen, since the war ended, before it was time for him to go.

In the organization called Esperanto, he met Monika Janusz with whom he feel in love and married. As a result he entered into the large family of her relations. Their marriage lasted 54 years.

Bad news arrived from his family in Poland. Euzebiusz's youngest brother was killed during the battles for independence and his father also died as a result of a difficult was experience.

The Zarnecki family is augmented by two daughters–Eugenia and Elaine. The basic means of maintaining the family at that time was a vegetable store which Euzebiusz had founded and which he ran successfully 'till the 1930s when the Depression forced him to close the store.

The enterprising Zarnecki, who now knew both languages well and had a wide acquantaceship with merchants, decided to organize a Polish radio program. Correctly concluding that the greatest majority of the Chicago Polonia came from non-urban locales, he decided to organize the program around folk music. And so a new Polish radio program arose in Chicago in 1935, called "Tance w stodole'" (Barn Dances), which Zeb Zarnecki produced. John Piwowarczyk's folk orchestra which played weddings in Poland played on the program. Marysia Data, "Cesia from America," and John Piwowarczyk sang folk songs.

Once a week, Zeb Zarnecki broadcast programs directly from the halls where the folk dances were taking place. The halls were alwyas packed. The popularity of these programs is testified to by the thousands of letters sent to the management every week. The "Barn Dance" became a part of the life of Chicago Polonia. Through these broadcasts, and also in the dance halls from which they were broadcast, hundreds of thousands of government bonds were sold and collections for worthy causes were made.

Zeb's program was broadcast on station WHFC at 1450 Kilocycles until 1945 when Zeb decided to put a new idea into operation. At that time, radio stations operated on short wave were becoming more and more popular. Zeb received permission from the FCC to build an FM station in Elmwood Park, a suburb of Chicago.

And so the first Polish radio station in metropolitan Chicago was built. Its call letters were WLEY-FM, operating on 107.1 kilocycles. The "Barn Dance" program was transferred to this station. From its inception, station WLEY-FM was plagued with financial difficulties. In order to receive this station, one needed to have a short wave radio. Years passed before factories began to manufacture radios which received both long and short wave transmissions. From lack of necessary finances, Zeb was the manager, director, announcer, advertising salesman, etc. He fought back adversity and lived to see better times.

His oldest daughter, Eugenia, after completing Roosevelt University, married Robert Brandt, a naval pilot instructor. From this marriage, came Zeb's first grandchild, Michael. The second daughter, Elaine, after completing the University of Illinois, worked as a teacher and married Walter Corvine. From that marriage, Zeb has two grandchildren, Jean Marie and Walter.

The year 1955 brought the Zarnecki family serious worries. Zeb's wife, Monika, began to lose her eyesight. Zeb was forced to sell the radio station and dedicate himself totally to his wife's care.

Zeb believed in education and the advantages which it brings; therefore, he saw to it that his daughters received a university education and then took care to see that his grandchildren should be educated. Michael, his oldest grandson, finished the University of Illinois and is an engineer for the State Highway Commission. His grandson Walter studied at the Jagiellonian University in Cracow for three years.

After his wife died in 1973, Zeb remained alone and consequently renewed tighter contact with his remaining family in Poland. During his visit, he learned about the fates of his nearest and dearest. His brother Zygmunt, a merchant in Kalisz, died of torture by the Nazis. His brother Heliodor, who had been a teacher was also dead. Remaining family from his half-sister, Jadwiga, is a daughter, Irene Wasilewski-Pomierna, who lives in Warsaw, where her two daughters, Wieslawa Kowalczyk and Danuta Wasilewski, also live. Heliodor's daughter and his grandchildren live in Kalisz.

Zeb lives alone at present, but his daughter and grandchildren live nearby and they take care of him as thoughtfully as he used to take care of them.

Based on written and oral narration of Euzebiusz Zarnecki's daughter, Eugenia Brandt, who lives in Chicago.

WALTER LESKIEWICZ

Walter Leskiewicz was born September 20, 1888, in the town of Wlodzimierz Wolynski, Poland. His parents ran a business dealing in farm produce. After completing the gymnasium, Walter studied at the University of Lwow. He never finished his studies there, choosing to come to the United States in 1909. First, he settled in New York, where be became a reporter and writer for the Polish press. He also worked in the same field in Newark, New Jersey and Cleveland, Ohio. In 1929, he came to Detroit as an actor in the theater and a writer of satiric couplets and songs on topical themes. Then he organized a touring theater company in which his wife, Stainlawa, his stepson, Benajmin Stawinski, and other Polish actors, in addition to himself, took part. This troupe gave performances in various Polonian centers all over the United States.

During the Depression, theater ceased being economically feasible. A number of Polish theaters were closed during this period. Polish theater actors seeking new possibilities of work found employment in Polish radio which was very popular at that time.

The enterprising Leskiewicz, along with his wife and Benjamin Stawinski, founded a Polish radio program called "Program rozmaitosci" (Variety Hour) in 1931 on station WEXL in Detroit. The program was presented every day of the week. From Monday through Saturday it was aired from 9:00 a.m. to 10:00 a.m. and on Sunday from 12:00 to 1:0 p.m. The content of these programs consisted of national and international news, commentaries, live dramatizations of stories and novels, songs, and satire. Whole programs were carried out by actors live. Władysław Leśkiewicz did not use recorded music during his broadcasts. He himself appeared in several "trademark" roles: one was "Dziadek Psia Pora" (Granddaddy Dog Age) and on the Sunday programs in the role of "Włoczęa" (Vagabond).

From 1932 to 1938 "The Variety Program was broadcast over WJBK. As a result of an illness Własysław Leśkiewicz was unable to perform and the program was suspended to six months in 1938. When the program was resumed in 1939 it was broadcast from WEXL from 8:00 p.m. to 9:00 p.m.

Leśkiewicz's wife, Stanisława, (nee Budzon, and her first husband's name was Stawiński) was born June 4, 1897, in the village of Maków Podhalańnski, Poland. She finished the gymnasium and the home of economics technical school and then taught in Krakow schools. She participated in various amateur theatrical groups and the theater attracted her more and more. Her father Stanisław was an assistant surgeon and he owned a mill in her native village.

In 1914, Stanisława came to the United States and settled in Detroit where she acted professionally in theater. In 1915 she married an actor named Stawiński from whom she was divorced in 1927. She married Władysław Leskiewicz in 1928. From the inception of "The Variety Program" Stanisława worked with her husband enacting various roles in the radio theater and in addition presenting her own characteristic segments "Polska Gośposia" (The Polish Homemaker) and "Głucha Barbara" (Deaf Barbara).

After the death of her husband May 21, 1939, she carried on the program with her son Benjamin Stawiński until the winter of 1947. From 1942 to 1947 Stanisława Leśkiewicz was also a distributor of Polish films. In 1947 she retired and moved to Arizona where she died August 2, 1967.

Both Leśkiewiczs were active in the Polish Artists Group of the Polish National Alliance in Detroit. Apart from their radio and stage work, they organized cultural programs for various Polish organizations on the occasion of meetings, banquets, and celebrations of national and similar occasions.

Benjamin Stawiński, Stanisława:s son from her first marriage, worked with the Leśkiewiczs on "The Variety Program." Benjamin was born in Detroit January 27, 1917. From 1938 to 1941 he studied aviation engineering at Wayne State University in Detroit. Near the end of 1941 he was mobilized by the Federal government to work on airplane construction at the Ford Motor Co. in Detroit as an engineer. After the end of the war in 1945 he entered the Merchant Marine where he served for one year. After his return to Detroit, he worked for General Motors in the automobile division until his retirement in 1970. Benjamin Stawiński is currently gathering materials relating to a history of Polish theater in the United States.

Based on oral interviews and the private papers of Benjamin Stawiński in Detroit, Michigan.

STANISLAW ZENON WACHTEL

Stanisław Wachtel was born May 10, 1887, in JarosŁaw, the son of Karol and Antonina nee Myczykowska. Stanisław was the fourth of six children; the four daughters perished during World War I, while the oldest brother Karol immigrated to the United States in 1906. Stanisław completed grammar school and high school in Jarosław, but received a degree of Engineer of Agronomy from the University of Lwów. After having completed officers training school, he served as an officer of the cavalry in the Austrian regiment of ulans in Lwów.

At the invitation of his brother Karol, who was at that time the chief editor of the "Dziennik Chicagowski" (The Chicago Daily) in Chicago, Stanisław arrived in the United States for a visit just before the outbreak of World War I in 1914.

After spending several months with his brother who was a prominent Polonian activits, Stanisław decided to remain in the United States permanently and took on employment. For six months he worked as a surveyor for the Florida Land Company, surveying land between Tampa and Orlando. However this work gave him no satisfaction and he resigned. Then he became an actor in the theater and stage plays, and subsequently a director of touring theatrical companies. He appeared on the stage in Newark, New York, Detroit, Cleveland, Philadelphia, Baltimore and Chicago.

Wachtel, the well-known pioneer of Polish theater in the United States, specialized in adapting stories and novels for use in "Radio's Little Theater." Among other adaptations for radio use, he made scenarios of many of Bartel's *Adventures of a Polish Detective* with the following titles–"The Ragpicker's Daughter," "The Kidnapped Child," "The Voice from the Grave," "The Sheik," "Mystery of the Cursed House," "The Eight Wives of Bluebeard."

Other works he prepared for radio include: J. Brandkowski's "Demon Woman"; A. Trohanowski's "Swamp Flower" and Harriet Beecher Stowe's *Uncle Tom's Cabin*.

Aside from reworking other authors, Wachtel wrote his own plays on patriotic, historic and folk themes, which were for use on the stage and also for radio. He also began writing operettas and musicals in 1924. One of his plays was published under the title "Cacusia" (The Plaything).

From the moment that he was engaged in radio work, first on other people's programs and from 1936 on his own radio program, Wachtel as a Polish theater actor, tied the theater to radio; he changed the theater audience to the considerably larger audience of listeners of the short stories and novels turned into radio dramas.

As a director of touring theater groups, he gave performances not only on theater stages located in the larger Polish–American settlements, but in vacation spots and parochial halls as well. In Cleveland, he worked with the actors Paul Faut and Joseph Dejroch.

In 1917, Wachtel volunteered in the Polish Army, which was later led in France and Poland by General Joseph Haller. Sent to the camp in Niagara On-The-Lake, in Ontario, Canada, he contracted pneumonia and had to return to the United States.

In 1930 and 1931, Wachtel lived in Buffalo where he set off with his acting troupse. He met his future wife, Gertrude Irene Wieckowski (born March 21, 1884) in Chicago at the theater. Gertrude studied at the Academy of the Felician Sisters where she learned Polish. Shw worked as a professional actress. She and C Wachtel were married August 10, 1914. they had one daughter, Estelle, born October 11, 1920, who became a gynecologist and lives in Holland, Michigan.

At the invitation of the director of a Polish radio program in Detroit, Thaddeus Zajac, Stanislaw Wachtel moved to Detroit with his family in 1923 and began working as a radio actor. From 1932 to 1936, he worked with three Polish radio programs in Detroit, namely with Thaddeus Zajac on station WEXL during an evening program; with Walenty Jarosz on station WMBC during a morning program; and with Walter Leskiewicz on station WJBK. He worked with Zajac for a long time.

In 1936, Wachtel started his own radio program on station WMBE in Detroit, presently station WJLB, and he carried on this program until

1948. It was called "The Morning Polish Program." In 1937, Gertrude began to work with her husband by introducing "Komentarz Kobiecy" (Woman's Commentary) which she worked out and she also sold the advertising for this portion of the program. During World War II, the Wachtels prepared a series of programs and took an active part in the efforts of Polonia to aid Poland.

In 1937, their daughter, Stanislawa, joined her parents' program and performed in "Treatrzyk Radiowy" (Radio's Little Theater) whenever it was a part of their program.

In the years 1937-1940, Stanislawa had her own radio program called "Przyjaciolka Stasia" (Your Friend Stasia) on station WMBC on Saturdays from 9 to 10. The content of her program was verse for children, little stories, contests and riddles. This program was extremely successful, and Stasia, a medical student gained a deserved popularity among the Polonia in Detroit.

The Wachtels belonged to a number of Polish-American organizations and worked diligently in their midst. For many years, Wachtel was the financial secretary of the Polish Artists Group of the Polish National Alliance in Detroit. He died June 13, 1950, in Detroit. After her husband's death, she b his wife became the President of the Polish Artists' Group of the Polish National Alliance and she kept this position for 14 years until her death. She worked for many years in the Polish Women's Alliance of American and also in the Polish Falcons, where she was a member of the administration in Detroit. She died January 31, 1976 in Detroit.

The personal documents of the Wachtel Family were donated to the Detroit Public Library and the Bruton Historical Lab.

Written on the basis of private papers and oral interviews of Dr. Estelle Torres nee Wachtel in Holland, Michigan, as well as two articles: Wachtel the Actor from the Daily Record–May 6, 1933 Leonora Leswon. Fredro Theater. Polish Heritage.

WALTER "LI'L WALLY" JAGIELLO
The Man Who Universalized the Polka

Walter Jagiello was born August 1, 1930, in Chicago to a family of Polish immigrants. They say that he is a man of many talents. He sings, writes lyrics to songs, arranges music, and plays various instruments. He began to sing when he was 8 years old and continues to do so. He is self-taught, having completed only the elementary school. He learned to sing from listening to his parents and friends sing during friendly get-togethers. He created his own orchestra with which he has played all across the United States; he has also played in Europe. He is known in Poland, where he has been a number o times with his group. In 1949, eight songs of his own compositions were recorded by him for Columbia Records. In 1951, he established his own record company under the label Jay-Jay, and it is the largest company producing Polka records. In 1958, he built his own studio to record albums, tapes and cassettes.

A recording by Jagiello in 1954 of a song sung in both Polish and English had a phenomenal success with the Polonia and with other nationalities as well. It was titles "Chcialbym byc znowu kawalerem," (I Wish I Were Single Again). In Chicago alone the record sales were 150,000 copies within a two-week period. More than six million copies of this song were sold on records and cassettes.

Lil Wally became the undeniable "Polka King." Presently he lives in Miami, Florida, where his production plant and studio are located.

Jagiello's orchestra called Li'l Wally and His Band played in the biggest dance halls in America, attracting thousands of enthusiasts of Polka-type music.

From 1950, Walter Jagiello has been broadcasting a Polka-type radio program over a number of radio stations, at first announced exclusively in Polish and then in Polish and English.

Based on written and oral narration of Walter Jagiello.

THE POINEERING ACTIVITIES OF THE PALUSZEK BROTHERS:

The First Polish Advertising Agency in the United States

The three Paluszek brothers–Adam, John and Ludwik–were born in the village of Lipnica near Kolbuszowa in the part of Poland designated as Little Poland (Maloposka). There father, John, was a wealthy farmer, who was highly respected by his neighbors and by the gentry. Several times, he was elected the head of the "Gmina"–the local community government. He was a passionate horsebreeder with a far-reaching reputation. His sons and neighbors from Lipnica who settled in the United States compared him to Boryna, an important character in Walter Remont's Nobel prize-winning novel *The Peasants*. While he was not stingy about educating his sons, he projected that Adam, the oldest son, would run the farm; that John would become a priest; and that Ludwig, the youngest, would have a career in the city. The boys, however, dreamt of countries beyond the seas to which leass wealthy inhabitants of Lipnica had emigrated. The father thwarted in his plans and was known to say: "Others will take over the ancestral ground; none of my sons will remain on our property." The mother quitely cried, having a foreboding of an lonely age. The first to leave home was Adam, who immigrated to the United States. For a brief time, he settled in Passaic, New Jersey, where some relatives lived, but before long, the call of the open road possessed him and he headed for the distant "Wild West." After his return in 1909, Adam settled in Chicago, got married and worked at the Home Bank. At a time when he was already the head of the advertising section of the "Dziennik Narodowy" (The National Daily), he brought his younger brother, John, over from Poland. John then also worked for a publication from 1911 to 1914. In the autumn of 1915, during their yearly convention which was held in Detroit, Adam was chosen to head up the advertising section of all publications of the Polish National Alliance.

Ludwig, the youngest brother, who had completed the gymnasium in Rzeszow, had (as his father often said) "become addicted to politics for good and all." When representatives of the "Polskie Stronnicstwo Ludowe" (Polish Peasant Party) would arrive in the diestrict, Ludwig would vanish from home and agitated for the cause. Evidently, this was not a passing fancy, since later in Chicago he belonged to the Circle of the Polish Peasant

Party, which had been organized by Stanislaus Mermel, who hailed from Dabrowa Tarnowski, a friend of Vincent Witos, a leader of the PSL.

In 1912, when the clouds of war were already gathering on the horizon over Europe, the father fearing that his son would be conscripted into the Austrian army, sent Ludwik to his brothers.

The Paluszek brothers joined into the current of Polish-American life in Chicago and held various offices in those groups where they were members. Ludwig Paluszek was extremely active in the "Towarzystwo Dramatyczno-Literackie 'Promień'" (The Literary Dramatic Society 'The Beam.') where he fulfilled the role of president and played various character roles in the amateur theatricals which the group presented.

In 1916, the Paluszek brothers established the first Polish advertsing agency in Chicago for Polish publications and called it "Paluszek Brothers Publishers Representatives. The establishment of the Paluszeks' advertising agency falls into the period of the greatest blossoming of Polish-American activity, particularly the expansion of the Polish press. In Chicago and other Polonian communities a number of Polish organizations and various Polish commercial firms came into being.

In Europe revolutionary trends began to seethe in the opressed countries, and the greatest efforts of preparing for battle for freedom were noted in Poland. The World War I broke out, and with the outbreak hopes rose for regaining the independence of Poland. The United States at first neutral entered the war. President Woodrow Wilson stating the aims of the war in point thirteen of the Declaration clearly presented the matter of independence of Poland. All of this mobilized the American Polonia, which actively engaged in the fight for Polish independence. The "Armia Błękitna" (The Blue Army) created by General Haller in France was strengthened by more than 30,000 Polish-American volunteers, who presented themselves well outfitted and well-trained from their training period in the Canadian camps. In Poland, the Legions fought under the leadership of Józef Piłsudski. And in Washington, D. C. Ignacy J. Paderewski was carrying on diplomatic activity for the cause of Polish independence.

One of the mass media of the time was the press. At that time in Chicago, the Polish press was numerous, since it was in great demand; a Polish newspaper was found in every Polish home. Everyone was interested in reading because important events were constantly occurring on the international scene. In Chicago four daily newspapers were printed: "The Alliance Daily" (Dziennik Związkowy), the Chicago Daily" (The

Chicago Daily), "The People's Daily," the organ of the Polish Socialists, (Dziennik Ludowy), and "The National Daily" (Dziennik Narodowy). Furthermore, three weeklies were published by large Polish-American organizations. There were also politically partisan weekly papers and a large number of special occasion papers printed to commemoraate national holidays and conventions. In addition, there was a humor publication.

Polish-American newspapers were published daily in Milwaukee, Detroit, Cleveland, Toledo, Buffalo, New York and Pittsburgh. Many weeklies were published in the less densely settled Polonian communities, and they were characteristically filled with American and Polish patriotism.

The basis for the existence of these Polonian publications was the profits received from selling the papers themselves and from the small advertisements received from Polish merchants and manufacturers. The well-paying advertisements of large American firms, allocated by advertising agencies called "placing agencies, were not given to Polonian publications. The few such advertisements which were placed in Polonian publications paid very little." A similar situation exists even today in the American advertising market.

In these very unprofitable conditions, the Paluszek brothers pioneering Polish advertising agency arose. The beginnings were quite modest; the whole agency was located in a simple room in the Home Bank Building, which is no longer standing, but which had been on the north-east corner of Ashland and Milwaukee Avenues. After six months, the Paluszek agency moved into a three-room suite in the Loop in the Advertising Building on Madison Avenue.

At first the personnel of the firm, except for the owners, consisted of Jan Dzibiszewski, an advertising salesman; Władysław Worzała, a copy writer; Irena Krzyczewska, a bookkeeper; and Marta Oszuscik, a stenographer. The agency began pioneering statistical work about Polonia. They prepared brochures with a map of the United States on which they showed the biggest Polish settlements where Polish papers were published. On the basis of income they figured out the buying power of the Poles. They also provided a list of trade and manufacturing companies which employed large numbers of Polish workers. Polish customs were described which were handed down from generation and still maintained here in America. National traditions and local customs were explained. In this way, the large advertising agencies were shown a market which had not been used hitherto. This resulted in capturing better-paying advertisements for the Polonian press.

At the beginning, the Paluszek's advertising agency represented three Polish-American newspapers, namely: "Ameryka Echo" (American Echo) from Toledo, Ohio; "Gwiazda Polarna" (The Polanr Star) from Stevens Point, Wisconsin;and "Kurier Polski" (The Polish Courier) from Milwaukee. Then other Polonian publications as well as other ethnic publications in the United States joined in.

Among the others who joined were Lithuanian, Ukrainian, Czechoslovakian, Russian, Italian, French and Spanish. There were also publications from Latin America.

Evaluating the activity of the Paluszek brothers' advertising agency from the perspective of time, one must say that it comprised an activity without precedent. The firm grew from day to day and just two years after its founding in April 1918, they opened a branch office in New York, which was the center of the most important placing agencies. At first they were located in the Woolworth Building on Nassau Street, but when the "Polska Komisjia Zakupów" (The Polish Trade Commission) was liquidated they took over their luxuriously furnished offices in the Aeolian Building on 42nd Street. From that time the New York office was the main office where 15 employees worked under the management of Adam Paluszek. The Chicago office with 12 workers was managed by Jan Paluszek, by then located in the Tower Building on Michigan Avenue. Ludwik Paluszek worked at both the New York and Chicago offices in rotation.

The Paluszek advertising agency was the first to gain advertisements for Polish-American publications from Lucky Strike, Chesterfield, Old Gold and Camel cigarettes. They also brought in the first automotive advertising from Ford and Dodge, advertisement from steamship lines and from Standard Oil Company of Indiana. They also negotiated a contract with publications from South America and with the important "La Prensa" and also created a special division from American export firms having personnel who spoke Spanish.

The advertising agency began to head for a fall when they accorded too large a credit for advertising in various Polonian publications to enterprises which began to arise in the Polonia for the purpose of trade with Poland. To the most important creditors belonged a banking firm which was trying to get a loan in the United States for Poland.

As a result of their difficulties in getting paid by their creditors, this first Polish advertising agency was liquidated and its particular type ceased to exist. Nonetheless Polish-American publications continued to profit from the pioneering effort of the Paluszeks. American businesses which had seen the value of advertising in Polonian publications continued to profit from their services. Afterwards other Polish advertising agencies arose but none of them reached the scope of the Paluszek brothers' agency.

After the advertising agency was dissovled, the Paluszek brothers went their separate ways to earn a living. Adam remained in New York when he established a factory which manufactured grease and oil for automobiles and airplanes. They used castor oil to produce these products. He managed this factory until his death in 1947. Jan Paluszek ran a cosmetics factory established by all three brothers for a short time. Then he was an editor for "Czas Brooklyński" (The Brooklyn Times). Afterwards he worked as the head of the advertising department on the "Dziennik Zjednoczenia" (The Daily Union) in Chicago where he died in 1929.

Ludwik Paluszek remained in the advertising field. At first he operated his own advertising agency in Chicago, then he became the head of advertising for the "Nowy Świat" (The New World) in New York. After Jan's death he returned to Chicago and assumed his position as "The Daily Union." He also worked in the classified ads department in the "Dziennik Związkowy" (The Daily Alliance). He died in 1952 as the head of the advertising department of the Chicago Daily.

Ludwik also belongs to the Polonian pioneers of radio. Already in 1929 he was broadcasting from station WBBM in Chicago. Soon he began a radio program sponsored by "The Daily Union" on station WGES. That was the first time that a Polonian newspaper publication was brought together with a radio audience. He also broadcast from stations WSBC, WEDC, and WHFC for the Chicago Merchants and Manufacturers.

The Paluszek brothers left a prominet mark on the history of American Polonia.

This material was drawn from the private collection of Halina Paluszek-Gawronska, Ludwik Paluszek's wife.

OUTSTANDING POLES IN RADIO AND TELEVISION IN THE UNITED STATES

Vincent Thomas Wasilewski attained a leading position in American radio broadcasting. In 1965, he was elected president of the National Association of Broadcasters, a nationwide association of the owners of radio and television stations. In this responsible position, he and various boards governing radio and television determined the general policies in operation of the country's broadcasting networks. He also also the spokesman regarding its interests.

In 1957, Joseph Tanski was awarded the Fellowship Award, a highly remunerative as well as honorary award, which is acknowledged as the highest achievement in the broadcast industry. Tanski, who is the director of a television station in Cleveland, Ohio, received this award for the unusually thought-provoking broadcasting of the presidental election.

The television dramatist and director Stanley Losak operated the television film chronicle division of the Columbia Broadcasting Company.

William Grayskey (Grajewski), a well-known actor, was a member of the permanent acting group of the National Broadcasting Company and won several awards for performances on radio programs.

One of the most important television writers is Paddy Chayefsky. Most of his television dramas have also been published as books. He has also won much acclaim for his dramas which have been produced on Broadway.

Lucyna Migala was the producer of a television news program on NBC-News. She received an award for producing a social-problem film for television.

Mrs. Halina Paluszek-Gawronska of Chicago, Illinois.

Mr. Zeb Zarnecki/Euzebiusz Żarnecki/of Chicago, Illinois.

Mr. Edward D. Oskierko of Indiana.

Mr. Francis K. Czyszewski of South Bend, Indiana.

Mr. Bruno Zielinski of Chicago, Illinois.

Mr. Walter Jagiello, known as Li'l Wally, of Chicago, Illinois.

Mr. Walter Jagiello, known as Li'l Wally, and his musical group known as the Harmony Boys.

LIDIA PUCIŃSKA

Mrs. Lydia Pucinski of Chicago, Illinois.

Walter Leskiewicz [*at far right*] pictured with his wife and son, of Detroit, Michigan.

Pictured left to right in the first row are: Stanley Z. Wachtel, Hedwig Furmaniak, Estelle Leskiewicz, Gertrude I. Wachtel, Walter Leskiewicz and, at the far right, Benjamin Stawinski [all of Detroit, Michigan].

Joseph and Slawa Migala, of Chicago, Illinois.

PART THREE

The Role of Radio in the Service of American Ethnic Groups

CHAPTER 16

A Study Based on the Application of Migala Communications Corporation of Chicago for an FCC License to Build an Ethnic Radio Station in Illinois

Among applicants who were attempting to get permission to broadcast over the 1450 kilocycles spot in Cicero, Illinois was the author of this book. He presented the problems of the Polish nationality group and the possibility of solving them through the aid of appropriately prepared radio broadcasts. An excerpt from the application for a license read as follows:

> The United States still does not have any ethnic radio station. There are stations which accept ethnic radio programs, although this is taking place more and more rarely. There are radio programs produced in various foreign languages by people who come from individual ethnic groups. However there is no radio station with a clearly defined presence and program serving ethnic groups exclusively. For example in Cicero, research has shown that the vast majority of the residents of this town are people who originated from white European ethnic groups and continue to use their original languages and maintain the culture and traditions of their countries of origin. A similar situation exists in neighboring towns like Berwyn, Stickney, South Chicago, Lombard and others. In the Chicago metropolitan area itslef 50% of the inhabitants trace their descents from various ethnic groups. The ethnics who have become permanent residents

or citizens of the United States have various problems like other residents which must be solved in a particular way.

When our family decided to apply for a license to broadcast over 1450 kilocycles in order to build an ethnic radio station in Cicero, and serving Cicero residents particularly, but also indirectly the residents of surrounding towns and residents of Chicago itself, we knew that we were deciding to undertake very serious work. The work does not have ready-made examples, since no pioneering work has been done. We evaluated out financial situation in a very detailed fashion, but we also thoroughly examined the possibilities of solving the difficult problem of working out the kind of programs which would benefit the great majority of the potential listeners within the hearing range of 1450 kilocycles.

Just as my autobiographical sketch and those of the whole family indicate, we were always concerned with important questions and we always reached our intended goal. Like me, the rest of the family members are also workoholics, and we especially love radio work, having a good influence on people, serving people and especially helping those who can't help themselves and are alone and about whom no one is concerned.

The capital which we would be investing in building the radio station would probably bring in greater returns if it were invested elsewhere, but it wouldn't give us the satisfaction which radio work does. When one believes in what one is doing, one can easily overcome any difficulties. Of course, we will not be alone, since already a number of ethnic groups are offering us their help and cooperation. People are evaluating our initiative and are enthusiastically awaiting the moment when they will be able to join with us in this wonderful and useful work. This undertaking will bring benefits to the country through quickly preparing new citizens to serve their country. It will bring benefits to the entire society which will learn of the value of citizens originating from various ethnic groups. The ethnic groups themselves will profit from making their beginning in a new country easier, by making them more aware of citizen's rights and obligations, by giving them advice and help in the first difficult period of assimilation in their new surroundings.

Why do we consider ourselves the most qualified to operate an ethnic radio station? By the fact that we ourselves are ethnics and therefore can best understand the needs and worries of people in ethnic groups. We ourselves experienced similar problems, and what is very important, we know how to solve them. That is our advantage over others. We garnered our experience in radio work over almost 30 years by running the most popular Polish radio program—"Głos Polonii"—(The Voice of Polonia). We began with a 30-minute program on a weekly basis; at present we broadcast for an hour and a half Monday through Friday and for two hours on Saturday. We have wide contacts among other directors of ethnic radio prgorams and they have offered their cooperation to us. Furthermore, and even more importantly, we were actively working among ethnic and American oranizations which gives us the possibility of probing public opinion on current issues of the day. We work with people, we play and pray with them. Our contact with society is lively and constant. A man with the best intentions cannot operative an ethnic radio station effectively unless he comes from an ethnic background and he himself has experienced the Gehenna of the newly arrived ethnic in the United States. Consequently, in all seriousness and responsibility I can affirm that none of the other applicants for 1450 kilocycles can offer as much to the community as my family and myself.

The quota of time given over to ethnic broadcasting is very small and in proportion to the number of ethnic groups living in the Chicago area is not in any way proportionally just. Not only is this state of affairs not increasing, but the time allotted is diminishing. Station WOPA in Oak Park, on which I work, which developed thanks to the programs of European ethnic groups has recently transferred its Polish radio programs broadcast during the morning hours to afternoon hours and created a 6-hour program—'Latinos.' A similar situation can be observed on other radio stations where programs for European ethnic groups are pushed into less desirable time frames or totally liquidated.

It is true that it is not easy to operate an ethnic radio station. Control is made difficult for the management by their not knowing other languages. If the management lay in the hands of ethnic groups knowing other languages, that problem would not exist.

Ethnics do not own a radio station. Our application is the first for running an ethnic station. . . . White ethnics need a radio station which will be partisan to their needs. People in numerous ethnic groups feel as if they are second class citizens. The language barrier and the lack of recognition in the mass media creates feelings of resentment which brings about non-beneficial relations of the citizens to local and national government. And these are people who are worthwhile, hard working and generous. Statistics indicate that the largest majority of soldiers from World War II was comprised of soldiers from ethnic groups. Only an ethnic radio station managed by people from ethnic groups, and thus knowing ethnic problems, can in English present to American society the value of individual citizens and ethnic groups in its true light, their contribution to the building of the country, and their contribution to the cultural and educational achivement taken in the broadest sense. Then white ethnics will be treated on the same level as other citizens, and will regain the respect from others and faith in themselves. In order to run an ethnic radio station with advantage for the public, one must have constant direct contact with a broad gamut of ethnic organizations. In addition one must be an organization which will cooperate closely with individual directors of ethnic radio programs and the management of the station.

Radio, which is a boon to humanity, transmits ideas and thoughts very rapidly and reaches where other mass media cannot reach, cannot be a boon only for privileged groups. White ethnic groups in metropolitan Chicago deprived of their own radio station do not possess the same opportunity as others for making their life vital. Our programs, which we listed in our application, and which will be given in ethnic languages and also in English, are directed as much as possible to the convictions of the leaders of many ethnic groups in Cicero and metropolitan Chicago as well. These directions were taken after many interviews with these leaders. Many of our programs are in answer to the needs and problems which are uppermost in the ethnic groups.

One of the basic difficulties in beginning life in the United States is the lack of knowing the English language. Teaching English via radio is most desirable and ought to be subsidized by the government.

Difficulties in finding work, especially in professions learned and practiced in Europe, also belong to the most difficult for the new arrival. Many of these people finished trade schools at a high school or university level, but they don't know how and where to have their diplomas verified. The radio job employment section, which we proposed, is an answer to solving these problems. With this problem is connected the necessity of further professional education in courses given in local trade schools, but with teachers who know the ethnic languages.

Another serious problem for new arrivals are high pressure door-to-door salesmen who sell various articles both necessary and unnecessary on the payment plan. These people sign sales contracts which they don't understand and then are obliged to pay installments. The new arrivals have serious problems in this regard when buying automobiles, furniture and other objects on the installment plan; they are manipulated and cheated. A radio segment dealing with legal advice in the ethnic languages run by civic-minded lawyers would help alleviate such problems a lot.

Another problem for the new arrivals is getting to a place of employment when it is located beyond the city where no public transportation exists. This forces the person to purchase his own auto and to apply for a driver's license. The insufficient knowledge of the language prevents knowing the driver's code of rules, therefore preparatory courses to the driver's exam ought to be given in the specific foreign languages. Ethnic radio programs can be of great help here by broadcasting the terms of the courses to those interested and also organizing talks on the radio with highway patrol officers.

People from various ethnic groups have serious problems when they wish to prepare themselves for their citizenship examinations. For that reason appropriate radio courses in foreign languages should be organized such as the ones which we offer in our programs. Various conflicts between the new arrivals and local authorities have their source in the former not knowing the laws and duties of permanent residents or citizens. Therefore periodic radio courses on this theme are very necessary.

Normal life for the new arrivals is also made more difficult by a lack of knowledge about the history of the United States, the government structure, the constitution, the participation of various ethnic groups in the origin and development of our country.

Many people from ethnic communities who wish to establish their own businesses complain that there are no trade courses in the foreign languages which would prepare them to operate a business. Representatives of all the ethnic groups complain that some professions are closed to them, for example: policeman, guard, local, county or state office worker. People from ethnic groups should be notified in time when recruiting for such positions is taking place along with the qualifications demanded etc. The ethnic radio station can also be of help here.

Every new arrival from Europe to this country yearning for his family, friends, the nilieu in which he lived and the cultural he knew, is the most faithful listener to ethnic programming on the radio. Poles yearn to hear Polish songs, the Polish language, news from Poland. For many, Polish radio is the only source of Polish culture. This is also the case for people from all ethnic groups.

During the "Voice of Polonia" broadcasts, I try to perform authentic old Polish songs. Often after the broadcast I get a telephone call which indicates that someone has been touched by what they heard. Thus, one example: a woman called to thank me for playing a song about a stream which flows through her native village in Poland. She said, "I've been in America for 60 years and this is the first time that I heard a song on the radio that I used to sing in Poland. Thanks from the bottom of my heart. Please play more like it." Or, for example, I might get a telephone call from a man who says that he is sorry that he speaks Polish badly, but he always listens to my broadcasts, because somehow the songs "talk" to him. He was listening with his mother, an old lady, who was very touched when she recalled the song which she used to sing as a young girl. He asks where he can buy the record with these songs as a present for his mother. In order to give people those affective emotions and joy an ethnic radio station is needed.

Another problem for people from ethnic groups who still don't know English well enough to be able to avail themselves profitably from mass media is the lack of enough news programs local, national and international in the ethnic languages. This problem is linked with another phenomenon, the diminishing ethnic press. This is occurring because thanks to population shifts in Chicago, ethnics no longer live, as they once did, in large concentrations, but are scattered over the whole of the Chicago metropolitan area. Because of this scattering, it does not pay to distribute daily newspapers over such a wide geographic area. Therefore a greater obligation falls on ethnic radio to provide the news. This burning need of informing about local, national and international occurrences can only be filled by ethnic radio which has a far reach.

A further problem for those living in the Chicago area is the lack of sufficient language schools where the children of the ethnic population can learn the language of their parents, something about the history of the country their parents came from, the national songs and dances. Such schools operated on Saturday and Sunday would keep the children off the street. For years within the framework of "The Voice of Polonia" broadcasts, Polish is taught on the radio. This was the first experiment of its sort in the United States and it met the test extremely well. Such programs should be broadened to include other ethnic groups.

Another serious problem is the conflict between new and old immigrants within the various ethnic groups. People from the new wave of immigration do not join very eagerly to organizations established and run by the older immigrants. This conflict arose on the basis of educational differences, cultural level, the level of wealth, and finally on political views. The new arrivals form their own organizations, while the old organizations, as a consequence of the lack of new and younger members, become less active.

Another problem within the Polonia is the activity of divisive provocateur groups determined to destroy the unity of organized Polonia. They besmirch without having any foundation for their accusation the leaders of Polonia in order to undermine the confidence of the majority in them. The aim of this divisive activity is ultimately to act on the disoriented masses for the interests of those who are paying for this ignoble work. One can only guess who is interested in destroying Polish American unity. Our programs confront these issues through the discussions on "Radio Forum." Radio discussion programs can adequately enlighten the masses by informing them about the aims of such activity and thereby effectively torpedoing the divisive activity. Through discussion on "Radio

Forum" some of the difference between the old and new immigrants can be smoothed over.

Yet another serious problem which reflects negatively on the organizational life of Polonia is the population shift. Many changes have taken place in the neighborhoods. Neighborhoods which until recently were inhabited by Poles are presently dominated by Blacks, Mexicans, and Puerto Ricans. The Poles lived in these neighborhoods and their own well maintained houses wieh enchantingly beautiful flower gardens that have now lost their financial value. Those who could afford it bought homes in the Northwest sections and left the former Polish sections. Not everyone could afford to do this and they had to remain in their former neighborhoods. Those people are now experiencing very difficult conditions. The new neighbors are an unstable element, who threaten the peace and safety. The older people are even afraid of going out in front of their house or into their backyard. They are simply prisoners in their own houses. The value of their homes, often the sum total of their life savings has fallen to a minimum.

Similar problems are being experienced by important Polonian organizations who had their establishments in the former Polish neighborhoods or where they are still located having impressive buildings with halls for meetings, performances, lectures, libraries etc. For example, the Polish National Alliance, a national organization of fraternal aid, having almost 350,000 members nationally, sold their building at Milwaukee and Division for the mere sum of $125,000. It cost almost one million dollars to build. The largest Polish organization of women the Polish Women's Alliance comprising almost 100,000 members nationally and owning their own building also in the now run down area of Ashland and Milwaukee Avenues is seeking a building in the northwest section of town since members returning from meetings are mugged, beaten and robbed.

Yet another example. The Alliance of Polish Clubs, a social organization with till recently more than 200 local clubs in the Chicago area as members owned a huge building with five large halls located in the same neighborhood that was sold for a mere $32,000. The building had to be sold, since no club wished to meet in that building any longer because of the muggings, vandalizing the automobiles etc. This organization which celebrated its 50th anniversary in May, 1978 and which during its half-century of activity did marvelous social work, after having lost its building, lost the basis of its existence. Through lacking it own building the Alliance of Polish Clubs is creating a series of problems for Polonia. One of them relates to the retirees of "Senior Citizens" a group which used to hold their bingo and social parties, their fairs etc. there. Any profits from these gatherings were given to charitable causes. These people have lost their reason for living, and they could have spent their old age in a pleasant way among their friends and benefitting society.

It is also necessary to mention other specific problems of ethnic Senior Citizens. They are not informed about various programs which the local government runs for them. There are state and federal programs run of their benefit as well, but since they are not informed about these programs, they do not participate. Some of these important programs are: Social Security, Medicare, Medicaid, Food Stamps, RTA Cards for reduced transportation costs, Rent or Tax Relief, Assistance in filing various government forms. I am well acquainted with these problems since I cooperate with "Project Senior Ethnic Find" which is jointly sponsored by the Illinois Department on Aging and Action in Chicago. I cooperate by providing information over the radio. Thanks to the information given on the above themes over "The Voice of Polonia" to Polish retirees, that organization received so many inquiries that because of a lack of personnel they were unable to take care of everyone. I was asked to cease broadcasting this information. To a great degree our programs take into account the concerns of senior citizens, since we know that only information given in ethnic languages will get to them.

A further problem for the old is the lack of religious services, especially when they are unable to attend church either because of bad weather or physical infirmity. Therefore we are proposing religious broadcasts in our program schedule.

The greatest problems of youth relate to drunkenness, using drugs, anti-social behavior, promiscuous sex and the veneral disease which may result, dropping out of school, poor relations with adults. Our programs also take such problems into account while proposing means to remedy them. Much can be done through informing parents and teachers about these problems and through them informing the youth and also informing directly by discussions with the young people themselves. However one should add that in ethnic families because of the prevalent religious upbringing and the strength of parental authority youth problems are not too drastic.

In the Chicago metropolitan area yet another problem plagues the life of ethnic groups, and that is the hostility which one group may have for another. Such feelings of resentment have their roots in events which occurred in Europe. For example, the Poles have bad feelings toward the Germans because the latter occupied their country and committed crimes there. Similarly, the Ukrainians and the Lithuanians retain bad feelings toward the Poles for incorporating territory after World War I into Poland which they considered belonged to them. Our programming speaks to these issues by proposing an ethnic "Radio Forum" where in open discussion these issues can be addressed.

A separate issue are the problems which ethnics have with the Bureau of Immigration and Naturalization. Almost every ethnic has some kind of matter to take care of with the Bureau of Immigration and Naturalization. For example, when someone wants to bring his parents or other relatives to this country, he must go through a lot of red tape. I can attest from my own personal experience while working with the Europe Travel Bureau, Inc. when I had frequent contact with the Immigration authorities that this is the worst organized federal agency. Concretely, when I would phone Immigration to ask for help in a particular matter I would speak to three officials and I would receive three diametrically opposing answers. When I was convinced that I had been badly informed, I tried to speak with the supervisor of the department. I was never connected with him, I was told to hang on and then the connection was broken. That service does not have qualified workers and the behavior of the bureaucrats to the clients is simply scandalous.

Settling a simple matter drags on for months and sometimes even for years. Any intervention is practically impossible. The clerks in Immigration don't want to talk with the clients who don't speak English well, they also don't want to speak to the relatives who want to help, they don't want to talk to travel agents who fill out the forms for people, they wish to speak to lawyers who for such intervention ask very steep prices, which most people cannot afford to pay.

Documents presented to Immigration disappear. Last year, I personally handed to Immigration the Polish passport of my cousin's daughter in connection with trying to get a change of status (she should be accorded American citizenship because her father was born here). When it was necessary to extend her passport, I asked that it be returned only to be told that they did not have the passport. They tried to tell me that I had never given them the passport. This year my wife had a similar incident with the passport of a client; the passport disappeared at Immigration and once again they said that they had never received it. This is difficult to prove since Immigration does not have a policy of providing a receipt that they have received documents at the time they are submitted.

A petitions for visas presented by ethnics on behalf of members of their families are taken care of after the lapse of a year, which causes various complications for them and for their lived ones in Poland.

The Immigration and Naturalization Service in Chicago ill treats human dignity of the ethnics who are obliged to deal with them and someone ought to investigate and expose these matters. These issues are appropriate for discussion on "Ethnic Forum".

The problems of people from ethnic groups who live in metropolitan Chicago are the same or fairly similar to ethnics who live in other towns like Cicero, Berwyn, Leon and others. Nonetheless there are specific problems which relate to Cicero alone.

Cicero is an old ethnic town which was established 125 years ago with a European style of architecture. Old homes require a lot of money for renovation. The mainstreet of the town, Cermak Road, requires a serious expenditure of money for renovation. The town needs new and more spacious parking places, particularly near the shopping areas.

One of the worries of Cicero residents is employment. Western Electric which employes 9,000 people intends to let 2,000 of them go this year and next year it plans to let go even more. White ethnic groups which now reside in Cicero fear that the areas bordering Chicago will be taken over by Blacks since they are now living along Austin Avenue to Cicero. Because of these two issues people have ceased to take good care of their homes and the section is deteriorating. The elements who do not care for cleanliness and who threaten the safety of long time residents are increasing.

Another problem relates to the east side of town where people have stopped investing in home repairs and are living in uncertainty, since for 10 years the proposed "cross-town expressway" has been projected which would cut through this section and would result in many homes being demolished. The lack of a clear decision in this matter causes the residents of the area serious problems, and the town is looking seedier.

There is an insufficient number of policemen in Cicero, due to a lack of funds. About 25,000 people live in this town who are living on Social Security benefits. Since their income is small, it is difficult to raise taxes, but the town needs funds for various programs.

People are also troubled by rowdy behavior in residential areas when the taverns close. Cicero needs new sporting facilities for its youth. The town has problems with the Metropolitan Sanitary District which creates a smoke problem when they are burning trash.

In addition Cicero has problems with drugs, particularly among the youth. Then too, there are gang related difficulties. While these problems are not at the critical stage they are in Chicago, they do exist and they are increasing.

Thus the leaders of each ethnic group and also the town government complain about the difficulties of their work which are enhanced because they get no support from the mass media. A broad, open discussion is imperative both between the governing body of the town and the general population as also among the various groups of people representing various interest groups. Leaders of ethnic organization throughout the whole Chicago metropolitan area also complain about the lack of interest of the mass media.

> This is all the more incomprehensible since more than 50% of the area originated from ethnic groups. The malicious say that the management of radio and television stations in metropolitan Chicago remember that ethnics exist only just before license renewal with the FCC, before elections and on a daily basis only with insulting jokes that make fun of Poles, Italians, or Jews.
>
> In conclusion, I maintain that without the personal involvement and dedication of the management, a radio station does not fulfill the hopes which it listeners invest in it. Personal involvement and dedication can only be expected from management which is rooted in ethnic groups and which is well acquainted with ethnic problems and wants to confront them.

The arguments presented to the FCC by the president of the Migala Communications Corporation, Jozef Migala, were acknowledged by the remaining five applicants as equitable and just.

As a result, after almost 6 years of endeavors and a very complicated procedure, the FCC awarded the Migala Communications Corporation a license to build a radio station to broadcast over 1450 kilocycles AM. For the first time in the history of American radio the FCC awarded a license to a corporation representing ethnic groups in the Chicago metropolitan area making it clearly understood that it should serve ethnic group interests.

As mentioned earlier Polish broadcasting in the United States is almost entirely the effort of independent producers who create individual programs aired on stations that sell bulk time to independent radio producers. Few stations have any real commitment to serving a particular ethnic group or other. The stations simply sell the airtime in bulk and oversee the programs as to compliance with FCC rules and station regulations. Many smaller stations took on what they still call "foreign language" programming, simply as a financial necessity. They could not attract any other segment of the metropolitan radio audience.

Since the 1920's ethnic language programs have appeared usually on lower powered stations of five thousand watts or less which carry multi-ethnic programming. In the 1970's, more and more of the smaller stations realized they could maximize profits by not remaining multi-ethnic, but by specializing in one or another of the major ethnic groups in their area. By the 1970's major advertising agencies began setting aside so-call "ethnic" or "minority" money–portions of advertising campaign budgets that were to be used to buy advertising on ethnic media. In most areas, this money was set aside for only the recognized minorities specifically for blacks and Hispanics.

However, major advertising agencies prefer to deal with radio stations rather than independent producers, because of communication problems with the producers and their often unprofessional billing practices. The agencies also prefer to place their advertising with stattions that could offer full-time or at least significantly long periods of programming aimed at a particular audience. They did not want to place advertising in, let's say, an Hispanic program of 3 or 4 hours duration, surrounded by other languages. They prefer a station that could offer 10, 12 or 24 hours of consecutive Hispanic broadcasting.

As a result radio stations that previously had aired a mix of languages, found it more profitable to air only one language, or serve only one group, such as black Americans. More and more stations expanded their Hispanic or black service, often creating station-produced programs, while moving other languages to less desireable airtimes, or dropping them entirely.

Independent ethnic producers had fewer and fewer stations from which to purchase good airtime. Producers who served smaller less recognized ethnic groups feared that they might be entirely locked out of the market and radio service for their communities would be a thing of the past. As one of those producers, aware of that trend, the author of this book, determined in the early 1970's to establish a station which would be committed to multi-ethnicity.

After a 6-year very costly process which included competitive hearings before a Federal Communications administrative law judge, my family company, Migala Communications Corporation, was granted the right to share the 1450 a.m. frequency in the Chicago metropolitan area with Midway Broadcasting Corporaration. Midway Broadcasting is a black partnership which airs black-oreinted programming 98 1/2 hours per week.

My company created station WCEV, which airs 69 1/2 hours a week. WCEV is specifically devoted to the concept of inter-ethnicity, that is, communication and cooperation among various ethnic groups. WCEV is also dedicated to servicing the many and large ethnic groups in greater

Chicago. WCEV's call letters in fact stand for "We're Chicagoland's Ethnic Voice."

WCEV covers the Chicago metropolitan area and is based in the west suburban town of Cicero, Illinois, one of the most ethnic communities in the nation. The station has a dual purpose: To provide quality broadcast service to the huge ethnic communities which are the majority in Chicagoland, but which are given little attention in most media; and to serve Cicero and surrounding suburbs.

In its 6 years of existence WCEV offered programs in various languages directed toward ten ethnic groups: Polish, Greek, Hispanic, Lithuanian, Italian, Serbian, Ukranian, Czechoslovak, Croatian, Irish, Sloveian, and Black. The programs often include popular and traditional music, national language newscasts as well as community news, interviews, literary features, radio theaters, conversation, and occasionally live-action sports. A few programs are bilingual.

WCEV is a member of Associated Press and carries English language newscasts on-the-hour, most hours, plus an impressive schedule of news and public affairs programs in English.

The inter-ethnic function of our station is fulfilled through daily ethnic feature reports in English which are aired within nearly all of our ethnic programs. The series is called "Who Are We." The reports spotlight ethnic facts, issues, histories, heroes and customs. They stress ethnic contributions and accomplishments. Such subjects are rarely discussed elsewhere on Chicagoland radio, especially not in English.

Who Are We reports serve not only as a means for ethnics to ear about issues important to them, but they also service as a means of learning more about one's enthicity and the traditions and customs of other ethnics.

The reports are written, produced, and voiced by my daughter Lucyna Migala, a broadcast journalist who served with NBC News for more then 12 years.

Lucyna also produces and voices our "Mosiac" interview programs. This weekly-half hour program concentrates on subjects of special interest to ethnic Americans. WCEV also concentrates on ethnicity organizations or on ethnic subjects are given priority on our station.

WCEV is operated by the members of my family, with direction from me and my wife, Estelle (Slawa) Migala. My daughter, Barbara Migala Holtzinger is office manager for WCEV. My daughter, Lucyna Migala, is

WCEV program director. Daughter number three, Diana Maria Migala, is business manager. My son George Migala, a well-known Polish American broadcaster, is station manager.

WCEV airs daily from 1 p.m. to 10 p.m, 1 p.m. to 8:30 p.m. on Saturdays, and from 5 a.m. to 10 p.m. on Sundays. Studio facilities are maintained in Chicago and Cicero and some programming is done from remote locations within ethnic communities. Operating at 1000 watts, non-directional, the station shares its 1450kc frequency with WVON, a black-oriented station. The transmitter and tower for both stations are located at 3350 South Kedzie Avenue in Chicago.

Six years of operating WCEV have taught me that a low power radio station can no longer truly serve any ethnic community in a metropolitan area such as Chicago. As ethnics become more affluent, they move farther and farther out into the suburbs in all directions. Even within city limits, there are few old ethnic neighborhoods. Meanwhile, newly arrived immigrants, who desparately need radio service in an ethnic language settle in the older, inner city neighborhoods. The result is that no ethnic group is limited to one neighborhood or one area of any city. In order to serve an entire ethinic community, a station must have a strong signal which can cover an entire ethnic metropolitan area. In the case of areas such as Chicago, which has ethnic communities as far north as Milwaukee, Wisconsin and as far south as South Bend, Indiana, only a strong regional station can really serve any ethnic community.

PART FOUR

Analysis of Response to a Public Opinion Survey About Polish Radio in the United States

CHAPTER 17

The Public Opinion Survey

1. The Organization of the Public Opinion Survey

The basis of the public opinion survey was three different questionaires, two of which dealt with existing or defunct Polish radio programs and one dealt with the opinion of the listeners about those programs. To make the identification of the kind of questionaire dealing with the programs easier, the following symbols were used:

Al - The questionaire about existing programs in Polish

Cl - the questionaire with the same content as Al in English

Bl - the questionaire about programs that have ceased being broadcast in Polish

Dl - the questionaire with the same content as Bl in English

In the questionaires dealing with existing radio programs Al and Cl, examples were included. The majority of them dealt with the contents of the programs and the personal characteristics of the professional producers. Of similar content were the questionares dealing with already defunct Polish radio programs, that is Bl and Dl, examples of which are also in the appendix. These questionaires were sent to producer-directors of Polish radio programs and addressed to them personally or to the radio station on which these programs were broadcast. The questionaires were accompanied by a letter explaining the aim of the research and a request for cooperation. An example of the letter is found in the appendix. All together some 200 inquiries were sent out; barely 25 were filled out and returned. The author, much disturbed by the small return, called a number of producer-directors for an explanation. It turned out that the small rate of return of the survey was the long and detailed list of questions which discouraged people from replying. As a result of this, a modified version of questionaires Al and Cl was prepared and the number of questions cut down to 16. An example of that version is in the appendix.

Another channel of information about Polish radio programs was the opinion research survey directed to listeners. An example is appended. The aim of this poll was to determine information about listener preferences. In order to reach the greatest number of listeners, the Polish press was used. The questionaire was placed in eight Polonian dailies and periodicals with an aggregate publication of 485,000 copies, which consisted of "Naród Polski," "Głos Polek," """Zgoda," "The Polish Weekly Straz," "Sokol Polski," "Gwiazda Polarna," "Dziennik Polski," and "Nowy Dziennik." The editors presented the questionaire with the following appeal: The editorial staff urges its readers to fill out his questionaire whose aim is to gather together materials for research about Polish radio programs in the United States." In addition to the author's efforts, about 500 questionaires properly filled out were obtained. The respondents remained anonymous.

2. Characteristics of Polish Radio Programs Based on the Poll

Peculiar to Polish radio is that one person is obliged to fullfil functions. He must be director, producer, editor, and advertising announcer. Polish radio programs do not bring in enough profits to allow additional people to be hired to fill each specific function. The one and only source of income on Polish radio are commercial announcements. From the received questionaires it turns out that for a 30 second advertisements the manger of the program receives an average of $8.33 on a national average, and $15.06 for a 60 second commercial. A radio station on the average for one hour of air time asks $135.71. During one hour, 18 minutes of commericals are permitted. However, the average number of advertisements during an ethnic program lasting an hour is only 15 minutes. From the received sum of $225.90 for commercials, after paying the radio station, only $90.19 remains for the program manager. However, this is not clear profit. From that sum, he must buy materials for the program like records, and tapes, he pust pay the 15% commission to the advertising agent and he must cover a number of other costs incurred with running the broadcast.

The quality of the Polish broadcasts goes hand in hand with the education of the producer-director. In contrast to radio broadcasts in English where music or information can be purchased ready-made, no companies produce Polish programming in part or whole. Furthermore there are not even examples of how to create programs. The Polish producer is left to his own creativity exclusively. He must know his listeners well and what their demands are and then meet them.

In order to deal with such problems educated people are necessary, people of culture who are in steady contact with their nationality group, and thus involved in working for the commonwealth. Generally speaking one must say that the average level of the Polish radio program in the United States is low. The level of the broadcast is equal to the level of the producer-directors educational level.

The best Polish musical broadcasting was created by managers who came from the Polish theater, while the best information programs are given by those who worked professionally as journalists on Polish dailies or weeklies. At present those Polish programs whose producer-directors have at least a high-school education or higher and who receive their broadcasting material from Polish Radio in Poland are on the highest level. To produce materials such as radio dramas or to dramatise novels or short stories for radio is totally impossible for the Americans working on Polish radio programs from several standpoints: it is financially too expensive, there is a lack of the necessary talent both in front of the microphone and behind it from the technological end.

The Polonian listener primarily demands a good informational service. "Głos Polonii," the longest existing Polish radio program in Chicago allots 25% of its time to this, giving local national and international news, news from Poland and about Poles all over the world. For very many Poles living in the heart of large cities, the radio news in their native language is their only source of information. News in the now continually diminishing Polish press is not presently accessible to the majority of Poles who not longer live in concentrated communities as they once did. Poles have moved from the center to the far edges of the city where it is not cost effective to distribute Polish newspapers in small quantities. The level of Polish radio programs in the United States is constantly rising. The listeners are becoming more and more demanding. Besides good music, they demand news, radio dramas, literary segments, interviews etc.

The managers of Polish radio programs state in the poll that they only receive moral support from Polonian organizations, although as far as these organizations benefit a great deal. A good Polish radio program broadcasts more non-paid organization announcements then paid commercials. The main Polish fraternal organizations like the Polish National Alliance, The Polish Roman Catholic Union, the Women's Alliance, The Polish National Union and others cannot arbitrarily dispense the funds of their membership and spend money for purposes not directly tied to their chartered activity. The numerous Polonian clubs or societies are working for ideological aims. Their funds come from membership dues or from profitable fund rasers like dances, bingos or picnics and they are designated for cultural-educational purposes. Consequently Polish radio programs also cannot count on any material help from these sources.

The one and only source of income for Polish radio programs is the advertising of merchandise or service companies. Getting good advertising contracts is, however, a difficult task. The advertising budgets of small Polish firms are low, while large firms, like chain stores, are not interested in advertising within the framework of Polish radio programs. This is the result of various reasons. The lack of knowing Polish causes difficulty for the managers of large firms as far as controlling the advertising which is broadcast. It also causes the necessity to hire sales people who speak Polish. Finally, the scattering of Poles over large metropolitan areas does not give those commercial results to the firms which are advertising that were easily reached when Poles lived in concetrated communities.

3. Analysis of Listeners' Preferences

The Polish community does not yet constitute a very demanding audience for quality radio programs. The majority of this audience comes from the older generation and they are people without much education who occupy a rather lowly place on the social and profession hieraracjhy. Also the intellectual level of the audience is not particularly high.

This situation, it is true, is changing for the better because more young people are seeking higher education and because of the influx of educated people from Poland, but the situation is still not totally satisfactory.

From the response in the poll it turns out that the structural preference in programming is differentiated by such elements as age, sex, employment, education, country of birth and the degree of connections with the country of origin. Many of these elements are tied together and they create an integrated power of influence on the arrangement and structure of preference. Thus for example birth in Poland has an influence on maintaining contact with Poland through correspondence. This is shown in the following:

Answers in Percentages

Born in Poland	Corresponds with Poland Yes	No
Yes	100.0	0
No	80.0	20.0

In order to check on the correctness of the influence an independent test was used X^2 and using the following equation:

$$X^2 = \frac{\Sigma / n_{ij} - \hat{n}_{ij} /^2}{\Sigma \hat{n}_{ij}}$$

where:

n_{ij} is the observed number of answers in line "i" and column "j"

$\hat{n}_{ij}$ is the counted number of answers in "i" and column "j".

The theoretical / counted / number of answers $\hat{n}_{ij}$ is obtained by multiplying the sum of answers in line i by the sum of answers in column j and dividing the number by the total number of answers. One obtains as a result of these numerical operations the obtained value of the test is $X^2 = 9.4737$. Because this value is higher than the critical value X^2 0.05 = 7.879 which is read from th table, we reject the hypothesis about there being no difference in the answers in the alternative affirmative hypothesis that the fact of the respondent having been born in Poland has an essential influence on maintaining contact with Poland via correspondence.

In turn the connection between being born in Poland and visiting one's native land was analyzed. The structure of replies according to this criterion is shown below.

Answers in Percentages

Born in Poland	Visits Poland Yes	No
Yes	68.9	31.1
No	66.7	33.3

The value of the test X^2 for these responses comes to $X^2 = 0.02567$ which compared to the critical value $X^2 0.05 = 7.879$ does not allow the hypothesis about no differences existing in the answers of the respondents to be rejected. Thus we affirm that birth in Poland does not influence the visiting of one's native land in an essential way.

Finally a key question was examining the existence of a tie between being born in Poland and listening to Polish radio programs. The responses according to this criterion is shown below.

Answers in Percentages

Born in Poland	Listens to Polish Programs Yes	No
Yes	84.4	15.6
No	53.3	46.7

The counted test $X^2 = 8.087$ exceeds the critical value $X^2 0.05 = 7879$ and allows us to affirm that the fact of birth in Poland has an essential influence on listening to Polish radio programs.

A further analysis of the answers of the respondents was the examination of their preferences in the sphere of individual kinds of programming. Those who were polled had to arrange their program preferences according to a point scale. This made possible finding the norm on the scale of preference. The scale is different for men and women listeners, indicating a different sequence of programs most willingly listened to. This is expressed in the following way:

Female Listeners

Music and popular songs	1.8
Operettas	2.1
Local news	2.2
News from Poland, about Poland and Poles	2.5
National news	2.7
Polka music	2.9
International news	3.0
Literary segments	3.8
Folk music	3.9
Popular music	4.5
Opera	4.7
Classical music	5.2
Announcements about organizations	5.4
Interviews	5.8
Sports	5.8
Dramatised stories	6.5
Dramas	6.5
Rock and roll music	7.8
Jazz	9.3

Male Listeners

Music and popular songs	1.5
Operettas	2.0
Local news	2.6
Opera	2.7
National news	2.0
News from Poland, about Poland and Poles	3.1
International news	3.2
Polka music	3.5
Rock and roll music	4.4

Popular music	4.5
Jazz	4.6
Literary segments	6.1
Folk music	6.1
Classical music	6.2
Interviews	6.2
Dramatized stories	6.4
Announcements about organizations	7.0
Dramas	8.8
Sports	9.4

Next to the names of the programs was placed the numerical ranking position of the individual programs according to the degree of their popularity. From the ranking it turns out that the decisive first place for both male and female respondents popular songs and music and operettas were preferred over local and national news. In the last place of preference for male listeners was jazz and rock and roll music, while female listeners put dramas and sports. The men prefer informational programs over musical ones, while it is the opposite with women who place music over information. Among both groups of respondents dramas and dramatized stories enjoy little popularity.

The next group analyzed were answers on the theme of the popularity of specific programs depending on various characteristics of the respondents. First the influence of the country of origin on the structure of preference will be examined. The results are given below.

Preference in Percentages

Type of Program	Born in Poland Yes	No
Local News	44.4	53.3
National news	57.8	20.0
International news	73.3	60.0
News from Poland, about Poland and Poles	84.4	80.0
Sports	22.2	26.7
Literary segments	44.4	33.3
Dramatized stories	33.3	13.3
Dramas	35.6	13.3
Interviews	40.0	33.3
Announcements of organizations	40.0	46.7
Folk music	37.8	60.0

Preference in Percentages (cont.)

Type of Program	Born in Poland Yes	No
Polka music	28.9	60.0
Popular songs and music	78.9	53.3
Operettas	57.8	46.7
Operas	26.7	26.7
Rock and roll music	13.3	6.7
Jazz	13.6	6.7

In comparing the structure of preferences it turns out that listeners born in Poland vastly prefer news about their native land and also place popular music above folk music or news. One also observes a disinclination to listen to Polka type music. On the other hand Poles born abroad willingly listen to the lively Polk-type music, as well as folk music.

The differentiation of program preference was also examined with the aid of the independent test X^2, whose amount turned out to be less than the critical value. The counted value of $X^2 = 11.883$ while the tabulated value was $X^2 0.05 = 26.296$, which allows us to affirm that the fact of birth in Poland does not influence in any essential degree changing the structure of preference in the sphere or programming. Only in individual cases was there a marked deviation, which was designated in the chart.

The further comparison deals with preferences in the sphere of radio programming depending on whether the Polonian listeners visit Poland. The results are found below.

Answers in Percentages

Type of Program	Visits Poland Yes	No
Local News	43.9	52.6
National News	48.8	78.9
International news	65.9	78.9
News from Poland, about Poland and Poles	82.9	84.2
Sports	24.4	21.1
Literary segments	39.0	47.4
Dramatized stories	29.3	26.3
Interviews	39.0	36.8

Announcements of organizations	46.3	31.6
Folk music	34.1	63.2
Polka music	34.1	42.1
Popular music and songs	82.9	73.7
Operettas	61.0	42.1
Operas	36.6	5.3
Rock and roll music	14.6	5.3
Jazz	17.1	5.3

In comparing the structuring of preferences it turns out that listeners who visit Poland listen to operas and operettas far more frequently than those who do not visit Poland where that cultural tradition is deeply rooted. On the other hand these latter listeners perfer news programs and folk music. Also among this group of listeners polka music is more popular.

The counted value of the test function X^2 even though larger than in the previous example also does not confirm an essential influence of visiting Poland by the listeners on a change in the structure of preferences. That value equals $X^2 = 15.103$ in relation to the critical value X^2 $0.05 = 26.296$ and thus the influence of visiting Poland although non-essential still turned out to be more significant that the fact of being born in Poland.

The following comparison deals with the effect of the frequency of listening to programs on the change of preferences with regard to programming. The results are shown below.

Preference in Percentages

Type of Program	Listens to the Program Yes	No
Local news	45.6	50.0
National news	54.3	71.4
International news	71.7	64.3
News from Poland, about Poland and Poles	87.0	71.4
Sports	23.9	21.4
Literary segments	43.5	35.7
Dramatized stories	28.3	28.6
Dramas	32.6	21.4
Interviews	43.5	21.4
Announcements of organizations	41.3	42.9

Folk music	41.3	50.0
Polka music	34.8	42.9
Popular music and songs	89.1	50.0
Operettas	28.3	21.4
Rock and roll music	15.2	-------
Jazz	17.4	-------

Comparing the structure of preference one notices that among people who listen to Polish radio programs all the time musical programs predominate, especially popular music and songs as well as the programs sporadically, news programs, particularly national news, dominates, while operettas and operas are listened to rarely and rock and roll and jazz not at all.

The counted value of the test function X^2 equals: 10.751 and is considerably lower than the tabulated $X^2 0.05 = 26.296$ which over and above a few individual examples designated in the table means that the frequency of listening to the programs does not effect an essential influence on the change of preferences in this sphere.

The next comparison is the preference programming from the point of view of the sex respondents. The results follow.

Answers In Percentages

	Sex	
Type of Program	Men	Women
Local news	45.0	50.0
National news	50.0	75.0
International news	67.0	75.0
News from Poland, about Poland and Poles	70.0	90.0
Sports	22.5	25.0
Literary segments	35.005.0	55.0
Dramatized stories	17.5	50.0
Dramas	25.0	40.0
Interviews	37.5	40.0
Announcement of organizations	37.5	50.0
Folk music	47.5	35.0
Polka music	35.0	40.0
Popular music and songs	87.5	65.0
Operettas	52.5	60.0
Operas	12.5	55.0
Rock and roll music	5.0	25.0
Jazz	7.5	25.0

The comparison of the preferences indicates that female listeners are greater devotees of serious music programs than male listeners who prefer light music and popular songs. Similarly dramatized stories and dramas are listened to more readily by women than by men. This rather large differentiation in preferences on the basis of sex did not find a confirmation in the counted value of the test function $X^2 = 19.6343$ which in comparison to the critical value $X^2 0.05 = 26.296$ is still of little significance to find out the sex by differentiating preferences in an essential way.

The next personal trait which could have an influence on the structure of preference in programming is age. The results observed do not allow for introducing a greater number of differentiated age groups than four, as presented in the chart.

Answers in Percentages

	Age				
Type of Program	Under 40	40-50	50-60	60-70	70 & up
Local news	83.3	41.7	50.0	41.2	28.6
National news	83.3	50.0	44.4	64.7	71.4
International news	66.7	75.0	55.6	76.5	85.7
News from Poland, about Poland and Poles	100.0	75.0	77.8	70.6	85.7
Sports	50.0	41.7	16.7	7.6	-------
Literary segments	50.0	58.3	38.9	29.4	42.9
Dramatized stories	33.3	50.0	22.2	17.6	28.6
Dramas	33.3	50.0	22.2	35.3	-------
Interviews	50.0	33.3	38.9	41.2	28.6
Announcement of organizations	16.7	50.0	38.9	41.2	57.1
Folk music	50.0	33.0	50.0	41.2	42.9
Polka music	33.3	33.0	33.3	47.1	71.4
Popular music and songs	100.0	83.3	77.8	82.4	28.6
Operettas	33.3	50.0	55.6	76.5	14.3
Operas	16.7	33.3	11.1	41.2	28.6
Rock and roll	33.3	33.3	-------	5.9	-------
Jazz	33.3	41.7	5.6	-------	14.3

In comparing structural indicators one notices that along with increasing age comes an increase of interest in serious music and announcements regarding organizational activities, and accompanied with a fall in new musical styles and sports or local news. Alslo popular music and songs cedes its place to the lively music of the Polka type. This can be clearly seen at the extreme limits designated in the chart.

Despite a rather large differentiation of preferences depending on age the counted value of the test function $X^2 = 29.131$ is lower than the tabulated value $X^2 0.05 = 83.675$ and does not allow formulating a proposition about the essential effect of age on changing programming predilictions. From the computation it turns out, however, that the groups which deviate the most from the established structure of preferences are the 40 to 50 group and the 70 and up group.

The next comparison will be the structure of preferences according to the level of education. The results are given in the chart below.

Answers in Percentages

	Education		
Type of Program	Elementary	High School	University
Local news	44.4	40.7	60.0
National news	50.0	63.0	60.0
International news	66.7	77.8	60.0
News from Poland, about Poland and Poles	88.9	88.9	66.7
Sports news	16.7	29.6	20.0
Literary segments	44.4	37.0	46.7
Dramatized stories	44.4	18.5	26.7
Dramas	38.9	25.9	26.7
Interviews	38.9	33.3	36.7
Announcements of organizations	22.2	40.7	66.7
Folk music	50.0	40.7	40.0
Polka music	38.9	37.0	33.3
Popular music and songs	83.3	85.2	66.7
Operettas	50.0	63.0	46.7
Operas	11.1	37.0	26.7
Rock and roll	– 4.8	14.8	20.0
Jazz	11.1	22.2	6.7

Comparing the indicators of the structured preferences one notices that as the level of education grow, interest in informational programs and news also increases. On the other hand interest in popular, folk and Polka type music diminishes. Interest in news from Poland also diminishes, while interest in local and national news augments. Dramatized stories and dramas are mist popular amoung listeners with lower educations levels, while interviews and information about organizations are most popular among listeners with higher education.

The effect of edcuation turned out, however, finally not to be essential in changing preferences since the tabulation of the test value equals $X^2 = 21.103$ whilw the tabulated value is $X^2 0.05 = 46.194$.

The last element which was taken into account in the analysis of preferences is profession.

Answers in Percentages

	Profession			
Type of Program	Worker	Clerk	Technician	Others
Local news	45.5	57.1	41.7	47.4
National news	50.0	57.1	50.0	68.4
International news	77.3	71.4	66.7	63.2
News from Poland, about Poland and Poles	86.4	85.7	91.7	68.4
Sports news	22.7	42.9	25.0	15.8
Literary segments	27.3	71.4	33.3	52.6
Dramtised stories	31.8	28.6	8.3	36.8
Dramas	31.8	57.1	8.3	31.6
Interviews	45.5	28.6	41.7	31.6
Announcements of organizations	27.3	57.1	33.3	57.9
Folk music	54.5	71.4	16.7	47.4
Polka music	40.9	57.1	25.0	31.6
Popular music and songs	81.8	100.0	91.7	63.2
Operettas	50.0	71.4	66.7	47.4
Operas	18.2	14.3	16.7	47.4
Rock and roll music	-------	28.6	16.7	15.8
Jazz	13.6	28.6	8.3	10.5

In comparing the indicators of preference it turns out that the smallest differentiation in the sphere of program preference in the professions is characterized by the blue collar workers, where one should emphasize a decided lack of interest in rock and roll music. In the white collar clerical group a somewhat greater differentiation of preferences appears, and in that category one must emphasize that a high interest in literary segments exists. In the technical group on the other hand the differentiation of preferences is very high; there the dominating position is the interest in news from Poland about Poland and Poles, while a decided lack of interest is apparent as far as dramas, for dramatized stories and folk music.

Despite the rather considerable differences in the preferences connected with professions, the value of the test function X^2 this time also turned out to be little significant reaching the value of $X^2 = 29.465$ in relation to the critical value $X^2 0.025 = 83.675$.

This analysis of listener preference with regard to programming can have great practical value for the producer-directors of Polish radio programs. Their broadcasting can be more responsive to the wishes and desires of the listeners.

CHAPTER 18

Characteristic Features of Polish Language Radio and Its Listeners

The overwhelming majority of Polish language programming in this country is is not produced by stations, but by independent producers, who purchase bulk time from radio stations as brokers. Most producers are individuals, some are two people working together, often a married couple, and occassionally a committee or small group.

In most cases, this producer or small group of producers must also served as the program's writers, editors, announcers and salesmen. Few Polish radio programs generate sufficient income to permit the employment of additional persons to carry out particular tasks. In most cases, the only source of proceeds for these programs are responses from advertisements. Responses to questionnaires sent out by the author in 1979-1980, indicate that, on the average, commercials the manager of a Polish program receives is $8.83, for a 30-second commercial–a tragically low amount; for a 60-second commercial–$15.06.

Nationwide, radio stations demand, on the average, $135.71 for one hour of bulk airtime. Until recently, the FCC limited the amount of advertising in one hour to 18 minutes. During that regulation, on-hour Polish programs average 15 one-minute commercials. If a producer was fortunate to sell all 15 commercials, he earned $225.90 per program. After paying the radio station for airtime, the manager of the program had only $90.19 left. This was not the profit. From this amount, the manager had to buy materials for his program, such as records, recording tape, pay advertising agency commissions (usually 15 percent), and cover all other costs connected with broadcasting the program. All in all, Polish radio programs in the United States are not profitable enterprise, but more a labor of love or idealism, or a vehicle for community prestige.

The quality of the Polish language programming depends on the education and talent of the manager-producer. For English radio programs, ready-made music programming or news or information segments can be purchased; There is no one in the United States producing ready-made Polish programs, or program segments for Polish language broadcasts (other than religious programs). Not only is there a lack of ready-made Polish program segments, there is also a lack of models for how such programs should be done. The producer of a Polish radio program can rely only on his or her own intuition or taste. He must know his listeners and their needs and meet their expectations. To meet those needs of its needs, Polish radio in the United States needs to attract educated, cultured people, who have regular contact with the Polish-American community, and who are devoted to community service.

Unfortunately, the quality of Polish radio programming in the United States is not high. The best Polish music programs are produced by those who were once themselves Polish artists and actors, while the best news programs are prepared by people who work or worked professionally as journalists in the numerous Polonia dailies and weeklies. Presently, the quality of those Polish radio programs whose producers have a high school degree or higher education do distinguish themselces from the average as do those programs that air material from Polish radio in Poland, which supplies various entertainment and informational program segments. The productions of radio plays, radio versions of popular novels or stories, in the conditions in which the producers of Polish programs in the United States work, is impossible, because of financial reasons as well as the lack of talented people and suitable technical conditions. Few producers have access to their own broadcast or recording studios or equipment.

What motivates these producers to undertake the production of Polish language programs?

For a few, this is work as any other, which can be a means of support for oneself and one's family, and obviously, satisfaction if the results suit the ambitions of the producer. However, there are also important social motivations to serve one's own community of which the author studied in 1979, when he took on the difficult task of starting an ethnic station in the Chicago area. The list of problems encountered by a large portion of the ethnic radio listeners is very long. Even a cursory review of these problems may shed some light on the social context in which ethnic radio operates, especially in big cities, such as Chicago.

The following is such a review, along with the author's suggestions for how ethnic radio can address and perhaps alleviate them, based on his 34-year experience in this field: A significant part of the Polish listening audience are new arrivals to his country from Poland.

One of the basic barriers for immigrants to the United States is their lack of the knowledge of English. The teaching of English through ethnic radio is thus a needed service, and should be subsidized by government.

Difficulties in finding work, especially in a professional learned and practiced in another country are among the most vital problems faced by new immigrants. Many of those people have completed vocational schools, sometimes on a technical or university level, but have no idea how or where to have their diplomas recognized in this country. An employment exchange, a listing of available jobs with information on diploma verification would be a very popular element of ethnic programming.

Another serious problem of new immigrants is ignorance of the law. Very often, immigrants are cheated when making purchases, especially by salesmen who offer them installment payments. Immigrants sign contracts of purchase which they do not understand. Radio segments offerieng legal advice by an attorney speaking the ethnic language would be very helpful.

Yet another difficulty of immigrants it is transportation to a job that is located far from the city, where no public means of transportation exists. This forces people to quickly obtain a car and a driver's license. People who do not know English well, encounter a barrier in learning about traffic laws. Few states offer driver's examinations in ethnic languages. Ethnic programs could air segments in traffic laws and preparation for driving tests.

Most immigrants want to become citizens as quickly as possible. Citizenship classes in English or in ethnic languages would be helpful. Many conflicts with local authorities have their sources in ignorance by immigrants of the rights and duties of permanent residents or citizens, hence regular radio courses covering these subjects are necessary.

More established ethnic listeners often complain that they are kept from joining such professions as police officer, fire officer, municipal or state officer. Through ethnic radio, ethnic groups could be informed at the right time of recruitment for such professions and given information on the required qualifications, etc.

New immigrants homesick for their native culture and ethnics seeking to retain or return to that culture are the most faithful listeners of ethnic radio. It is natural for Poles to want to hear Polish music, the Polish language, news of Poland. Ethnic radio fulfills these needs.

New immigrants do not have a sufficient knowledge of English to benefit from regular mass media. They require information and news in their own language, yet the daily ethnic press is now on the decline, a fact that reflects ethnic migration patterns. Ethnics no longer live in neighborhoods as was once the case, but are scattered throughout metropolitan communities. The cost of distribution across such wide areas has forced many ethnic daily newspapers to cut their service area or to publish less often. This, plus the rising cost of paper have caused many dailies to fold. Ethnic radio must fulfill this information gap. The author's own Polish program "Voice of Polonia" devotes 25 percent of its airtime to informational elements: local news, national and international news from Poland, news about Poles and Polonia around the world.

Another vital problem is the lack of a sufficient number of supplemental schools teaching ethnic languages, especially in suburban area, where children can learn notonly the language of their ancestors, but also history, literature, national dances and songs. Again, ethnic radio can serve splendidly in this area.

One of the serious problems causing disunity within ethnic groups are conflicts between the old and new immigrants. This phenomenon is quite obvious in the Polish community. People from recent waves of immigration are reluctant to join organizations that were founded and run by earlier immigrants. This conflict is caused by differences in age, education, cultural level, affluence and finally, political views. People from the newer immigration set up their own organizations, while the older organizations, as a result of no influx of new blood, become less active. This is reflected also in radio service, with some programs serving only a specific immigration, a specific political point of view, a certain age group.

Because of migration of various ethnic groups to the older, inner-city areas of American cities, many Polish-American organizations found themselves with headquarters buildings, often large and expensive facilities, that were in neighborhoods that were no longer Polish and were considered unsafe by their members. Members, especially older ones, could no longer attend meetings and functions there, no longer visit the libraries and reading rooms. Often, Polish organizations were forced to sell such facilities at a great loss to the organization and move to better neighborhoods, often in the suburbs. Such moves created further problems, as segments of the Polish population, especially the poor, the elderly and the newest immigrants, could not reach the new headquarter buildings because of sporadic public transportation in these "better" neighborhoods.

This situation put even more pressure on Polish radio to fill the entertainment and information function that these former meeting places provided.

A significant percentage of those listening to Polonian programs are elderly people, a majority of whom have little education and occupy lower positions on the socio-economic scale. Younger listeners are often from the newer immigrations from Poland, comprising more educated people. Also, more and more children from Polish-American families today receive better education, and they too are listeners.

Not surprisingly, an analysis of the questionnaire sent out by the author to listeners of Polonian radio indicates that there exists a close link between the fact of being born in Poland and the listenership of Polish-American radio. A full 84.4 percent who declared themselves listeners of Polonia programs were born in Poland.

Most popular program elements among listeners according to the questionnaire are pop music, operettas and local news.

Ethnics born in the United States are often polka fans and like authentic Polish folk music, too. Many elderly people are also great fans of polka music. People below forty are equally interested in jazz and rock music, radio plays, dramatized novels, as well as polka music. Thirty-three and one-third percent of listeners responding in this age bracket expressed interest in those elements of Polish radio programs.

Every category of listener expressed great interest in information from and about Poland.

AFTERWARD

Conclusions and Proposals

A number of Polish radio programs in the larger Polonian communities via special broadcasting have in the past and also at present broadened a consciousness of their national heritage among the Polonia. In turn causeries on the occasion of important national commemorations teach the listeners the history of Poland and raises their morale. Monetary collections among the American Polonia were organized via Polish radio programs for the National Defense Fund (Fundusz Obrony Narodowej) just before World War I. During World War II Polish radio programs in the United States took an active part in rasing material help for throngs of refugees who found themselves dispersed in various countries. The Polish American Coucil (Rada Polonii Amerykanskiej) and its numerous chapters organized collections of clothing and food for the refugees through the help of Polish radio programs. The president of the main administration and the chapter presidents often spoke on these programs and led appeals to the listeners for generosity on behalf of the refugees. The directors of radio programs stood at the head of collection committees, or they themsleves organized drives via the radio.

Enormous charitable aid was brought to their compatriots by the many clubs and societies which belonged to the Headquarters of the Alliance of Clubs of Małopolska (Centralia Związku Klubów Małopolskich). In the Chicago territory the Radio Hour of the Alliance of Clubs of Małopolska directed by the author of his work was the leader.

From the beginning of its history Polish radio programs had an important influence in forming public opinion among the Polonia in various aspects of life, and they mobilized public opinion and guided its development. Community work initiatives in many instances came from the directors of Polish radio program. They not only gave the inspiration but also took an active part in bring projects to fruition.

The larger Polish programs eagerly carry on interviews with representatives of Polish science, culture or art. The Copernicus commemorations in the United States began from a series of interviews of the author with the Rector of the Mikolaj Kopernik University in Toruń, Professor Łukaszewicz.

Similarly, the collections for the building fund of the King's Palace in Warsaw started from a series of twelve interviews of his author with Professor Stanisław Lorenc, the curator of the National Museum in Warsaw, also within the framework of "The Voice of Polonia" radio program in Chicago. The twenty-minute interview conducted by Jerzy Migała with Cardinal Karol Wojtyla after the Eucharistic Congress in the United States in which the distinguished guest imparted his impressions of meeting with Polonia in various Polonian groups was repeated on the "Voice of Polonia" on the day that Karol Wojtyla was elected Pope. The rebroadcast naturally elicited great enthusiasm.

From these few examples we see that Polish radio programs are an integral part of the community life of Polonia in the United States.

However, the situation of Polish radio programs in the United States does not belong to the easiest. The directors of these programs struggle with severe difficulties. Polish radio programs like radio programs of other ethnic groups of European origin are clearly discriminated against by the chain stores from the point of view of advertising revenues. Therefore to win the position owing to them in American broadcasting and to participate in the advertising budget of large firms, the necessity exists of creating a professional organization of directors of Polish radio programs. A very real need exists to organize an ethnic advertising bureau which professionally and persistently would try to get paid advertising for ethnic programs.

As a result of Poles settling not only in the suburbs but also in small towns and villages across the United States a very urgent need exists to build ethnic radio stations with a powerful range which would be able to reach Polish families within a radius of hundreds of miles. It is necessary at this very moment to mobilize public opinion in regard to this idea via radio talks in English and in articles in the American press. Before long, conditions will exist for allotting new frequency bands for radio stations with a wide range, then it will be necessary to turn to the Federal Communications Commission with an appropriate application.

The role of Poland in the adequate development and the correctly fulfilling the role of Polish radio programs in the United States is a large one. One of the most important factors is the systematic provision to Polish radio programs of needed materials. Folk music or popular music, dramas, dramatized stories, interviews, news of cultural events are materials without which one could not dream of preparing good Polish broadcasts. Polish radio has accomplished a great deal in this field, but the needs are ever greater.

Various departments of centralized export trade which are trying to promote their goods for sale in American markets could help their own interests and the cause of Polish radio here by advertising Polish goods over Polish radio. Except for Polish hams advertised as goods coming from Poland, one does not hear advertisements on radio or television about Polish goods. This can be attributed to the Polish exporter who in negotiations with the American distributor allows him at least 5% of the whole sum for the advertising of their goods. The distributors use this money for advertising their own firm and not for the Polish goods. A consumer gets attached to a particular brand if the quality is to his taste, and he asks for that brand, which forces the store manager to stock that brand of goods in large quantities.

NOTES

Notes to Introduction

1. A. Miklaszewski, J. Serwański: Polonia chicagowska w latach siedemdziesiątych. *Chicago Polonia in the 1970's* "Przegląd Zachodni 3/1980, p. 128: Polish Guide to Chicagoland 1978, Chicago 1978, p. 55.
2. A. Paczkowski: Prasa polska w latach 1918-1939 *Polish Press between 1918-1939*, Warsaw 1980, p. 387.
3. B. Lewandowski: Propaganda radiowa w USA *Radio propaganda in the USA*, Warsaw 1981.
4. Stan i potrzeby badań nad zbiorowo/*ciami poloijnymi State and needs of studies into Polonian communities,* edited by H. Kubiak and A. Piloch, Wrocław 1976, p. 13.
5. J. Drohojowski: Polacy w Ameryce *Poles in America,* Warsaw 1976.
6. Poles in the history and culture of the United States of America, Wrocław 1979.
7. J.A. Wytrwal: Poles in American History and Tradition, Detroit 1969; The Poles in America, Minneapolis 1974.
8. L. Pilarski: They came from Poland. The stories of famous Polish-Americans, New York, 1969.
9. T. Polzin: The Polish American: Whence and Wither, Pulaski, Wisconsin 1973.
10. H. Znaniecki Lopata: Polish Americans. Status Competition in an Ethnic Community, New Jersey 1976, p. 65.
11. N.C. Sandberg: Ethnic Identity and Assimilation: The Polish-American Community. Case Study of Metropolitan Los Angeles. New York 1974, p. 22.

Notes to Chapter One

1. Data on number of radio stations differs, for example, Family Encyclopedia of American History, New York 1975, p. 921 states that between 1922-1927 the number of radio stations increased from 30 to 732, while the number of radio sets from 60,000 to 6,500,000.
2. Samuel L. Rothafeld, Raymond Francis Yates: Broadcasting, Its New Day, New York 1925, p. 53.
3. J. Fred MacDonald: Don't Touch That Dial. Radio Prgramming in American Life from 1920 to 1960, Chicago, p. 21.
4. Edgar A. Grunwald: Program–Production History, 1929-1937 Variety Radio Directory, 1937-1938 New York 1937, p. 19.
5. J. Fred MacDonald, op. cit. p. 36.
6. Charles A. Siepmann: Radio, Television and Society, New York 1950, pp. 48-49.
7. Hanely Captril: The Invasion from Mars: A Study in the Psychology of Panic, Princestin 1940.
8. Erik Brooouws: The Golden Web, A History of Broadcasting in the United States, 1933-1953 New York 1958, pp. 241-42.
9. Raymond Gram Wing: "Good Evening!" A Professional Memoir New York 1964, pp. 225-26.
10. J. Fred MacDonald, op. cit. p. 88.

Notes to Chapter Two

1. Broadcast Dureau Publication 8310-100, FCC, Washington, D.C. October 1979: Telecommunications and Interdisciplinary Survey ed. by L. Lewin, Washington 1980, p. 44; J. Danecki, E. Machut-Mackdecka, B. Wrona: Radio and Television in the USA, Warsaw 1975, p;9.
2. The FCC in Brief "Information Bullitin" 1/79 Washington, D.C.
3. Ibid., 10/79 Washington, D.C.
4. Ibid., 10/70 Washington, D.C.
5. Ibid., 1/79 Washington, D.C.

Notes to Chapter Four

1. Written report by Władysław Jagiełło dated March 10, 1980.

2. Carol Trzebiatowski: Looking Back, International Polka Association, Ed. Bock Wilwaukee 1978.

Notes to Chapter Six

1. Halina Paluszek-Gawrońska: Gawcda o polskich godzinach radiowych w Chicago *Story of Polish Radio Hours in Chicago,* "Dziennik Związkowy of January 22, April 29 and May 7, 1977 and personal report.
2. "Dziennik Związkowy" dated October 25, 1929.
3. Ibid., December 21, 1930.
4. Ibid., December 21, 1930.
5. Ibid., April 4, 1930.
6. Ibid., June 9, 1929.
7. Ibid., December 5, 1929.
8. Ibid., December 11, 1930.
9. Ibid., April 1, 1930.
10. Ibid., May 21, 1930.
11. Ibid., June 9, 1930.
12. Ibid., February 18, 1931.
13. Ibid., May 17, 1931.
14. Ibid., September 19, 1931.
15. Ibid., October 28, 1932.
16. Ibid., December 19, 1932.
17. Ibid., May 10, 1933.
18. Ibid., July 5, 1933.
19. Ibid., May 22, 1933.
20. Ibid., November 21, 1934.
21. Ibid., February 2, 1935.
22. Ibid., April 9, 1936.
23. Ibid., January 20, 1937.
24. Ibid., October 21, 1937.
25. Ibid., November 13, 1937.
26. Ibid., February 20, 1938.
27. Ibid., January 21, 1939.
28. Written Report by Robert Lewandowski in "Dziennik Związkowy" dated November 21, 1955.
29. "Dziennik Związkowy" dated October 21, 1955.

30. Ibid., December 1, 1955.
31. Ibid., January 27, 1956.
32. Ibid., January 27, 1956.
33. Ibid., October 26, 1958.
34. Ibid., December 20, 1958.
35. Ibid., December 20, 1958.
36. Archives of the "Voice of Polonia"
37. "Dziennik Związkowy" dated October 6, 1964.
38. Ibid., July 1, 1967.
39. Ibid., July 1, 1967.
40. Ibid., November 5, 1974.
41. Ibid., October 9, 1974.
42. Ibid., July 1, 1976 and December 11, 1979.

Notes to Chapter Seven

1. "Nowy Dziennik" New York, July 15, 1979.

Notes to Chapter Eight

1. Written report by director of WSBT radio station in South Bend, Joe W. Kelly dated August 17, 1979.
2. "Dziennik Związkowy" dated October 25, 1929.
3. Ibid., April 4, 1930.
4. Ibid., April 24, 1930.

Notes to Chapter Nine

1. Written by director of WRYM station Barry A. Kursman dated July 16, 1970.
2. Written report by director of WCNX station Cindy Walsh dated July 20, 1970.
3. Written report received from the WGCH station on August 15, 1979.
4. Written report of Casimir Majewski from WVOP station on January 21, 1980.

Notes to Chapter Ten

1. Robert E. Moody, "The Adam Mickiewicz Polonia Literary Society, written report dated January 26, 1980.
2. Written report by Irene Stryjewski of August 19, 1979.
3. Robert F. Moody, The Adam Mickiewicz Polonia Literary Society, written report of January 26, 1980.

Notes to Chapter Eleven

1. Private collection of Benjamin Stawiński from Detroit, Michigan.
2. Ibid.
3. Ibid.
4. Ibid.
5. Ibid.
6. Collection of Dr. Estelle Torres -nee Wachtel of Holland., Michigan.
7. Personal report of Dr. Estelle Torres -nee Wachtel of Holland, Michigan.
8. Based on private collection of Dr. Estelle Torres -nee Wachtel of Holland, Michigan, and Benjamin Stawiznski of Detroit, Michigan.
9. "Dziennik Polski" dated March 21, 1980.
10. "Dziennik Polski" dated March 22, 1980 and written report of Jerzy Rózalski

Notes to Chapter Twelve

1. Wrriten report by Ignacy Morawski of May 19, 1980.
2. 1980 Polish Broadcasting Corporation, Radio Programs B. Rosalka
3. "Nowy Šwiat" dated November 18, 1959.
4. Written report by director of WKNT station Joseph E. Shuler of August 18, 1979.
5. Written report by Stanely Jasiński of September 13, 1979.

Notes to Chapter Thirteen

1. Written report by Peter Garnowski of August 21, 1979.

2. Written report by Johnny Kotrick of August 27, 1979.

Notes to Chapter Fourteen

1. "Gwiazda Polarna" dated June 25, 1977.
2. Ziggy Gordon: A Proud Polish-Jew Tells It Like It Is, "Post Eagle" dated May 24, 1978.
3. Polish-American Club Diary of Miami, Florida, 1978.
4. Personal report by Eugenin Kasperkowiak.
5. "Gwiazda Polarna" dated April 5, 1980.
6. Written report by Father Zbigniew Kaszubski dated February 8, 1980.
7. Written report from WJDM station of August 31, 1979.
8. Written report received from WSUS station of August 27, 1979.
9. Book of the Silver Jubilee of the Polish Veterans Circle in Milwaukee, 1952-1977, Milwaukee 1978.

Notes to Chapter Fifteen

1. Written report by Father Kornelian Dende dated February 15, 1980.
2. Fr. Justin Rosary Hour Program, Publication November 4, 1979.

Notes to Chapter Sixteen

1. Broadcasting Publication Inc., Washington, D.C. 1980.

SOURCE MATERIAL

Literature:

Arne Sigrid: One-Time Matinee Idol Polish Arts Mentor Hero "The Cleveland News" March 11, 1959.

Budakowska E.: Polskie programy radiowe w USA "Krajowa AGencja Informacyjna" nr 12/948, 20-26 III 1978.

Burbage R., Cazemajon J., Kaspi A.: Presse, Radio et Television aux Etats-Unis Paris 1972.

Burnouw E.: A Tower in Babel/vol. I, 1933./A History of Broadcasting in the United States, New York 1966.

Burnouw E.: The Golden Web/vol. II, 1933-1953./A History of Broadcasting in the United States, New York 1968.

Burnouw E.: The Image Empire/vol. III, 1953./A History of Broadcasting in the United States, New York, 1970.

Coffin E., Lindia J., Baiman M.: Strangers into Customers New York, 1955.

Culbert David Holbrook: News for Everyman; Radio and Foreign Affairs in Thirties, America Westport, Conn. 1976.

Crozier M.: Broadcasting/Sound and Television/London, 1958–The Home University Library of Modern Knowledge 235.

Czerwiński M.: Telewizja, radio, ludzie Warszawa, 1979.

Danecki J., MachutOMandecka E., Wrona B.: Radio i telewizja w USA Warszawa, 1975.

Drohojowski J.: Polacy w Ameryce Warszawa, 1976.

Dunning J.: Tune-In Yesterday. The Ultimate Encyclopedia of Old-Time Radio/1925-1976/Englewood Cliffs, N.J. Prentice-Hall, 1976.

Family Encyclopedia of American History New York, 1975

Grunwald A. Edgar: Program-Production History 1929-1937, Variety Radio Directory 1937-38, New York, 1937

Hanley Cantril: The Invasion From Mars: A Study in the Psychology of Panic, Princeton 1940

Hermes Bound. The Policy and Technology of Telecommunications by Mogillen and William P. McLauchlen, Purdue University, West Lafayette, Indiana 1978

Historia Progamu Radioego SPK w Milwaukee. Pamiętnik, Srberny Jubileusz SPK, Milwaukee 1952-77, Milwaukee 1978

Kenrick A.: Prime Time; The Life of Edward R. Murrow Boston, 1969

Lewandowski B.: Propaganda radiowa w USA Warszawa, 1981

Lidia Pucińska w pracy dla sprawy polskiej, Chicago 1963

McDonald J. Fred: Don't Touch That Dial; Radio Programing in American Life from 1920 to 1960 Nelson Hall, Chicago

Martin J.: The Wired Society New Jersey, 1978

Migala L.: Program Book Cleveland, 1976

Mihali J.: Radio Stations Here Lead in Old World Music Programs "The Cleveland News" March 29, 1935

Miklaszewski A., Serwański J.: Polonia chicagowska w latach siedemdziesiątych. Wybrane zagadnienia "Przegląd Zachodni" nr 3, 1980

Miszczak St.: Radifonia i Telwizja w XXV-leciu Warszawa, 1969

Osetyński: List z podrózy "Ameryka Echo" 23 XII 1962

Paczkowski A.: Prasa polska w latach 1918-1939 Warszawa, 1980

Paluszek-Gawrońska H.: Gawęda o Poskich Godzinach Radiowych w Chicago "Dziennik Związkowy" Chicago, 22 and 29 IV, as well as 7 V 1977

Pamiętnik, Srebrny Jubileusz Koła Polskich Kombatant2w w Milwaukee 1952-77 Milwaukee, 1978

Pamiętnik, Polsko-Amerykańskiego Klubu w Miami, Florida, 1978

Pamiętnik. Związek Kloubów Małopolskich Chicago, 1978

Pilarski L.: They Came From Poland. The Stories of Famous Polish-Americans New York, 1969

Poles in the History and Culture of the United States of America Wrocław, 1979

Polskie programy radiowe w USA "Narodowiec"/France/1 IV 1978

Polzin T.: The Polish Americans: Whence and Whither Pulaski, Wis. 1973

Prasa, radio i telewizja w swiecie./Edited by Bartłomiej Golka/Warszawn, 1980

Rothafeld L. Samuel, Yates R. Francis: Broadcasting, Its New Day New York, 1925

Sandberg W.C.: Ethnic Identity and Assimilation; The Polish-American Community. Case Study of Metropolitan Los Angeles, New York, 1974

Schramm W.: Mass Media and National Developing Countries UNESCO, 1964

Seltzer Bob: Polish Star Shines Here "The Cleveland News" 1964

Sltzer Bob: He Is The Voice of Poland Here "The Cleveland News" 1971

Siepman A. Charles: Radio, Television and Society New York 1950

Spot Radio, Rates and Data. A Monthly publication of Standard Rate and Data Service, Inc. Skokie, Illinois 1980

Stan i potrzeby Badań nad zbiorowościami polonijnymi/Edited by H. Kubiak and A. Pilch/Wrocław 1976

Stolarczyk E. and J.: Zjazd KPA a Programy Radiowe "Dziennik Związkowy" Chicago, 4 XI 1972

Trzebiatowski C.: Looking Back, International Polka Association Ad Book, Milwaukee 1978

Telecommunications and Interdisciplinary Survey/ed. by L. Lewin/ Washington, 1980

Wing R. Gram: "Good Evening." A Professional Memoir, New York 1964

Wijtrwal J.A.: The Poles in America, Minneapolis 1974

World Almanac and Book of Facts 1975

Znaniecki H. Lopata: Polish American. Status Competition in an Ethnic Community New Jersey, 1976

Periodicals:

Broadcasting Yearbook, Broadcasting Publication, Washington D.C. for years 1958-80

"The Adam Mickiewicz Polonia Literary Society" 1980

"The Cleveland News" 1935, 1964, 1971

"Diennik Chicagowski" 1937, 1963

"Dziennik Polski" 1977, 1979, 1980

"Dziennik Związkowy" 1929-1939, 1955-1956, 1958, 1964, 1967, 1972, 1974, 1976-77, 1979

"The FCC in Brief. Information Bulletin" 1979
"Gwiazda Polarna" 1977, 1980
"Nowy Dziennik" 1979
"Post Eagle Polish Weekly Newspaper" 1978

Unpublished Sources:

Oral reports:
Damska Maria - President of the Polish American Club in Miami, Florida
Jagiełło Władysław - creator of polka show style programs Miami, Florida
Kasperkowiak Eugenia - social worker, Miami, Florida
Zieliński Brosisław - veteran of Polish radio broadcasting in Illinois

Written reports:
Bauer Joseph - manager of WZAK station in Cleveland, Ohio
Bejlovec Pat - manager of WTAQ station in La Grange, Illinois
Close, E.H. - manager of WKNE station
Flynn Bill - Bill Flynn Productions, Johnson City, New York
Garnowski Peter - Erie, Pennsylvania
Jagiełło Władysław - see oral report
Jasiński Stanley - manager of WXRL station, Lancaster, New York
Kelly Joe W. - manager of WSBT station in South Bend, Indiana
Kowalski Daniel - Cleveland, Ohio
Kursman Barry A. - manager of WRYM station in Wewington, Conn.
Liszka Edmund - manager of radio program
Majewski Kazimierz - Millford, Conn.
Moody Robert F. - member of the "Adam Mickiewicz Literary Society," editor of "The New England Polish American Digest"
Morawski Ignacy - journalist, New York
Ross Ray - manager of WKOP station in Binghamton, New York
Schuh James P. - manager of station in Stevens Point, Wis.
Shuller Joseph E. - manager of WKNY station in Kingston, N.Y.
Sierakowski Joseph - Peterson, New York
Stolarczyk Jerzy and Eugenia - Cleveland, Ohio
Summers Florence - former manager of WHPC station in Cicero, Illinois
Walsh Cindy - manager of WCNX station in Middletown, Conn.
Zieliński Bronisław - see oral report

Private Collections:

Archives of the "Voice of Polonia"/Author's collection/Editor Józef Białasiewicz, Chicago, Ill - press clippings

Editor Halina Paluszek-Gawrońska, Chicago, Ill. - private press articles and clippings

Jerzy and Eugenia Stolarczyk, Cleveland, Ohio - press clippings and written reports

NAME INDEX